Your Study of
The New Testament
Made Easier, Third Edition

Part 1

Matthew, Mark, Luke, and John

© 2022 David J. Ridges
All rights reserved.

No part of this book may be reproduced in any form whatsoever, whether by graphic, visual, electronic, film, microfilm, tape recording, or any other means, without prior written permission of the publisher, except in the case of brief passages embodied in critical reviews and articles.

This is not an official publication of The Church of Jesus Christ of Latter-day Saints. The opinions and views expressed herein belong solely to the author and do not necessarily represent the opinions or views of Cedar Fort, Inc. Permission for the use of sources, graphics, and photos is also solely the responsibility of the author.

ISBN 13: 978-1-4621-4419-8

Published by CFI, an imprint of Cedar Fort, Inc.
2373 W. 700 S., Springville, UT 84663
Distributed by Cedar Fort, Inc., www.cedarfort.com

Library of Congress Control Number: 2022939322

Cover design by Shawnda T. Craig
Cover design © 2022 Cedar Fort, Inc.

Printed in the United States of America

10 9 8 7 6 5 4 3 2 1

Printed on acid-free paper

GOSPEL STUDIES SERIES

Your Study of
The New Testament
Made Easier, Third Edition

Part 1

Matthew, Mark, Luke, and John

David J. Ridges

CFI
An imprint of Cedar Fort, Inc.
Springville, Utah

Books by David J. Ridges

The Gospel Study Series

- *Your Study of The Book of Isaiah Made Easier, Second Edition*
- *The New Testament Made Easier, Third Edition, Part 1*
- *The New Testament Made Easier, Third Edition, Part 2*
- *The New Testament Made Easier, Third Edition, Part 3*
- *Your Study of The Book of Mormon Made Easier, Part 1*
- *Your Study of The Book of Mormon Made Easier, Part 2*
- *Your Study of The Book of Mormon Made Easier, Part 3*
- *Book of Mormon Made Easier, Family Deluxe Edition, Volumes 1 and 2*
- *Your Study of The Doctrine and Covenants Made Easier, Second Edition, Part 1*
- *Your Study of The Doctrine and Covenants Made Easier, Second Edition, Part 2*
- *Your Study of The Doctrine and Covenants Made Easier, Second Edition, Part 3*
- *The Old Testament Made Easier, Third Edition, Part 1*
- *The Old Testament Made Easier—Selections from the Old Testament, Third Edition, Part 2*
- *The Old Testament Made Easier—Selections from the Old Testament, Third Edition, Part 3*
- *The Old Testament Made Easier—Selections from the Old Testament, Third Edition, Part 4*
- *Your Study of the Pearl of Great Price Made Easier*
- *Your Study of Jeremiah Made Easier*
- *Your Study of The Book of Revelation Made Easier, Second Edition*

Our Savior's Life and Mission to Redeem and Give Hope

Mormon Beliefs and Doctrines Made Easier

The Proclamation on the Family: The Word of the Lord on More than 30 Current Issues

Using the Signs of the Times to Strengthen Your Testimony

Doctrinal Details of the Plan of Salvation: From Premortality to Exaltation

Introduction

Welcome to the third edition of Your Study of the The New Testament Made Easier. This third edition is a substantial expansion of the second edition and is a three-volume set. It contains numerous additional notes and explanations, plus many additional verses from the Joseph Smith Translation of the Bible, which were not included in the second edition.

In Part 1, we will study the life of our Savior as taught in the Four Gospels—Matthew, Mark, Luke, and John, as found in the King James version of the Bible as published and used by The Church of Jesus Christ of Latter-day Saints. (It is interesting to note that only 31 days of the Savior's life and ministry are covered in the Four Gospels.) Part 2 and a portion of Part 3 are a study of Acts through Revelation. Parts 1, 2, and 3 include every verse in the New Testament. The remainder of Part 3 consists of the book *Our Savior's Life and Mission to Redeem and Give Hope* by David J. Ridges. It is a pleasant and fairly easy read of the Savior's life and mission to cleanse, heal, and make exaltation available to us. This book makes use of Matthew, Mark, Luke, and John as it helps you better understand and appreciate the Savior's mortal mission and Atonement and how His marvelous, infinite Atonement can fill your life with richness, confidence, and peace.

Note: Here in Part 1, I have used bold font for many words and phrases in Matthew, Mark, and Luke as an example of ways you might highlight or mark your own scriptures and also to point things out to you for teaching purposes. Beginning with the Gospel of John, I do not use bold, except for occasional emphasis, and particularly to point out the JST changes to Bible verses. By the way, I often use "we" rather than "I" when making my comments. The reason is simple. My parents taught me to avoid "I trouble."

—David J. Ridges

The JST References in Study Guides by David J. Ridges

Note that some of the JST (The Joseph Smith Translation of the Bible) references I use in my study guides are not found in the King James English-speaking edition of the Bible, published by the Church, in the footnotes or in the Joseph Smith Translation section in the reference section in the back. The reason for this, as explained to me while writing curriculum materials for the Church, is simply that there is not enough room to include all of the JST additions and changes. As you can imagine, as was likewise explained to me, there were difficult decisions that had to be made by the Scriptures Committee of the Church as to which JST contributions were included and which were not.

The Joseph Smith Translation of the Bible in its entirety can generally be found in or ordered through bookstores or online. It was originally published under the auspices of the Reorganized Church of Jesus Christ of Latter Day Saints in Independence, Missouri. The version of the JST that I prefer to use is a parallel column version, *Joseph Smith's "New Translation" of the Bible*, published by Herald Publishing House, Independence, Missouri, in 1970. This parallel column version compares the King James Bible with the JST side by side and includes only the verses that have changes, additions, or deletions made by the Prophet Joseph Smith.

By the way, some members of the Church have wondered whether or not we can trust the JST since it was published by a breakaway faction from our Church. They worry that some changes from Joseph Smith's original manuscript might have been made to support doctrinal differences between us and the RLDS Church. This is not the case. Many years ago, Robert J. Matthews of the Brigham Young University Religion Department was given permission by leaders of the RLDS Church to go to their Independence, Missouri, headquarters and personally compare the original JST document word for word with their publication of the JST. Brother Matthews was thus able to verify that they had been meticulously true to the Prophet's original work.

Contents

Foreword ix
The Gospel of Matthew 1
The Gospel of Mark 152
The Gospel of Luke 232
The Gospel of John 369
Sources 479
About the Author 485

Dedication

*To my wife and eternal companion, Janette,
who has encouraged and supported me
every step of the way.*

Foreword

In many years of teaching in the Church and for the Church Educational System, I have found that members of the Church encounter some common problems when it comes to understanding the scriptures. One problem is understanding the language of the scriptures themselves. Another is understanding symbolism. Another is how best to mark scriptures and perhaps make brief notes in them. Yet another concern is how to understand what the scriptures are actually teaching. In other words, what are the major messages being taught by the Lord through His prophets?

This study guide is designed to address each of the concerns mentioned above for the Gospels of Matthew, Mark, Luke, and John in the New Testament. The Bible text of the Gospels is included in its entirety and serves as the basic text for this work.

The format is intentionally simple, with some license taken with respect to capitalization and punctuation in order to minimize interruption of the flow. The format is designed to help readers to:

- Quickly gain a basic understanding of these scriptures through the use of brief explanatory notes in brackets within the verses as well as notes between some verses.

- Better understand the beautiful language of the scriptures. This is accomplished in this study guide with in-the-verse notes that define difficult scriptural terms.

- Mark their scriptures and put brief notes in the margins that will help them understand now and remember later what given passages of scripture teach.

- Better understand the symbolism of the parables of Jesus as well as many other passages where symbolism is used.

- Get a feel for the background and setting in which events and teachings take place. A basic understanding of Jewish culture in the days of the Savior is vital. Notes between verses help with these issues.

Over the years, one of the most common expressions of gratitude from my students has been, "Thanks for the notes you had us put in our scriptures." This book is dedicated to that purpose.

Sources for the notes given in this work are as follows:

- The standard works of The Church of Jesus Christ of Latter-day Saints.

- Footnotes in the Latter-day Saint version of the King James Bible.

- The Joseph Smith Translation of the Bible.

- The Bible Dictionary in the back of the Latter-day Saint version of the Bible.

- Various dictionaries.

- *Strong's Exhaustive Concordance of the Bible*, shown as [*Strong's* # or Strong's #].

- Various student manuals provided for our institutes of religion, including the New Testament student manual, Religion 211, *The Life and Teachings of Jesus and His Apostles*.

- James E. Talmage, *Jesus the Christ*, Deseret Book, 1982.

- Various translations of the Bible, including the Martin Luther edition of the German Bible, which Joseph Smith said was the most correct of any then available.

- *Doctrinal New Testament Commentary*, volumes 1, 2, and 3, by Apostle Bruce R. McConkie.

- *Teachings of the Prophet Joseph Smith*, 1976.

- *Understanding the Book of Revelation*, by Jay A. Parry and Donald W. Parry.

- *New International Version of the Bible*, Zondervan Publishing House, 1984.

- Other sources as noted in the text and in the "Sources" section.

I hope that this study guide will serve effectively as a "teacher in your hand" to members of the Church as they seek to increase their understanding of the life of the Savior during His mortal ministry and to strengthen their testimony of Him. Above all, if this work serves to bring increased understanding and testimony of the Atonement of Christ, all the efforts to put it together will have been far more than worth it. A special thanks goes to my wife, Janette, to whom this study guide is dedicated, and my children who have encouraged me every step of the way.

The Gospel According to
St Matthew

The JST (Joseph Smith Translation of the Bible) calls this "The Testimony of St Matthew." The Gospel of Matthew was written by the Apostle Matthew. He was sometimes called Levi (Mark 2:14; Luke 5:27). He lived in Capernaum, in Galilee, and worked as a tax collector, or "publican" until he was called by the Savior to follow Him. Matthew wrote primarily to a Jewish audience. In order to appeal to the Jews, who placed great emphasis on the Old Testament, he placed particular emphasis on how the Savior's life fulfilled Old Testament prophecy. For more information about Matthew, see Bible Dictionary (in the back section of your Bible), under "Matthew."

You will often see words in italics in the King James Version of the English-speaking Bible. King James, of England, assembled a group of scholars to make a new translation of the Bible. It was completed in A.D. 1611. We will quote from the Bible Dictionary as it explains this use of italics:

Bible Dictionary—Italics
"In the KJV, italics identify words that are necessary in English to round out and complete the sense of a phrase, but were not present in the Hebrew or Greek text of the manuscript used. Such additions were necessary because in some instances the manuscript was inadequate, and the translators felt obliged to clarify it in the translation. In other instances italics were necessary in cases where the grammatical construction of English called for the use of words that were not needed to make the same thought in Hebrew or Greek. Italics thus represent the willingness of the translators to identify these areas. It appears that generally, though not always, their judgment was justified in their choice of italicized words."

We will include several changes made in the JST (the Joseph Smith Translation of the Bible). You will find many of them in your English edition of the Scriptures by way of footnotes. However, since all JST changes and additions are not included in our Bible, because of space limitations, you will see that we have included some which are not in your Bible. If you would like to, you could purchase a copy of the complete JST at almost any religious-oriented bookstore or online. One other thing that you will notice is that the verse numbers of the JST are often different than those of the King James Version of the Bible. This is because the Prophet Joseph Smith added missing verses, combined verses, rearranged verses, and corrected things as needed.

MATTHEW 1

1 **The book of the generation** [*genealogy*] **of Jesus Christ**, the son of [*descendant of*] David, the son of [*who was a descendant of*] Abraham.

> The genealogy of Christ, given here by Matthew, is that of the legal successors to the throne of David, not a strict father-to-son genealogy. It includes living successors such as grandson, nephew, etc. Luke's genealogy of the Savior, as given in Luke 3:23–38, is a strict father-to-son genealogy. Since Joseph and Mary were cousins (see the New Testament student manual, p. 22), Joseph's genealogy is essentially Mary's genealogy and thus, the Savior's.

> We will use **bold** to point out the genealogy as given by Matthew.

2 **Abraham** begat [*was the father of*] **Isaac**; and Isaac begat **Jacob**; and Jacob begat **Judas** [*Judah—see Genesis 29:35*] and his brethren;

3 And Judas begat **Phares** and Zara of Thamar; and Phares begat **Esrom**; and Esrom begat **Aram**;

4 And Aram begat **Aminadab**; and Aminadab begat **Naasson**; and Naasson begat **Salmon**;

5 And Salmon begat **Booz** [*Boaz, Ruth's husband—see Ruth 4:13*] of Rachab; and Booz begat **Obed** of Ruth; and Obed begat **Jesse** [*King David's father*];

> You've no doubt noticed that some of the names here are spelled differently than you are used to from the Old Testament. What is happening here is that the New Testament is using Greek forms of the names, which sometimes differ from the Hebrew. Thus, Ruth's husband, Boaz, is listed here (in verse 5, above) as "Booz," and Judah was listed as "Judas" (in verses 2 and 3, above).

6 And Jesse begat **David** the king; and David the king begat **Solomon** of her [*Bathsheba*] that had been the wife of Urias;

7 And Solomon begat **Roboam**; and Roboam begat **Abia**; and Abia begat **Asa**;

8 And Asa begat **Josaphat**; and Josaphat begat **Joram**; and Joram begat **Ozias**;

9 And Ozias begat **Joatham**; and Joatham begat **Achaz**; and Achaz begat **Ezekias**;

10 And Ezekias begat **Manasses**; and Manasses begat **Amon**; and Amon begat **Josias**;

11 And Josias begat **Jechonias** and his brethren, about the time they were carried away to Babylon:

12 And after they were brought to Babylon, Jechonias begat **Salathiel**; and Salathiel begat **Zorobabel**;

13 And Zorobabel begat **Abiud**; and Abiud begat **Eliakim**; and Eliakim begat **Azor**;

14 And Azor begat **Sadoc**; and Sadoc begat **Achim**; and Achim begat **Eliud**;

15 And Eliud begat **Eleazar**; and Eleazar begat **Matthan**; and Matthan begat **Jacob**;

16 And Jacob begat **Joseph the husband of Mary**, of whom was born **Jesus**, who is called Christ [*Greek: the "Anointed One"*].

JST Matthew 1:4
4 And after they were brought to Babylon, Jechonias begat Salathiel; and Salathiel begat Zorobable; and Zorobable begat Abiud; and Abiud begat Eliakim; and Eliakim begat Azor; and Azor begat Sadoc; and Sadoc begat Achim; and Achim begat Eliud; and Eliud begat Eleazar; and Eleazar begat Matthan; and Matthan begat Jacob; and Jacob begat Joseph, the husband of Mary, of whom was born Jesus, **as the prophets have written**, who is called Christ.

As you can see, the JST combines Bible verses 12–16 into one verse, JST verse 4. I have bolded the phrase "as the prophets have written" near the end of the verse to make it easier for you to pick out the change Joseph Smith made. We know, of course, that Jesus was literally the Son of God, not the son of Joseph. In tracing this genealogy, Matthew points out that Joseph, the Savior's wonderful stepfather, would have been the political king of the Jewish nation at this time if the Romans had not been in power. And Joseph's legal successor to the crown would have been Jesus. See *Jesus the Christ*, p. 87.

17 So all the generations from Abraham to David are fourteen generations; and from David until the carrying away into Babylon are fourteen generations; and from the carrying away into Babylon unto Christ are fourteen generations.

Next, Matthew summarizes the birth of the Savior. Many people use the word "engaged" to explain "espoused," as used in verse 18, next. Among the Jews, being espoused was a much more serious obligation than our "engagement." During the espousal period, the bride-to-be lived with her family or friends, and communication between her and her husband-to-be was carried on by a friend.

18 ¶ **Now the birth of Jesus Christ was on this wise** [*happened this way*]: When as his mother **Mary was espoused to Joseph**, before they came together [*before they married and had intimate relations*], **she was found with child of the Holy Ghost.**

In Jewish culture at this time, an unmarried woman found to be expecting a child was subject to being stoned to death.

19 Then Joseph her husband, being a just [*righteous; fair; strict in truly living the gospel*] **man,** and not willing to make her a publick example [*which would protect his own reputation, but could subject Mary to humiliation and even execution by stoning*], **was minded to put her away privily** [*privately, so as to avoid embarrassing her, and to avoid putting her life in danger*].

20 But while he thought on these things, behold, **the angel of the Lord appeared unto him** in a dream, saying, Joseph, thou son of David [*descendant of David*], **fear not to take unto thee Mary thy wife** [*don't be afraid to marry her*]: **for that** [*the child*] **which is conceived in her is of the Holy Ghost.**

Luke clarifies what is meant at the end of verse 20, above, where it says that Mary's child was "of the Holy Ghost." He says, in effect, that the Holy Ghost came upon Mary so that the divine conception could be accomplished. Luke wrote:

Luke 1:35
35 And the angel answered and said unto her, **The Holy Ghost shall come upon thee**, and **the power of the Highest** [*the Father*] **shall overshadow thee**: therefore also **that holy thing** [*the Christ child*] which shall be **born of thee shall be** called **the Son of God.**

Elder James E. Talmage, of the Quorum of the Twelve, further explained: "That Child to be born of Mary was begotten of Elohim, the Eternal Father, not in violation of natural law but in accordance with a higher manifestation thereof; and, the offspring from that association of supreme sanctity, celestial Sireship, and pure though mortal maternity, was of right to be called the 'Son of the Highest.' In His nature would be combined the powers of Godhood with the capacity and possibilities of mortality; and this through the ordinary operation of the fundamental law of heredity declared of God, demonstrated by science, and admitted by philosophy, that living beings shall propagate—after their kind. The Child Jesus was to inherit the physical, mental and spiritual traits, tendencies, and powers that characterized His parents— one immortal and glorified— God, the other human—woman" (*Jesus the Christ*, p. 81).

21 And she shall bring forth a son, and thou shalt call his name JESUS: for he shall save his people from their sins [*in other words, Mary is expecting the promised Messiah*].

It is interesting to note that the angel came and put Joseph's mind at ease *after* he made the decision to be merciful to Mary.

22 Now all this was done, that it might be fulfilled [*that Isaiah's prophecy would be fulfilled—see*

Isaiah 7:14] which was spoken of the Lord by the prophet, saying,

23 Behold, **a virgin shall be with child, and shall bring forth a son**, and they shall call his name Emmanuel, which being interpreted is, God with us.

24 **Then Joseph** being raised from sleep did as the angel of the Lord had bidden him, and **took unto him his wife** [*Joseph obeyed the angel immediately, no doubt with great relief and joy, and married Mary*]:

25 And **knew her not** [*had no sexual relationship, so that Jesus was born to a virgin, as prophesied*] **till she had brought forth her firstborn son**: and he called his name JESUS.

Joseph and Mary went on to have at least six children of their own. See Mark 6:3. In fact, the Greek text of that verse indicates that there were at least three sisters plus the four brothers mentioned.

MATTHEW 2

The Wise Men Come

1 Now **when Jesus was born in Bethlehem** of Judæa in the days of Herod the king [*see Bible Dictionary, pp. 700–701, for background information on Herod the Great*], behold, **there came wise men** [*no doubt inspired men of God; perhaps prophets*] from the east to Jerusalem,

2 **Saying, Where is he that is born King of the Jews?** for **we have seen his star** in the east, and are come to worship him..

JST Matthew 3:2

2 Saying, Where is **the child** that is born, **the Messiah** of the Jews? for we have seen his star in the east, and **have** come to worship him.

3 When **Herod the king** had heard these things, he **was troubled**, and **all Jerusalem with him** [*this stirred up much discussion in Jerusalem*].

4 And when **he** had **gathered all the chief priests and scribes** [*the Jewish religious leaders and scholars*] of the people **together, he demanded of them where Christ should be born.**

5 **And they said** unto him, **In Bethlehem** of Judæa: **for thus it is written** by the prophet [*Micah 5:2*],

6 And thou Bethlehem, in the land of Juda, art not the least among the princes of Juda: for **out of thee shall come a Governor** [*Christ*], **that shall rule my people Israel.**

JST Matthew 3:4–6

4 And when he had gathered all the chief priests, and scribes of the people together, he demanded of them, saying, **Where is the place that is written of by the prophets, in which Christ should be born? For he greatly feared, yet he believed not the prophets.**

5 And they said unto him, **It is written by the prophets, that he should be born in Bethlehem of Judea**, for thus have they said,

6 **The word of the Lord came unto us**, saying, And thou Bethlehem, which lieth in the land of Judea, in thee shall be born a prince, which art not the least among the princes of Judea; for out of thee shall come the Messiah, who shall save my people Israel.

7 **Then Herod**, when he had privily [*privately*] **called the wise men**, enquired of them diligently what time the star appeared.

8 And he **sent them to Bethlehem, and said**, Go and search diligently for the young child; and **when ye have found him, bring me word again, that I may come and worship him also** [*Herod is lying. He secretly wants to kill the child*].

9 When they had heard the king, **they departed**; and, lo, **the star**, which they saw in the east, **went before them, till it came and stood over where the young child was.**

By the time the wise men arrived in Jerusalem, enquiring about the birth of Christ, Jesus was already a young child. Joseph and Mary had apparently decided to stay in Bethlehem for a while, after the Savior's birth, and had settled in a house there. You can see that this is implied in verse 11, which informs us that He was now living in a house in Bethlehem. Thus, the pictures we see of the wise men and shepherds visiting baby Jesus in a stable are a composite of two separate events.

10 When they saw the star, they rejoiced with exceeding great joy.

11 **And when they were come into the house, they saw the young child with Mary his mother**, and fell down, **and worshipped him**: and when they had opened their treasures, **they presented unto him gifts; gold**, and **frankincense**, and **myrrh** [*frankincense and myrrh were costly gifts, as was gold, and were highly prized for their use as incense in this culture where sanitation was a concern and incense helped mask unpleasant odors; it may well be that these gifts from the wise men helped pay expenses for the trip to Egypt, mentioned in verse 13*].

Remember that the wise men had been requested by King Herod to report back to him when they found Jesus, so that he also could worship Him. They are warned not to do so.

12 And **being warned of God in a dream that they should not return to Herod, they departed into their own country** another way.

Righteous Joseph is also warned by an angel. He is told to take Mary and Jesus to Egypt, where the child will be out of reach of Herod.

Matthew 2

13 And when they were departed, behold, **the angel of the Lord appeareth to Joseph** in a dream, **saying, Arise, and take the young child and his mother, and flee into Egypt**, and be thou there until I bring thee word: **for Herod will seek the young child to destroy him**.

14 When he arose, **he took the young child and his mother by night, and departed into Egypt** [*this would be a long and difficult journey, of about 200–300 miles, depending on where they stayed in Egypt, but Joseph and Mary were obedient*]:

15 **And was there until the death of Herod**: that it might be fulfilled which was spoken of the Lord by the prophet [*Hosea 11:1*], saying, Out of Egypt have I called my son.

> By way of information, the paragraph mark (¶) you see in your Bible (if it is the King James version, published through the Church) indicates a change in topic.

16 ¶ **Then Herod**, when he saw that he was mocked of the wise men, **was exceeding wroth** [*very angry*], **and sent forth, and slew all the children** [*Greek: male babies*] **that were in Bethlehem, and in all the coasts thereof** [*the area surrounding Bethlehem*], **from two years old and under**, according to the time which he had diligently enquired of the wise men.

John the Baptist was also a small child at this time, just six months older than Jesus (Elizabeth was six months along with John—see Luke 1, verses 26 and 36—when Mary visited her, right after Gabriel told her she would be the mother of Jesus). He lived in the vicinity of Bethlehem when Herod gave his murderous order to kill all the babies two years old and younger in the Bethlehem area. John the Baptist's father, Zacharias, was killed—see Matthew 23:35—because he would not tell where he had sent John and his mother to hide. The Prophet Joseph Smith gives us more information about this. "When Herod's edict went forth to destroy the young children, John was about six months older than Jesus, and came under this hellish edict, and Zacharias caused his mother to take him into the mountains, where he was raised on locusts and wild honey. When his father refused to disclose his hiding place, and being the officiating high priest at the Temple that year, was slain by Herod's order, between the porch and the altar, as Jesus said" (*Teachings of the Prophet Joseph Smith*, p. 261).

In verse 17, next, we see another example of Matthew emphasizing that Jesus was the fulfillment of numerous Old Testament prophecies.

17 **Then was fulfilled that** [*the prophecy given in Jeremiah 31:15*] **which was spoken by Jeremy** [*Jeremiah*] **the prophet, saying,**

18 In Rama [*a place northwest of Jerusalem where the Jewish captives were assembled prior to being taken to Babylon—see Bible Dictionary, under "Rachel"*] was there a voice heard, **lamentation,** and **weeping**, and great **mourning, Rachel** [*Jacob's wife, the mother of Joseph and Benjamin; she died giving birth to Benjamin—see Genesis 35:16–20*] **weeping for her children**, and would not be comforted, because they are not.

Thus, according to Matthew, the deaths of the male children in the Bethlehem area, because of Herod's edict, were yet another fulfillment of the prophecy given by Jeremiah. Rachel's tomb is located near the northern entrance to old Bethlehem, and we can picture her in our minds weeping for the slain children in the Bethlehem area.

After Herod died, an angel appeared in a dream to Joseph, who was still living with his little family in Egypt, and told him to bring Mary and Jesus back to Israel. Their stay in Egypt may have been relatively short, since Herod died just a few months after he issued the order to slay the male infants in Bethlehem—see Bible dictionary, under "Herod."

19 But **when Herod was dead,** behold, **an angel** of the Lord **appeareth** in a dream **to Joseph in Egypt,**

20 Saying, **Arise, and take the young child and his mother, and go into the land of Israel**: for they are dead which sought the young child's life.

21 And **he arose, and took the young child and his mother, and came into the land of Israel.**

It is likely that Joseph and Mary had determined to return to their home in Bethlehem at this time, but fear of Herod's son, Archelaus, who now ruled Judea, caused them to be afraid. An angel confirmed Joseph's concerns and instructed him to take his family back to Nazareth, where they had been living prior to coming to Bethlehem where Jesus was born—see Luke 2:4–5.

22 **But when he heard that Archelaus did reign in Judæa in the room of** [*in place of*] **his father Herod, he was afraid** to go thither [*there*]: notwithstanding, **being warned of God in a dream, he turned aside into the parts of Galilee:**

23 **And he came and dwelt in a city called Nazareth**: that it might be fulfilled which was spoken by the prophets, He shall be called a Nazarene [*we don't know where this prophecy is; it is one of the lost scriptures*].

The JST adds three verses which fit here and are not found in the Bible.

JST Matthew 3:24–26
24 And it came to pass that Jesus grew up with his brethren, and waxed strong, and

waited upon the Lord for the time of his ministry to come.

25 And he served under his father, and he spake not as other men, neither could he be taught; for he needed not that any man should teach him.

26 And after many years, the hour of his ministry drew nigh.

MATTHEW 3

John the Baptist Comes Preaching

1 **In those days came John the Baptist, preaching in the wilderness** of Judæa [*a desert area, west of the Dead Sea*],

2 And **saying, Repent ye: for the kingdom of heaven is at hand** [*is near; the gospel of Jesus Christ is now available to you*].

3 For **this is he that was spoken of by the prophet Esaias** [*Isaiah*], **saying,** The voice of one crying in the wilderness, Prepare ye the way of the Lord, make his paths straight.

As you will see, the Prophet Joseph Smith made a change in verse 3 which changes the whole meaning:

JST Matthew 3:29

29 For **I am he** who was spoken of by the prophet Esaias, saying, The voice of one crying in the wilderness, Prepare ye the way of the Lord **and** make his paths straight.

4 And the same **John had his raiment** [*clothing*] **of camel's hair** [*coarse cloth woven from camel's hair*], and a leathern girdle about his loins; **and his meat** [*food*] **was locusts and wild honey.**

The Bible generally uses the word "meat" to mean any kind of food. The word "flesh" is used when referring to meat, such as beef, chicken, lamb, etc.

Elder Bruce R. McConkie explained the importance of John the Baptist and his mission. He said: "This miraculously born son of Zacharias was the last legal administrator of the old dispensation, the first of the new; he was the last of the old prophets, the first of the new. With him ended the old law, and with him began the new era of promise. He is the one man who stood, literally, at the crossroads of history; with him the past died and the future was born. He was the herald of the Messianic age, the messenger, fore-runner, and Elias who began the great restoration in the meridian of time and on whose secure foundation the Son of Man himself built the eternal gospel structure. His ministry ended the preparatory gospel; Messiah's commenced again the era of gospel fulness" (*Doctrinal New Testament Commentary*, p. 113).

Next, we see that there was great excitement about John the Baptist throughout the region.

5 Then went out to him Jerusalem, and all Judæa, and all the region round about Jordan [*i.e., people from all over came to the Jordan River to see John the Baptist*],

6 And were baptized of [*by*] **him** in Jordan [*the Jordan River*], confessing their sins.

Verses 5 and 6, above, remind us that John the Baptist was baptizing by immersion. It was necessary for people to come over twenty miles from Jerusalem to a place where there was "much water" (John 3:23). The word "baptize" itself comes "from a Greek word, meaning to dip or immerse" (see Bible Dictionary, under "Baptism").

Have you noticed in reading these verses that no one was bothered by the idea of baptism? That is because baptism itself was a familiar ordinance. It had been practiced in Old Testament times, in fact, since the time of Adam (Moses 6:64–66), whenever the gospel of Jesus Christ was available. We will quote from the Bible Dictionary:

Bible Dictionary—Baptism

"Baptism has always been practiced whenever the gospel of Jesus Christ has been on the earth and has been taught by men holding the holy priesthood who could administer the ordinances. Although there is some obscurity in the Bible as to the antiquity of baptism before the time of Jesus, from latter-day revelation it is clear that Adam was baptized (Moses 6:64–68) and that the patriarchs and prophets since his time have taught the gospel and administered the ordinances that pertain to the gospel. This includes both water baptism and the laying on of hands for the Holy Ghost (Moses 8:23–24). The Book of Mormon shows also that baptism was taught and practiced long before the coming of Jesus Christ (2 Ne. 31; Mosiah 18:8–17)."

Verse 7, next, mentions Pharisees and Sadducees. These were religious groups among the Jews of the day, and many of them were hypocrites. Pharisees believed in the resurrection. Sadducees did not. Consequently, there was much arguing and disagreement between the two groups.

7 But when he saw many of the Pharisees and Sadducees come to his baptism, **he said unto them, O generation of vipers, who hath warned you to flee from the wrath to come?**

8 Bring forth therefore fruits meet [*necessary*] **for repentance:**

9 And think not to say within yourselves, We have Abraham to our father [*as our ancestor*]: **for I say unto you, that God is able of these stones to raise up children** [*descendants*] **unto Abraham.**

The JST adds to and makes changes in verses 8–9, above. The verse numbering is different because Joseph Smith combined Matthew chapters 2 and 3 together as chapter 3 in the JST. You will see that he added an entire verse before verse 8 in the King James version (the one we use) of the Bible. (By the way, as previously mentioned in this study guide, all of the changes made by the Prophet Joseph Smith are not contained in our Bible. There is simply not room enough for them. Thus, some of the changes mentioned in this study guide are only found in the complete text of the JST, which is available at most Latter-day Saint book stores.)

JST Matthew 3:34–36

34 **Why is it that ye receive not the preaching of him whom God hath sent? If ye receive not this in your hearts, ye receive not me; and if ye receive not me, ye receive not him of whom I am sent to bear record; and for your sins ye have no cloak**.

35 **Repent**, therefore, and bring forth fruits meet for repentance;

36 And think not to say within yourselves, We are the children of Abraham, and **we only have power to bring seed unto our father Abraham** [*in effect, saying we are the only ones who can be saved*]; for I say unto you that God is able of these stones to raise up children into Abraham.

It helps to understand the above verses if you are aware that the Jews had a belief that, since they were direct descendants of Abraham, they were automatically entitled to the highest position in heaven in the afterlife, and, that all other people, no matter how good they were, could attain only second-class status in heaven. As you noticed, John spoke strongly against this false belief in verse 9, above, and will continue to do so in verse 10, next.

10 And now also the axe is laid unto the root of the trees [*trees often represent people in the scriptures*]: therefore **every tree which bringeth not forth good fruit** [*every person who does not live righteously*] **is hewn** [*cut*] **down, and cast into the fire** [*in other words, the wicked, no matter who they are, will be destroyed, punished according to the law of justice, if they do not repent when given a fair chance to do so*].

Next, in verse 11, John humbly directs the people's attention to the Master.

11 I indeed baptize you with water unto repentance: but **he** [*Christ*] **that cometh after me is mightier than I, whose shoes I am not worthy to bear**: he shall baptize you with the Holy Ghost, and with fire:

Note: In the scriptures, the Holy Ghost is often compared to fire. The symbolism comes from the use of fire to purify gold. The gold ore is put in a container (a crucible) and fire is used to heat it. The ore melts, the impurities float to the top, and the pure gold settles to the bottom. The impurities are then discarded and pure gold remains. Thus, the gold is purified by fire. Similarly, the Holy Ghost purifies us, if we allow it. Example: We commit sin. The Holy Ghost points it out and causes our conscience to burn within us. We respond by repenting. The Atonement of Christ cleanses us. Thus we are purified, bit by bit.

12 **Whose fan** [*used to blow the chaff away from the kernels of wheat on the threshing floor*] **is in his hand**, and he will throughly purge [*cleanse*] his floor [*the earth*], and gather his wheat [*the righteous*] into the garner [*the barn*]; but he will burn up the chaff [*the wicked*] with unquenchable fire.

The JST makes changes in verses 11–12, above.

JST Matthew 3:38–40

38 I indeed baptize you with water, **upon your repentance**; and when he of whom I bear record cometh, who is mightier than I, whose shoes I am not worthy to bear **(or whose place I am not able to fill), as I said, I indeed baptize you before he cometh, that when he cometh he may baptize you with the Holy Ghost and fire.**

39 **And it is he of whom I shall bear record,** whose fan shall be in his hand, and he will thoroughly purge his floor, and gather his wheat into the garner; but **in the fulness of his own time** will burn up the chaff with unquenchable fire.

40 **Thus came John, preaching and baptizing in the river of Jordan; bearing record, that he who was coming after him had power to baptize with the Holy Ghost and fire.**

The Baptism of Jesus

13 ¶ **Then cometh Jesus from Galilee to Jordan unto John, to be baptized of** [*by*] **him.**

14 **But John forbad him**, saying, I have need to be baptized of thee, and comest thou to me?

15 **And Jesus** answering **said unto him, Suffer** [*allow*] **it to be so now:** for thus it becometh us to fulfil all righteousness [*to do the will of the Father*]. Then he suffered him.

The JST makes changes to verses 14–15, above.

JST Matthew 3:42–44

42 But John **refused** him, saying, I have need to be baptized of thee, and **why comest thou to me?**

43 And Jesus, answering, said unto him, **Suffer me to be baptized of thee**, for thus it becometh us to fulfill all righteousness. Then he suffered him.

44 **And John went down into the water and baptized him.**

16 And Jesus, when he was baptized, went up straightway **out of the water** [*evidence that He was baptized by immersion*]: **and, lo,**

the heavens were opened unto him, and he [*John the Baptist*] saw the Spirit of God [*the Holy Ghost*] descending like a dove, and lighting upon him [*the Savior—see JST quoted below*]:

17 And lo **a voice from heaven, saying, This is my beloved Son, in whom I am well pleased**.

The Joseph Smith Translation (JST) gives verses 16–17 as follows (remember, the numbering is sometimes different in the JST):

JST Matthew 3:45–46

45 And Jesus when he was baptized, went up straightway out of the water; and **John saw**, and lo, the heavens were opened unto him, and he saw the Spirit of God descending like a dove and lighting upon **Jesus**.

46 And lo, **he heard** a voice from heaven, saying, This is my beloved Son, in whom I am well pleased. **Hear ye him**.

Because of these and other verses in the scriptures, some people have come to believe that the Holy Ghost occasionally turns into a dove. Such is not the case. The Prophet Joseph Smith taught that the Holy Ghost does not transform himself into a dove. He said:

"The Holy Ghost is a personage, and is in the form of a personage. It does not confine itself to the *form* of the dove, but in *sign* of the dove. The Holy Ghost cannot be transformed into a dove; but the sign of a dove was given to John to signify the truth of the deed, as the dove is an emblem or token of truth and innocence" (*Teachings of the Prophet Joseph Smith*, pp. 275–76).

MATTHEW 4

The JST (the Joseph Smith Translation of the Bible) makes many changes to this chapter. You will see a number of them referenced in footnotes in your Latter-day Saint printing of the Bible. (Remember, as we mentioned previously, several JST changes are not contained in our Bible simply because they would take up too much space. Therefore, some JST changes that we give in this study guide are not found in your Bible.)

We see a significant change to verse 1, next. We will quote the JST after we read verse 1 as it stands in our Bible. We will use **bold** to help you see the difference.

1 Then was Jesus led up of the Spirit into the wilderness **to be tempted of the devil**.

JST Matthew 4:1

1 Then Jesus was led up of the Spirit, into the wilderness, **to be with God**.

As you can see, in the JST verse quoted above, the Prophet Joseph Smith teaches us that the Savior went into the wilderness to be with His Father. From this we learn that He did not go specifically to confront the devil nor to be tempted by him.

Perhaps one of the things we can learn from this is that we should not deliberately put ourselves in a position to be tempted. In fact, the Savior said, "lead us not into temptation" (Matthew 6:13). And if you look at Matthew 6:13, footnote b, in your Bible, you will see that "do not let us enter into temptation" is given as another translation of this phrase.

Thus we understand that temptation will come to us as a result of being here on earth, but we should not deliberately place ourselves in tempting circumstances.

As we move ahead now in this chapter, we note that the Savior was subjected to temptation by the devil. Likewise, God does not constantly protect us from the temptations of the devil and his evil followers because we need opposition in order to exercise our agency. This principle is taught in the Book of Mormon as follows:

2 Nephi 2:11
For it must needs be, that there is an opposition in all things.

The JST provides important additions to verse 2, next.

The Devil Tempts Jesus
2 And **when he had fasted forty days and forty nights, he was** afterward an **hungred**.

JST Matthew 4:2
2 And when he had fasted forty days and forty nights, **and had communed with God**, he was afterwards an hungered, **and was left to be tempted of the devil**.

Paul taught us why the Savior was tempted. He said:

Hebrews 2:18, 4:15
18 For in that he himself hath suffered being tempted, **he is able to succour** [*help, nourish*] **them that are tempted**.

15 For we have not an high priest [*Jesus is sometimes referred to as the "Great High Priest"*] which cannot be touched with the feeling of our infirmities [*in other words, we do not have a Savior who is unable to sympathize with our weaknesses*]; but **was in all points tempted like as we are**, *yet* without sin.

As we continue, we will see that the devil tempted the Savior in three major areas in which he likewise tempts us.

1. Physical appetites (verse 3).

2. Vanity and pride (verse 6).

3. Materialism and power (verse 9).

But you will see another form of temptation associated with

the above temptations. It is the word "if" in verses 3 and 6. The devil challenged Jesus to prove that He was indeed the Son of God. This "if" challenge can be a very effective tool for Satan as he likewise challenges us to "prove it." People often find themselves committing sin or taking foolish chances in order to respond to someone who is suggesting that they are not what they claim to be.

3 And when the tempter [*Satan*] came to him, he said, **If** thou be the Son of God, command that these stones be made bread [*temptation to yield to physical appetite*].

4 **But he answered** and said, It is written [*in Deuteronomy 8:3*], **Man shall not live by bread alone, but by every word that proceedeth out of the mouth of God**.

5 Then the devil taketh him up into the holy city [*Jerusalem*], and setteth him on a pinnacle of the temple,

JST Matthew 4:5
Then Jesus was taken up into the holy city and **the Spirit setteth him on the pinnacle of the temple**.

6 And saith unto him, **If** thou be the Son of God, cast thyself down: for it is written [*in Psalm 91:11–12*], He shall give his angels charge concerning thee: and in their hands they shall bear thee up, lest at any time thou dash thy foot against a stone [*temptation to yield to vanity, pride*].

JST Matthew 4:6
6 **Then the devil came unto him** and said, If thou be the Son of God, cast thyself down, for it is written, He shall give his angels charge concerning thee, and in their hands they shall bear thee up, lest at any time thou dash thy foot against a stone.

7 Jesus said unto him, It is written again [*in Deuteronomy 6:16*], **Thou shalt not tempt the Lord thy God**. [*Note that Jesus answers each temptation with a scriptural quote. This is a reminder of the power of the scriptures to safeguard us against successful temptation.*]

8 Again, **the devil taketh him up into an exceeding high mountain, and sheweth him** all the kingdoms of the world, and the glory of them;

JST Matthew 4:8
8 And again, **Jesus was in the Spirit, and it taketh him up into an exceeding high mountain, and showeth him** all the kingdoms of the world and the glory of them.

9 And saith unto him, All these things will I give thee, if thou wilt fall down and worship me [*temptation to yield to materialism and power*].

JST Matthew 4:9
9 **And the devil came unto him again**, and said, All these things will I give unto thee, if thou wilt fall down and worship me.

10 Then saith Jesus unto him, **Get thee hence** [*leave Me*], **Satan**: for it is written [*in Deuteronomy 6:13*], **Thou shalt worship the Lord thy God, and him only shalt thou serve.**

11 **Then the devil leaveth him,** and, behold, angels came and ministered unto him.

The topic now changes to John the Baptist, who has been imprisoned by Herod (see Mark 6:17).

John the Baptist in Prison

12 Now when Jesus had heard that John [*the Baptist*] was cast into prison, he departed into Galilee;

The JST makes some changes in verses 10–12, above, and verse 13, below. Among other things, we learn that the angels spoken of in verse 11 were actually sent by the Savior to minister to John the Baptist, who had been put in prison.

JST Matthew 4:10–12

10 Then said Jesus unto him, Get thee hence, Satan; for it is written, Thou shalt worship the Lord thy God, and him only shalt thou serve. **Then the devil leaveth him.**

11 **And now Jesus knew that John was cast into prison, and he sent angels, and, behold, they came and ministered unto him.**

12 **And Jesus departed into Galilee, and leaving Nazareth, in Zebulun, he came and dwelt in Capernaum,** which is upon the seacoast, in the borders of **Nephthalim,**

13 And leaving Nazareth, he came and dwelt in Capernaum, which is upon the sea [*Sea of Galilee*] coast, in the borders of Zabulon and Nephthalim [*the area where Zebulon and Naphtali, two of the twelve tribes, settled when Joshua brought the children of Israel into the promised land*]:

You will see yet another example, beginning with verse 14, next, of the emphasis by Matthew that Jesus was the fulfillment of Old Testament prophecies concerning the Messiah.

14 **That it might be fulfilled** which was spoken by Esaias [*Isaiah*] the prophet [*in Isaiah 9:1–2*], saying,

15 The land of Zabulon, and the land of Nephthalim, by the way of the sea, beyond Jordan, Galilee of the Gentiles;

16 **The people which sat in darkness** [*spiritual darkness*] **saw great light** [*the Savior and His gospel*]; and to them which sat in the region and shadow of death [*spiritual darkness*] light is sprung up.

17 **From that time Jesus began to preach** [*Jesus now begins His formal ministry*], and to say, **Repent: for the kingdom of heaven is at hand** [*salvation is now being made available to you*].

Watch, now, as the Savior begins calling the men who will later become Apostles. Note how humbly and quickly they left their worldly pursuits in order to follow Him.

Jesus Calls Men Who Will Become Apostles

18 **And Jesus**, walking by the sea of Galilee, **saw two brethren** [*brothers*], Simon called **Peter, and Andrew** his brother, casting a net into the sea: for they were fishers [*fishermen; they earned their living by fishing*].

19 **And** he **saith** unto them, **Follow me, and I will make you fishers of men.**

20 **And they straightway** [*immediately*] **left their nets, and followed him.**

Remember that the JST verse numbers are not always the same as the verse numbers in the Bible. This is because Joseph Smith sometimes added verses left out of the Bible. He also combined them and rearranged them at times.

JST Matthew 4:18–19

18 And he **said** unto them, **I am he of whom it is written by the prophets**; follow me, and I will make you fishers of men.

19 And they, **believing on his words**, left their **net**, and straightway followed him.

From the JST changes given above, we can glean that Peter and Andrew knew the scriptures and the prophecies about the coming Messiah. They recognized what He was saying because they knew the scriptures. This can remind us, among other things, of the great value of reading and studying the scriptures ourselves.

21 And going on from thence [*from that place*], **he saw other two brethren, James** the son of Zebedee, **and John** his brother, in a ship with Zebedee their father, mending their nets; **and he called them.**

22 **And they immediately left the ship and their father, and followed him.**

Luke gives more detail about the calling of these humble fishermen. You may wish to put a cross reference in your scriptures by Matthew 4:18, which sends you to Luke 5:1–11.

23 **And Jesus went about all Galilee, teaching** in their synagogues [*church buildings*], and **preaching** the gospel of the kingdom, and **healing** all manner of [*all kinds of*] sickness and all manner of disease among the people.

The JST adds an important lesson to the end of verse 23, above, about the necessity of believing. (Also, just a reminder that the verse numbering in the JST is sometimes different than in the King James Version of the Bible, which we use as a Church for English speaking areas of the world.)

JST Matthew 4:22
22 And Jesus went about all Galilee teaching in their synagogues, and preaching the gospel of the kingdom; and healing all manner of sickness, and all manner of diseases among the people **which believed on his name**.

In a significant way, the Savior's healing of physical illnesses is symbolic of His power and desire to heal our spiritual illnesses. For example, when He healed the blind, literally, it was symbolic of His ability to heal our spiritual blindness. When He healed the lame, it can be considered symbolic of His ability to heal our inability to walk along the strait and narrow path toward salvation in celestial glory.

24 **And his fame went throughout all Syria: and they brought unto him all sick people** that were taken with [*who had*] divers [*various*] diseases and torments, and those which were possessed with devils, and those which were lunatick, and those that had the palsy; **and he healed them**.

It would have taken a significant amount of time for Jesus to travel and preach and heal throughout "all Galilee" (verse 23, above). Thus, at this point in time, the first year of the Savior's three year formal mortal mission is drawing to a close. He has become tremendously popular by this time and crowds from all over the area are constantly following Him around.

25 And **there followed him great multitudes of people** from Galilee, and from Decapolis, and from Jerusalem, and from Judæa, and from beyond Jordan.

MATTHEW 5

The Sermon on the Mount

At this point in Matthew, we are with the Savior in Galilee and are at the beginning of the second year of His formal three-year ministry. Matthew chapters 5, 6, and 7 are known as "The Sermon on the Mount." Many Christians consider these chapters to contain a series of desirable ethical behaviors, and indeed they do. But they are much more than this. As explained in 3 Nephi as well as in the JST (the Joseph Smith Translation of the Bible), the righteous behaviors stressed here by the Master are among those which enable baptized members of the Church to obtain celestial glory and exaltation. You may wish to make a cross reference in the heading to Matthew, chapter 5, in your Bible, which sends you to 3 Nephi 12:1–2, wherein we are told that the sermon which follows in 3 Nephi (basically, the Sermon on the Mount as given to the Nephites) is addressed to baptized members of the Church and is a series of instructions for continuing after baptism to the point of qualifying for celestial glory.

Likewise, the JST teaches this fact, as you will see when we quote it after Matthew 5:2, below.

We will now begin Matthew, chapter 5, joining the multitude which has gathered on a hillside in Galilee to listen to the Savior.

1 And **seeing the multitudes, he went up into a mountain**: and **when he was set**, his disciples came unto him:

2 And **he opened his mouth, and taught them, saying,**

The JST adds two complete verses to Matthew 5:1–2 which are not found in the Bible.

JST Matthew 5:1–4
1 And **Jesus**, seeing the multitudes, went up into a mountain; and when he was set **down**, his disciples came unto him;

2 And he opened his mouth, and taught them, saying,

3 Blessed are they who shall believe on me; and again, more blessed are they who shall believe on your words, when ye shall testify that ye have seen me and that I am.

4 Yea, blessed are they who shall believe on your words, and come down into the depth of humility, and be baptized in my name; for they shall be visited with fire and the Holy Ghost, and shall receive a remission of their sins [which *leads to celestial glory—see D&C 76:52, which is talking about the celestial kingdom*].

The Beatitudes
(How to continue on to exaltation after baptism)

Verses 3–12 are often referred to as the "Beatitudes," meaning "to be happy or blessed" (see Matthew 5, footnote 3a, in your Bible). Notice that verses 3, 5, 8, 9, 10, and 12 all refer to heaven (celestial glory) in one way or another.

3 **Blessed are the poor in spirit** [*who come unto me. 3 Nephi 12:3*]: **for theirs is the kingdom of heaven** [*celestial glory*].

JST Matthew 5:5
5 Yea, blessed are the poor in spirit, **who come unto me**; for theirs is the kingdom of heaven.

From the JST addition to verse 3, above, we are taught, among other things, that those who recognize that they are "poor in spirit," (in other words, who recognize that they are poor in spirituality) who repent and come to Christ, can obtain celestial glory.

Verse 4, next, can have several meanings, including mourning for the loss of a loved one and being comforted by the Holy Ghost. But in the context of verse 3, above, dealing with repenting of sins, one possible interpretation is that verse 4 is continuing the theme of repenting, and the necessity of being truly sorry for sins committed.

4 Blessed are they that mourn [*for their sins; in other words, those who repent*]: **for they shall be comforted** [*by the Holy Ghost*].

5 Blessed are the meek: for they shall inherit the earth [*this earth will become the celestial kingdom; see D&C 130:8–9*].

6 Blessed are they which do hunger and thirst after righteousness: for they shall be filled [*with the Holy Ghost; 3 Nephi 12:6*].

JST Matthew 5:8
8 **And** blessed are **all** they **that** do hunger and thirst after righteousness; for they shall be filled **with the Holy Ghost**.

Have you noticed that when you truly "hunger and thirst after righteousness" the commandments are a joy rather than a burden?

Verse 7, next, is, in effect, a "formula." Based on how we treat others, the script is basically being written for the day when we appear before God to be judged ourselves.

7 Blessed are the merciful: for they shall obtain mercy.

8 Blessed are the pure in heart: for they shall see God [*including when they are in the celestial kingdom*].

9 Blessed are the peacemakers: for they shall be called the children of God [*another term for those who inherit the celestial kingdom*].

The phrase "children of God," in verse 9, above, can also refer to faithful followers of Christ right here on earth—see Mosiah 5:7, which, of course, is another way of saying that they ultimately attain celestial glory.

10 **Blessed are they which are persecuted for righteousness' sake: for theirs is the kingdom of heaven** [*celestial glory*].

11 **Blessed are ye, when men shall revile you** [*mock you, ridicule you for your righteous beliefs and lifestyle*], **and persecute you, and shall say all manner of evil against you falsely, for my sake** [*because you follow the Savior*].

12 **Rejoice**, and be exceeding glad: **for great is your reward in heaven** [*celestial glory*]: for so persecuted they the prophets which were before you [*who lived before you came to earth*].

JST Matthew 5:14
14 **For ye shall have great joy**, and be exceeding glad; for great **shall be** your reward in heaven; for so persecuted they the prophets which were before you.

13 **Ye are the salt of the earth**: but if the salt have lost his savour [*its ability to improve flavor, symbolic of the good the righteous can do to improve the lives of others*], wherewith shall it be salted [*how will others here on earth be helped*]?

it is thenceforth good for nothing, but to be cast out, and to be trodden under foot of men.

JST Matthew 5:15

15 **Verily, verily, I say unto you, I give unto you to be** the salt of earth; but if the salt shall lose its savor, wherewith shall **the earth** be salted? the salt shall thenceforth be good for nothing, but to be cast out, and to be trodden under foot of men.

14 **Ye are the light of the world.** A city that is set on an hill cannot be hid.

JST Matthew 5:16

16 **Verily, verily, I say unto you, I give unto you to be the** light of the world; a city that is set on a hill cannot be hid.

It is helpful to know that in the Holy Land, cities were built upon the hills, saving valuable land in the valleys for agricultural and pasture use.

The wording in JST Matthew 5:16, above, reminds us of the responsibility of those who are given the blessings of Abraham, Isaac, and Jacob (as often stated in patriarchal blessings) to take the gospel and accompanying blessings of the priesthood to all the world—see Abraham 2:9–11.

15 **Neither do men light a candle, and put it under a bushel** [*a bushel basket*]**, but on a candlestick; and it giveth light unto all** that are in the house.

JST Matthew 5:17

17 **Behold, do men light a candle and put it under a bushel? Nay**, but on a candlestick; and it giveth light to all that are in the house.

16 **Let your light so shine before men, that they may see your good works, and glorify your Father which is in heaven.**

JST Matthew 5:18

18 Therefore, let your light so shine before **this world**, that they may see your good works, and glorify your Father who is in heaven.

The topic now changes, starting with verse 17, next, to the Savior's role with respect to the Law of Moses. Misunderstanding of this issue, or deliberate refusal to accept Jesus as the fulfillment of Old Testament prophecies about the Messiah, led the Jewish religious leaders to demand that the Master be crucified.

17 **Think not that I am come to destroy the law** [*of Moses*]**, or the prophets** [*the Old Testament*]: I am not come to destroy, but to fulfil.

Old Testament Atonement Symbolism

The Savior was accused by the Jews of trying to destroy all the laws and teachings of the Law of Moses. In fact, the rituals, teachings, and animal sacrifices taught by the Law of Moses all were designed by God to point people's minds toward the Savior and His Atonement. A good example of this Old Testament Atonement symbolism is found in Leviticus 14:1–9. We will take the time here to examine these verses and make notes about such symbolism in them. Keep in mind that symbolism allows for many meanings and interpretations. What we present is one possible approach to these verses in Leviticus.

Leviticus 14:1–9

The message and symbolism here is the power of the Atonement of Christ to cleanse and heal people from very serious sins. Leprosy is described in Webster's New World Dictionary, Second College Edition, as follows: "a chronic infectious disease . . . that attacks the skin, flesh, nerves, etc.; it is characterized by nodules, ulcers, white scaly scabs, deformities, and wasting of body parts."

1 And the LORD spake unto Moses, saying,

2 This shall be **the law of the leper** [*the rules for being made clean; symbolic of serious sin and great need for help and cleansing*] **in the day of his cleansing** [*symbolic of the desire to be made spiritually clean and pure*]: **He shall be brought unto the priest** [*authorized servant of God; bishop, stake president, who holds the keys of authority and judgment to act for God*].

3 And **the priest shall go forth out of the camp** [*the person with leprosy did not have fellowship with the Lord's people and was required to live outside the main camp of the children of Israel; the bishop, symbolically, goes out of the way to help sinners who want to repent and return to good standing in the Church*]; and **the priest shall look, and, behold, if the plague of leprosy be healed in the leper** [*the bishop serves as a judge to see if the repentant sinner is ready to return to full membership privileges*];

4 Then shall the priest command to take for him that is to be cleansed [*the person who has repented*] **two birds** [*one represents the Savior during His mortal mission, the other represents the person who has repented*] alive *and* clean, and **cedar wood** [*symbolic of the cross*], and **scarlet** [*associated with mocking Christ before his crucifixion, Mark 15:17*], and **hyssop** [*associated with Christ on the cross, John 19:29*]:

5 And the priest shall command that **one of the birds** [*symbolic of the Savior*] be **killed in an earthen vessel** [*Christ was sent to earth to die for us*] **over running water** [*Christ offers "living water," the gospel of Jesus Christ—John 7:37–38, which cleanses us when we come unto Him*]:

6 **As for the living bird** [*representing the person who has repented*], **he** [*the priest; symbolic of the bishop, stake*

president, one who holds the keys of judging] **shall take it** [*the living bird*], **and the cedar wood**, and the **scarle**t, and the **hyssop** [*all associated with the Atonement*], **and shall dip them and the living bird in the blood of the bird *that was* killed over the running water** [*representing the cleansing power of the Savior's blood which was shed for us*]:

7 And he shall **sprinkle upon him that is to be cleansed from the leprosy** [*symbolically, being cleansed from sin*] **seven times** [*seven is the number which, in Biblical numeric symbolism, represents completeness, perfection*], **and shall pronounce him clean** [*he has been forgiven*], **and shall let the living bird** [*the person who has repented*] **loose into the open field** [*representing the wide open opportunities again available in the kingdom of God for the person who truly repents*].

8 And **he that is to be cleansed shall wash his clothes** [*symbolic of cleaning up your life from sinful ways and pursuits—compare with Isaiah 1:16*], and **shave off all his hair** [*symbolic of becoming like a newborn baby; fresh start*], and **wash himself in water** [*symbolic of baptism*], **that he may be clean** [*cleansed from sin*]: and **after that he shall come into the camp** [*rejoin the Lord's covenant people*], and shall tarry abroad out of his tent seven days.

9 But it shall be on the seventh day, that he shall shave all his hair off his head and his beard and his eyebrows, even all his hair he shall shave off [*symbolic of being "born again"*]: and he shall wash his clothes [*clean up his life—clothing is often used in scripture to symbolize our lives; thus, cleansing our clothing or garments from sin is a way of saying that our lives are made clean through the blood of Christ—see 1 Nephi 12:10*], also he shall wash his flesh in water [*symbolic of baptism*], and he shall be clean [*a simple fact, namely that we can truly be cleansed and healed by the Savior's Atonement*].

Such Atonement symbolism and teaching is found much in the Old Testament. We will now return to Matthew, chapter 5, and continue with verse 18 as the Savior continues to explain how His coming fulfills the Law of Moses.

Jesus Fulfills the Law of Moses

18 For verily I say unto you, Till heaven and earth pass, **one jot or one tittle** [*tiny bit*] **shall in no wise pass from the law** [*Law of Moses*], **till all be fulfilled.**

JST 5:20
20 For verily I say unto you, **Heaven and earth must pass away**, but one jot or one tittle shall in no wise pass from the law, **until** all be fulfilled.

19 **Whosoever** therefore **shall break one of these least commandments, and shall teach men so, he shall be called the least in the kingdom of heaven** [*will not*

receive a great reward on Judgment Day; in other words, will be punished]: **but whosoever shall do and teach them, the same shall be called great in the kingdom of heaven** [*will gain a great reward in the celestial kingdom*].

Remember that the JST verse numbering is often different than the verse numbering in the Bible.

JST Matthew 5:21
21 Whosoever, therefore, shall break one of these least commandments, and shall teach men so **to do**, he shall **in no wise be saved** in the kingdom of heaven; but whosoever shall do and teach **these commandments of the law until it be fulfilled**, the same shall be called great, **and shall be saved in the kingdom of heaven**.

In verse 20, next, the Master points out that the religious leaders of the Jews at the time claim to be living the laws of God, as embodied in the Law of Moses, but are actually wicked men.

20 For I say unto you, That **except your righteousness shall exceed the righteousness of the scribes** [*Jewish religious leaders who explain and interpret the scriptures*] **and Pharisees** [*a particular group of Jews who adhered very strictly to the Law of Moses*], **ye shall in no case enter into the kingdom of heaven.** [*This was a direct blow to the hypocritical scribes and Pharisees*]

The Law of Moses had been given as a "schoolmaster" (see Galatians 3:24) to bring the people to the point where they could accept Christ and His higher gospel. Beginning with verse 21, next, we see the Savior teaching to help the people make this transition.

The Law of Moses Was a "Schoolmaster"

21 Ye have heard that it was said by them of old time, Thou shalt **not kill**; and whosoever shall kill shall be in danger of the judgment [*punishments of God*]:

22 **But I say unto you, That whosoever is angry with his brother** without a cause [*both the JST and 3 Nephi 12:22 omit the phrase "without a cause"*] **shall be in danger of the judgment:** and whosoever shall say to his brother, **Raca** [*a term of derision, such as "You stupid idiot!" See Matthew 5, footnote 22d, in your Bible*], shall be in danger of the council: but **whosoever shall say, Thou fool, shall be in danger of hell fire.** [*In other words, don't put others down, as if you didn't have any imperfections yourself.*]

JST Matthew 5:24
24 But I say unto you that whosoever is angry with his brother, shall be in danger of **his** judgment; and whosoever shall say to his brother, Raca, **or Rabcha,** shall be in danger of the council; and whosoever shall say **to his brother,** Thou fool, shall be in danger of hell fire.

Some people believe that the word "fool" should never be used, because of the warning in verse 22, above. However, it appears from the scriptures that it is the behavior of demeaning people as if we had no faults or imperfections ourselves, that is referred to here, since the Savior uses the word in Matthew 23:17 and Luke 24:25. Also, the Apostle Paul uses it in Romans 1:22 as well as in other places, and Nephi, son of Helaman, uses it in Helaman 9:21.

23 **Therefore if thou bring thy gift to the altar, and there rememberest that thy brother hath ought against thee** [*you have contention with someone close to you*];

JST Matthew 5:25
Therefore, **if ye shall come unto me, or shall desire to come unto me, or** if thou bring thy gift to the altar, and there rememberest that thy brother hath aught against thee,

24 Leave there thy gift before the altar, and go thy way; **first be reconciled to** [*make peace with*] **thy brother**, and then come and offer thy gift.

JST Matthew 5:26
26 Leave **thou** thy gift before the altar, and go thy way **unto thy brother, and** first be reconciled to thy brother, and then come and offer thy gift.

25 **Agree with thine adversary** [*make peace with the person you have contention with*] **quickly**, whiles thou art in the way with him [*while you have the opportunity*]; **lest** at any time the adversary deliver thee to the judge, and the judge deliver thee to the officer, and **thou be cast into prison.** [*If you don't try to make peace, it does a lot of damage to you, yourself.*]

26 Verily I say unto thee, **Thou shalt by no means come out** thence [*from the prison you put yourself into*], **till thou hast paid the uttermost farthing.** [*You pay dearly for holding grudges etc. in terms of lack of peace for yourself.*]

27 **Ye have heard that** it was said by them of old time [*in the Law of Moses*], **Thou shalt not commit adultery:**

28 **But I say unto you, That whosoever looketh on a woman to lust after her hath committed adultery with her already in his heart.**

The JST adds an entire verse here that is not found in the Bible.

JST Matthew 5:31
31 Behold, I give unto you a commandment, that ye suffer none of these things to enter into your heart, for it is better that ye should deny yourselves of these things, wherein ye will take up your cross, than that ye should be cast into hell.

29 And **if thy right eye** [*symbolic*

of specific temptation, bad environment, friends, bad habit, specific sin, etc.] **offend thee** [*puts you in spiritual danger*], **pluck it out, and cast it from thee**: for it is profitable for thee that one of thy members should perish, and not that thy whole body should be cast into hell.

> Body parts in verses 29 and 30 are symbolic of choices, behaviors, associations with friends, etc., which could cause you to lose salvation.

30 And **if thy right hand offend thee, cut it off**, and cast it from thee: for it is profitable for thee that one of thy members should perish, and not that thy whole body should be cast into hell.

> The JST adds a verse here that is not found in the Bible.

JST Matthew 5:34
And now this I speak, a parable concerning your sins; wherefore, cast them from you, that ye may not be hewn down and cast into the fire.

31 **It hath been said, Whosoever shall put away** [*divorce*] **his wife, let him give her a writing of divorcement** [*a legal divorce*]:

32 **But I say unto you, That whosoever shall put away** [*divorce*] **his wife, saving for** [*except for*] **the cause of fornication**, causeth her to commit adultery: and whosoever shall marry her that is divorced committeth adultery. [*See notes, next.*]

Verses 31 and 32 deal with divorce. Clearly, marriage and family involve sacred promises which are very serious. In an ideal society, there would seldom if ever be a divorce. In cases where divorce has taken place, verse 32 can sometimes be misunderstood to teach that anyone who gets a divorce and then remarries is now living in adultery, except where fornication was involved in leading up to the divorce.

Follow the Brethren
A very important principle about following the Brethren, our First Presidency and Quorum of the Twelve, can be taught here. The principle is: The current practice of the Brethren, under the direction of the Lord, constitutes the correct interpretation of the scriptures. Even if you don't completely understand verse 32, you can understand the Brethren. The principle is: What do the Brethren do? Do they ever allow a worthy divorced person to be sealed to another spouse, in the temple? Answer: Yes. Would they allow such a thing if such sealing led automatically to adultery? Answer: No. It would be a mockery of most sacred ordinances. Conclusion: There must be some things we don't understand about verse 32.

With this in mind, we might wonder at the meaning of specific words in verse 32. For instance, the word "fornication" is usually used with respect to sexual sin between unmarried individuals.

Why, then, is it used in this verse where married people are involved? One possibility is that the word "fornication" is often used in the scriptures to mean total disloyalty, breaking covenants, etc. See, for example, Revelation 14:8, 17:2, 19:2.

The word "adultery" is likewise often used in the sense of total disloyalty to God, apostasy, etc. This is mentioned in the Bible Dictionary, in the back of your Latter-day Saint Bible, under the topic "Adultery," where it says: "While adultery is usually spoken of in the individual sense, it is sometimes used to illustrate the apostasy of a nation or a whole people from the ways of the Lord, such as Israel forsaking her God and going after strange gods and strange practices" (Exodus 20:14; Jeremiah 3:7–10; Matthew 5:27–32; Luke 18:11).

33 Again, ye have heard that it hath been said by them of old time, **Thou shalt not forswear thyself** [*commit perjury; make false or insincere promises*], **but shalt perform unto the Lord thine oaths** [*keep your word*]:

34 **But I say unto you, Swear** [*make contracts, promises, etc.*] **not at all**; neither **by heaven**; for it is God's throne:

35 **Nor by the earth**; for it is his footstool: **neither by Jerusalem**; for it is the city of the great King.

36 **Neither** shalt thou swear **by thy head**, because thou canst not make one hair white or black.

It was common among the Jews to make agreements, contracts, and such, so complex that they were easy to get out of, legally. For instance, if one promised "by the full moon" that a chariot for sale was in top shape, and it wasn't, one could later say to the irate customer that the moon wasn't actually a full moon on the day of the contract; rather, was a day or two away from its full phase. Thus, the one giving his word was legally exempt from keeping it.

37 But **let your communication be, Yea, yea; Nay, nay**: for whatsoever is more than these cometh of evil. [*In other words, if you make a promise, keep it.*]

38 Ye have heard that it hath been said, An **eye for an eye, and a tooth for a tooth**:

This could be considered a rather high law, as given in Exodus 21:24–25, Leviticus 24:20, etc. In effect, it meant "Only one eye for an eye, only one tooth for a tooth, only one cow for a cow, only one sheep for a sheep." Many people tended to get revenge, kill off a whole village in retaliation for the death of a sheep or other wrong against themselves. Now, the Savior will give a much higher law, a law requiring even more self-control and forgiving. Keeping such higher laws develops Christ-like qualities in us. These higher laws are designed by the Lord to lead us along the path toward exaltation, as stated in verse 45, "That ye may be the children of (successful followers of) your Father which is in heaven." In other words, this is a vital part of our education toward becoming gods.

39 But I say unto you, That ye resist not evil: but **whosoever shall smite thee on thy right cheek, turn to him the other also.**

40 And **if any man will sue thee at the law, and take away thy coat, let him have thy cloke also.**

41 And **whosoever shall compel thee to go a mile, go with him twain.**

> Note: Often, we tend to look at these verses and think in terms of extremes. For instance, if attacked by a mob, intent on severely harming or killing us, we might be hesitant to give them a head start by "turning the other cheek." In fact, D&C 98:31 seems to give different instructions for situations where life is in immediate danger. If we look at the Savior's words in terms of daily living, we see and experience that exercising self-control on our part, returning good for evil, does much good in our relationships with others.

42 **Give to him that asketh thee, and from him that would borrow of thee turn not thou away.**

43 **Ye have heard** that it hath been said, Thou shalt **love thy neighbour, and hate thine enemy.**

44 **But I say unto you, Love your enemies, bless them** that curse you, **do good to them** that hate you, and **pray for them** which despitefully use you, and persecute you;

45 **That ye may be the children of your Father** which is in heaven [*that you may be received into celestial glory and become gods*]: for he maketh his sun to rise on the evil and on the good, and sendeth rain on the just [*the righteous*] and on the unjust [*the wicked*]. [*He shows love and kindness for all.*]

46 For **if ye love them which love you, what reward have ye?** do not even the publicans the same? [*Publicans were Jews who worked for the Roman government as tax collectors. They were hated by the Jews and were excommunicated when they accepted such employment. See Bible Dictionary, under "Publicans."*]

47 And **if ye salute your brethren only, what do ye more than others?** do not even the publicans so?

> As we become more successful in developing the Christlike qualities given in the above commandments, we draw closer to fulfilling the startling yet wonderful commandment given next in verse 48.

48 **Be ye therefore perfect, even as your Father which is in heaven is perfect.** [*The word "perfect," as*

used here, means complete, finished, fully developed, as stated in Matthew 5:48, footnote b. This denotes our actively pursuing the path leading to exaltation, eventually becoming "fully developed," and thus makes this commandment attainable for us.]

JST Matthew 5:50
Ye are therefore commanded to be perfect, even as your Father **who** is in heaven is perfect.

MATTHEW 6

The Sermon on the Mount (continued)

Proper Motives
1 **Take heed that ye do not your alms** [*righteous deeds; contributions to the poor, etc.*] **before men, to be seen of them** [*your main motive for doing them*]: otherwise ye have no reward of your Father which is in heaven.

2 Therefore **when thou doest thine alms, do not sound a trumpet before thee, as the hypocrites** [*people who want to look righteous but do not want to be righteous*] **do** in the synagogues and in the streets, that they may have glory of men. Verily I say unto you, They have their reward [*the reward of having people think they are righteous*].

3 **But when thou doest alms** [*give offerings for the poor, etc.*], **let not thy left hand know what thy right hand doeth**:

4 **That thine alms may be in secret**: and thy Father which seeth in secret himself shall reward thee openly.

5 And **when thou prayest, thou shalt not be as the hypocrites are**: for they love to pray standing in the synagogues [*church buildings where the Jews worshipped*] and in the corners of the streets, that they may be seen of men. Verily I say unto you, They have their reward.

6 **But thou**, when thou prayest, enter into thy closet, and when thou hast shut thy door, **pray to thy Father which is in secret**; and thy Father which seeth in secret shall reward thee openly.

7 But **when ye pray, use not vain** [*useless, meaningless, ineffective*] **repetitions**, as the heathen [*non-Jews, non-Christians*] do: for they think that they shall be heard for their much speaking.

8 **Be not ye therefore like unto them**: for your Father knoweth what things ye have need of, before ye ask him.

> The Savior now gives us what is commonly known as "The Lord's Prayer." It is a beautiful example of prayer and may be considered to be one example of appropriate prayer, rather than a rigid form to be followed without deviation.

The Lord's Prayer

9 After this manner therefore pray ye: Our Father which art in heaven, Hallowed [*sacred, holy*] **be thy name.**

10 Thy kingdom come. Thy will be done in earth, as it is in heaven.

11 Give us this day our daily bread.

12 And forgive us our debts [*sins, faults, offenses—see Matthew 6:12, footnote a*], **as we forgive our debtors.** [*This is an important formula for our obtaining forgiveness for our own sins.*]

13 And lead us not into temptation [*we should avoid purposely putting ourselves into temptation*], **but deliver us from evil: For thine is the kingdom, and the power, and the glory, for ever. Amen.**

Forgiving Others

14 For if ye forgive men their trespasses [*their sins against you*], **your heavenly Father will also forgive you:**

15 But if ye forgive not men their trespasses, neither will your Father forgive your trespasses. [*This is a very simple guide to obtaining forgiveness ourselves.*]

> The Savior now reminds us again that our internal motives are what really count in pursuing the path to exaltation.

16 Moreover when ye fast, be not, as the hypocrites [*people who want to look righteous but don't want to be righteous*], **of a sad countenance: for they disfigure their faces, that they may appear unto men to fast.** Verily I say unto you, They have their reward [*their reward is that people look at them and think that they are righteous*].

17 But thou, when thou fastest, anoint thine head, and wash thy face;

18 That thou appear not unto men to fast, but unto thy Father which is in secret: and thy Father, which seeth in secret, shall reward thee openly.

> Another reminder about priorities is presented now.

Priorities

19 Lay not up for yourselves treasures upon earth, where moth and rust doth corrupt, and where thieves break through and steal:

20 But lay up for yourselves treasures in heaven, where neither moth nor rust doth corrupt, and where thieves do not break through nor steal:

> In the Book of Mormon, Jacob 2:17–19, we find the following counsel about obtaining personal wealth which can go along with these teachings of the Savior in the Sermon on the Mount:

Jacob 2:17–19

17 Think of your brethren like unto yourselves, and be familiar

with all and free with your substance, that they may be rich like unto you.

18 But before ye seek for riches, seek ye for the kingdom of God.

19 And after ye have obtained a hope in Christ ye shall obtain riches, if ye seek them; and ye will seek them for the intent to do good—to clothe the naked, and to feed the hungry, and to liberate the captive, and administer relief to the sick and the afflicted.

21 For **where your treasure is, there will your heart be also.**

22 **The light of the body is the eye: if therefore thine eye be single** [*Matthew 6:22, footnote b, healthy, sincere, without improper motives*], **thy whole body shall be full of light.** [*What you watch, read, intentionally look at, etc., strongly affects your spiritual well-being.*]

JST Matthew 6:22
22 The light of the body is the eye; if therefore thine eye be single **to the glory of God**, thy whole body shall be full of light.

23 **But if thine eye be evil** [*intentionally takes in evil things*], **thy whole body shall be full of darkness.** If therefore the light that is in thee be darkness, how great is that darkness [*spiritual darkness*]!

24 ¶ **No man can serve two masters**: for either he will hate the one, and love the other; or else he will hold to the one, and despise the other. **Ye cannot serve God and mammon** [*worldly sins, pleasures, desires*].

We learn from the wording in the JST that the Savior now turns from the multitude and addresses JST verses 25–27 and Bible verses 25–34 specifically to His Apostles and some disciples, telling them how they will be taken care of by the Father while on their missions. If you do not understand this, you might mistakenly consider some of the counsel in the Bible verses 25 to 34 to apply to all people. For instance, you might quit working and trust the Lord to take care of you, thinking that if you have sufficient faith, all your needs will be taken care of. Some people and groups have misapplied these verses with sad results.

Instructions to the Apostles

The JST adds three verses here that are not in the Bible.

JST Matthew 6:25–27
25 And, again, I say unto you, Go ye into the world, and care not for the world; for the world will hate you, and will persecute you, and will turn you out of their synagogues.

26 Nevertheless, ye shall go forth from house to house, teaching the people; and I will go before you.

27 And your heavenly Father will provide for you, whatsoever things ye need for food, what ye shall eat; and for raiment, what ye shall wear or put on.

25 **Therefore I say unto you** [*the Savior's Apostles and disciples, who are now being given instructions to take the gospel to all the world*], **Take no thought for your life, what ye shall eat, or what ye shall drink; nor yet for your body, what ye shall put on.** Is not the life more than meat [*food (in our Bible's language, "meat") means food in general, "flesh" means meat as we use the word*], and the body than raiment [*clothing*]?

26 **Behold the fowls of the air**: for they **sow not** [*don't plant crops*], **neither do they reap** [*harvest crops*], nor gather into barns [*nor store grain in barns*]; **yet your heavenly Father feedeth them. Are ye** [*the Savior's Apostles and disciples*] **not much better than they?**

JST Matthew 6:30
30 Wherefore take no thought for these things, but keep my commandments wherewith I have commanded you.

27 Which of you by taking thought can add one cubit [*about 18 inches*] unto his stature [*physical height*]?

28 And why take ye thought for raiment [*clothing*]? **Consider the lilies of the field**, how they grow; they toil not, neither do they spin [*weave cloth*]:

29 And yet I say unto you, That **even Solomon in all his glory was not arrayed** [*dressed*] **like one of these.**

30 Wherefore, **if God so clothe the grass of the field**, which to day is, and to morrow is cast into the oven, **shall he not much more clothe you**, O ye of little faith?

31 **Therefore take no thought** [*don't worry about your physical needs while on missions, etc.*], **saying, What shall we eat?** or, What shall we **drink?** or, **Wherewithal shall we be clothed?**

32 (For after all these things do the Gentiles seek:) for **your heavenly Father knoweth that ye have need of all these things.**

JST Matthew 6:36–37
36 Why is it that ye murmur among yourselves, saying, We cannot obey thy word because ye have not all these things, and seek to excuse yourselves, saying that, After all these things do the Gentiles seek.

37 Behold, I say unto you that your heavenly Father knoweth that ye have need of all these things.

33 But **seek ye first the kingdom of God, and his righteousness**; and all these things shall be added unto you. [*Cross-reference this with Jacob 2:17–19 as given*

between verses 20 and 21 above.]

JST Matthew 6:38
38 **Wherefore, seek not the things of this world** but seek ye first **to build up the kingdom of God, and to establish** his righteousness, and all these things shall be added unto you.

34 **Take therefore no thought for the morrow: for the morrow shall take thought for the things of itself** [*in other words, the Lord will take care of the Apostles' physical needs while they are on missions*]. **Sufficient unto the day is the evil thereof** [*The New International Version of the Bible translates this sentence to read, "Each day has enough trouble of its own." In other words, the Apostles and disciples are being told that they will have enough daily troubles in preaching the gospel, without the distraction of worrying about their physical needs.*]

MATTHEW 7

The Sermon on the Mount (continued)

Judging
1 **Judge not, that ye be not judged** [*judged harshly on Judgment Day, etc.*].

Obviously, there are situations in which we must judge, or we would constantly be victims of foolishness and deceit. The JST adds important clarity to this verse, as follows (JST verse 1 is not in the Bible):

JST Matthew 7:1–2
1 **Now these are the words which Jesus taught his disciples that they should say unto the people.**

2 Judge not **unrighteously**, that ye be not judged; **but judge righteous judgment**.

2 **For with what judgment ye judge, ye shall be judged:** and with what measure ye mete [*give out to others*], it shall be measured to you again.

3 And **why beholdest thou the mote** [*tiny speck; imperfection*] that **is in thy brother's eye, but considerest not the beam** [*large wooden beam; symbolic of shortcomings, faults*] **that is in thine own eye?**

4 **Or how wilt thou say to thy brother, Let me pull out the mote out of thine eye; and, behold, a beam is in thine own eye?**

5 **Thou hypocrite**, first cast out the beam out of thine own eye; and then shalt thou see clearly to cast out the mote out of thy brother's eye.

JST Matthew 7:4–8
4 **And again, ye shall say unto them,** Why **is it that thou** beholdest the mote that is in thy brother's eye, but considerest not the beam that is in thine own eye?

5 Or how wilt thou say to thy brother, Let me pull out the mote out of thine eye; and canst not behold a beam in thine own eye?

6 **And Jesus said unto his disciples, Beholdest thou the scribes, and the Pharisees, and the priests, and the Levites? They teach in their synagogues, but do not observe the law, nor the commandments; and all have gone out of the way, and are under sin.**

7 Go thou and say unto them, Why teach ye men the law and the commandments, when ye yourselves are the children of corruption?

8 **Say unto them, Ye hypocrites,** first cast out the beam out of thine own eye; and then shalt thou see clearly to cast out the mote out of thy brother's eye.

Cautions about Sharing Sacred Things
6 **Give not that which is holy unto the dogs, neither cast ye your pearls before swine** [*be careful with whom you share sacred things*], **lest they trample them under their feet, and turn again and rend you** [*they may turn on you and try to destroy you*].

JST Matthew 7:10–11
10 **And the mysteries of the kingdom ye shall keep within yourselves; for it is not meet to give** that which is holy unto the dogs; neither cast ye your pearls **unto** swine, lest they trample them under their feet.

11 **For the world cannot receive that which ye, yourselves, are not able to bear; wherefore ye shall not give your pearls unto them,** lest they turn again and rend you.

The Lord next invites us to feel free to ask for help from Him.

Ask, Seek, Knock
7 **Ask, and it shall be given you; seek, and ye shall find; knock, and it shall be opened unto you:**

JST Matthew 7:12
12 **Say unto them, Ask of God;** ask, and it shall be given you; seek, and ye shall find; knock, and it shall be opened unto you.

The words "ask," "seek," and "knock" remind us that work is required on our part.

8 For **every one that asketh receiveth; and he that seeketh findeth; and to him that knocketh it shall be opened.**

JST Matthew 7:13–17
13 For every one that asketh, receiveth; and he that seeketh findeth; and **unto** him that knocketh, it shall be opened.

14 **And then said his disciples unto him, They will say unto us, We ourselves are righteous, and need not that any man should teach us. God, we know, heard Moses and some of the prophets; but us he will not hear.**

15 And they will say, We have the law for our salvation, and that is sufficient for us.

16 Then Jesus answered, and said unto his disciples, Thus shall ye say unto them,

17 What man among you, having a son, and he shall be standing out, and shall say, Father, open thy house that I may come in and sup with thee, will not say, Come in, my son; for mine is thine, and thine is mine?

9 Or **what man is there of you, whom if his son ask bread, will he give him a stone?**

10 **Or if he ask a fish, will he give him a serpent?**

11 If ye then, being evil, know how to give good gifts unto your children, **how much more shall your Father which is in heaven give good things to them that ask him?**

The Savior gives what is known as "The Golden Rule" in the next verse.

The Golden Rule

12 Therefore **all things whatsoever ye would that men should do to you, do ye even so to them**: for this is the law and the prophets [*the "law" means the first five books of the Old Testament, and the "prophets" means the inspired writings of Old Testament prophets; the meaning of the phrase "for this is the law and the prophets" is that a major focus of the law and the prophets was to teach us to be good to each other*].

13 **Enter ye in at the strait** [*spelled this way, the word "strait" means narrow, reminding us that this gate has limited access, and requires focus, faith, repentance, baptism, and personal righteousness for entrance*] **gate**: for wide is the gate, and broad is the way [*there are many ways to be wicked*], **that leadeth to destruction**, and many there be which go in thereat:

In the next verse we find the words "strait" and "narrow" used together. This is often referred to as "the strait and narrow path," meaning, in effect, the "narrow and narrowing path." The message here is that the more righteous you become, the more you restrict your behaviors away from evil and toward personal righteousness. The imagery is that the less you wander back and forth toward the outer edges of the path, seeing how close you can get to temptation and evil, the "narrower" your chosen path becomes. There is a bit of a caution here: As you become more righteous, you discover inappropriate personal behaviors which you didn't even notice before. Sometimes, faithful Saints become discouraged and think, "It's no use. I'll never be perfect!" as these so-called "smaller" imperfections come to light. Actually, you might want to rejoice in the fact that your path has become sufficiently "narrow" that you notice these imperfections. Then, go ahead and work on overcoming them.

14 Because **strait is the gate, and narrow is the way, which leadeth unto life** [*eternal life, exaltation*]**, and few there be that find it.**

"By Their Fruits Shall Ye Know Them"
15 **Beware of false prophets** [*anyone who teaches false philosophies, behaviors, etc., by word, example, deed, or whatever*]**, which come to you in sheep's clothing** [*they seem harmless*]**, but inwardly they are ravening** [*very dangerous*] **wolves.**

16 **Ye shall know them by their fruits** [*what they ultimately produce*]. Do men gather grapes of thorns, or figs of thistles [*can you harvest good food from weeds*]?

17 Even so **every good tree bringeth forth good fruit; but a corrupt tree bringeth forth evil fruit.**

"Tree" is used here to symbolize people.

18 **A good tree cannot bring forth evil fruit, neither can a corrupt tree bring forth good fruit.**

19 **Every tree that bringeth not forth good fruit is hewn down, and cast into the fire** [*symbolic of the burning of the wicked at the Second Coming; also symbolic of the final judgment*].

20 Wherefore [*therefore*] **by their fruits ye shall know them.**

The Master now emphasizes again that the gate is "strait" (narrow). In other words, we must keep the commandments in order to enter celestial glory.

21 **Not every one that saith unto me, Lord, Lord, shall enter into the kingdom of heaven** [*celestial glory*]**; but he that doeth the will of my Father which is in heaven.**

The JST adds another verse here that is not found in the Bible.

JST Matthew 7:31
31 For the day soon cometh, that men shall come before me to judgment, to be judged according to their works.

22 **Many will say to me** in that day [*judgment day*]**, Lord, Lord, have we not** prophesied in thy name? and in thy name have cast out devils? and in thy name **done many wonderful works**?

23 And then will I profess unto them, **I never knew you**: depart from me, ye that work iniquity [*commit sin; disobey the laws of God*].

JST Matthew 7:33
And then will I **say, Ye never knew me.**

House Built on the Rock
24 **Therefore whosoever heareth these sayings of mine, and doeth them, I will liken him unto a wise man, which built his house** [*symbolic of his life*] **upon a rock** [*symbolic of Christ, who is the "rock"*

of our salvation. See, for example, Hymn #258]:

25 **And the rain descended, and the floods came, and the winds blew** [*trials and difficulties of life*], **and beat upon that house** [*his life*]; **and it fell not: for it was founded upon a rock** [*Christ*].

House Built on Sand

26 And **every one that heareth these sayings of mine** [*in other words, who is accountable*], **and doeth them not, shall be likened unto a foolish man, which built his house upon the sand** [*worldly ways, priorities etc.*]:

27 **And the rain descended, and the floods came, and the winds blew, and beat upon that house** [*his life*]; **and it fell: and great was the fall of it.**

> Did you notice that the "rain descended, and the floods came, and the winds blew and beat upon" both houses? In other words, trials and tribulation are a part of mortality for the righteous as well as the wicked. The outcome for us is determined by the foundation upon which we build.

28 And it came to pass, **when Jesus had ended these sayings, the people were astonished at his doctrine:**

JST Matthew 7:36
36 And it came to pass when Jesus had ended these sayings **with his disciples**, the people were astonished at his doctrine;

29 **For he taught them as one having authority,** and not as the scribes [*the main teachers and interpreters of the law among the Jews who rose in great opposition to the Savior. See Bible Dictionary, under "Scribes"*].

JST Matthew 7:37
37 For he taught them as one having authority from God, and **not as having authority from the scribes**.

MATTHEW 8

The Master now continues His ministry and teaching in Galilee. His popularity has resulted in large crowds following Him.

1 **When he was come down from the mountain** [*after giving the Sermon on the Mount*], **great multitudes followed him.**

The Healing of a Leper

2 And, behold, **there came a leper** and worshipped him, **saying, Lord, if thou wilt, thou canst make me clean** [*heal me*].

> Leprosy is described in Webster's New World Dictionary, Second College Edition, 1980, as follows: "A chronic infectious disease . . . that attacks the skin, flesh, nerves, etc.; it is characterized by nodules, ulcers, white scaly scabs, deformities, and wasting of body parts."

3 And Jesus put forth his hand, and touched him, saying, I will; be thou clean. And immediately his leprosy was cleansed.

> Every time you read of a physical healing of the sick, performed by the Savior, you can consider it symbolic of His ability to heal us spiritually, through His Atonement. Thus, every healing will remind you of the Master's power to heal you spiritually, through your repentance and His forgiving you. In this case of the healing of a leper, leprosy could be symbolic of very serious sin which can gradually destroy us spiritually.

4 **And Jesus saith unto him** [*the leper who had been healed*], **See thou tell no man** [*keep this spiritual experience very private*]; but go thy way, **shew thyself to the priest, and offer the gift that Moses commanded, for a testimony unto them** [*keep the requirements of the Law of Moses with respect to the cleansing of lepers*].

Healing of the Centurion's Servant

5 And when Jesus was entered into Capernaum, **there came unto him a centurion** [*a Roman soldier in charge of 100 soldiers*], **beseeching him,**

> The Romans were Gentiles, and thus were considered by the Jews to be inferior in the eyes of God, compared to the Jews, who considered themselves to be God's only chosen people. All others, despite their best efforts, were considered to be second class citizens in the Kingdom of God.

6 And **saying, Lord, my servant lieth at home sick of the palsy,** grievously tormented.

7 And **Jesus saith** unto him, **I will come and heal him.**

8 The **centurion** answered and said, Lord, **I am not worthy that thou shouldest come under my roof: but speak** the word only, **and my servant shall be healed.**

9 For I am a man under authority, having soldiers under me: and I say to this man, Go, and he goeth; and to another, Come, and he cometh; and to my servant, Do this, and he doeth it.

10 When **Jesus** heard it, he marvelled, and **said** to them that followed, **Verily I say unto you, I have not found so great faith, no, not in Israel.**

JST Matthew 8:9–10

9 **And when they that followed him, heard this, they marveled.** And **when Jesus heard this**, he **said unto** them that followed,

10 Verily I say unto you, I have not found so great faith; no, not in Israel.

11 And I say unto you, That **many shall come from the east and west** [*many foreigners, including Gentiles*], **and shall sit down with Abraham, and Isaac, and Jacob,**

in the kingdom of heaven [*will be saved along with Abraham, Isaac, and Jacob in celestial glory*].

12 But the children of the kingdom [*those Jews who considered themselves to be elite, above all other people*] **shall be cast out into outer darkness** [*probably not meaning into perdition, with Satan, rather, in the spirit world prison, as explained in Alma 40:11–13*]: there shall be weeping and gnashing of teeth.

13 And Jesus said unto the centurion, Go thy way; and as thou hast believed, so be it done unto thee. And his servant was healed in the selfsame hour.

Peter's Mother-in-law Healed

14 And when Jesus was come into Peter's house, he saw his wife's mother laid, and sick of a fever [*Peter's mother-in-law was very ill*].

15 And he touched her hand, and the fever left her: and she arose, and ministered unto them [*attended to their needs*].

Many Others Healed

16 When the even [*evening*] was come, they brought unto him many that were possessed with devils: and **he** cast out the spirits with his word, and **healed all that were sick** [*symbolic of the Atonement's power to cleanse and heal*]:

17 That it might be fulfilled which was spoken by Esaias [*Isaiah*] **the prophet, saying, Himself** [*Christ*] **took our infirmities, and bare our sicknesses** [*see Isaiah 53:5, Alma 7:12*].

From the above verse and cross-references, we learn that the Savior's Atonement works not only for our sins, but also for our infirmities, meaning our shortcomings, imperfections, etc., as we strive to live righteously.

18 Now **when Jesus saw great multitudes about him, he gave commandment to depart unto the other side** [*of the Sea of Galilee*].

19 And **a certain scribe** [*a leader among the Jews*] **came, and said** unto him, **Master, I will follow thee whithersoever thou goest**.

20 And Jesus saith unto him, The foxes have holes, and the **birds** of the air **have nests; but the Son of man hath not where to lay his head** [*in other words, following the Savior can require difficult personal sacrifices*].

21 And **another of his disciples** [*followers*] **said** unto him, Lord, **suffer me** [*allow me*] **first to go and bury my father**.

22 But Jesus said unto him, Follow me; and let the dead bury their dead [*there is probably more to the story here, but the message is clear, that following the Savior requires real commitment to Him and His instructions*].

"Master, the Tempest Is Raging"

23 And when he was entered into a ship, his disciples followed him.

We now read of the experience during the storm which was the inspiration for Hymn #105, *Master the Tempest Is Raging*. In these next verses we will again be clearly taught that Christ has power over the elements.

24 And, behold, **there arose a great tempest** [*storm*] in the sea, insomuch that the ship was covered with the waves: but he [*the Savior*] was asleep.

One can imagine the stress on the disciples in the ship, being in such danger while the Master slept. Also, we are reminded that the Savior could get very, very tired and weary. In Mosiah 3:7, we read: "And lo, he shall suffer temptations, and pain of body, hunger, thirst, and fatigue, even more than man can suffer, except it be unto death." We might also imagine the dilemma faced by the frightened disciples, knowing how tired the Savior was, in deciding which one of them should attempt to awaken the sleeping Master.

25 **And his disciples** came to him, and **awoke him, saying, Lord, save us: we perish.**

26 And he saith unto them, Why are ye fearful, O ye of little faith? **Then he arose, and rebuked the winds and the sea; and there was a great calm.**

27 But **the men marvelled, saying, What manner of man is this, that even the winds and the sea obey him** [*the disciples are still learning about the Savior and who He really is*]!

Two Possessed by Devils

28 And **when he was come to the other side** into the country of the Gergesenes [*an area on the eastern side of the Sea of Galilee; see* Talmage, *Jesus the Christ, pp. 323–24*], **there met him two possessed with devils**, coming out of the tombs, exceeding fierce, so that no man might pass by that way.

29 And, behold, **they** [*the evil spirits*] cried out, saying, What have we to do with thee, Jesus, thou Son of God? art thou come hither to torment us before the time?

There are many things that can be learned about evil spirits, based on this incident. Apostle Bruce R. McConkie summarized these things as follows:

"(1) That evil spirits, actual beings from Lucifer's realm, gain literal entrance into mortal bodies;

"(2) That they then have such power over those bodies as to control the physical acts performed, even to the framing of the very words spoken by the mouth of those so possessed;

"(3) That persons possessed by evil spirits are subjected to the severest mental and physical sufferings and to the basest sort of degradation—all symbolical of the eternal torment to be imposed upon those who fall under Satan's control in the world to come;

"(4) That devils remember Jesus from pre-existence, recognize him as the One who was then foreordained to be the Redeemer, and know that he came into mortality as the Son of God;

"(5) That the desire to gain bodies is so great among Lucifer's minions as to cause them, not only to steal the mortal tabernacles of men, but to enter the bodies of animals;

"(6) That the devils know their eventual destiny is to be cast out into an eternal hell from whence there is no return;

"(7) That rebellious and worldly people are not converted to the truth by observing miracles; and

"(8) That those cleansed from evil spirits can then be used on the Lord's errand to testify of his grace and goodness so that receptive persons may be led to believe in him." (*Doctrinal New Testament Commentary*, p. 311)

2,000 Swine Drown

30 And **there was a good way off from them** an herd of **many swine** [*pigs*] feeding.

31 So **the devils besought** [*asked*] him, saying, If thou cast us out, suffer [*allow*] **us to go away into the herd of swine.**

32 And **he said unto them, Go.** And when they were come out, **they went into the herd of swine:** and, behold, **the whole herd of swine ran violently down a steep place into the sea**, and perished in the waters.

33 **And they** [*the herdsmen*] **that kept them** [*the pigs*] **fled**, and went their ways into the city, **and told every thing**, and what was befallen to the possessed of the devils.

34 And, behold, **the whole city came out to meet Jesus**: and when they saw him, **they besought** [*asked*] **him that he would depart out of their coasts** [*they asked Jesus to leave*].

It is sad that the people of the city asked the Savior to leave, rather than inviting Him to stay and teach them His gospel. Perhaps they didn't want another economic disaster—Mark 5:13 tells us there were 2,000 swine.

MATTHEW 9

In this chapter, Matthew tells us that the Savior now went to His own home town of Nazareth. Watch how He is treated by those who knew Him as He was growing up.

1 And **he entered into a ship**, and passed over [*went back over to the west side of the Sea of Galilee*], **and came into his own city** [*Nazareth*].

Healing of the Man with Palsy

2 And, behold, **they brought to him a man sick of the palsy**, lying on a bed: and **Jesus seeing their faith said** unto the sick of the palsy; Son, **be of good cheer** [*cheer up*]; **thy sins be forgiven thee.**

3 And, behold, certain of **the scribes** [*religious leaders among the Jews who claimed the right to interpret the scriptures and had great power in the Jewish culture*] **said within themselves, This man blasphemeth** [*is acting with total disrespect for God and sacred things; a crime punishable by death in the Jewish society*].

4 And **Jesus knowing their thoughts** [*the scribes' thoughts*] **said, Wherefore** [*why*] **think ye evil in your hearts?**

5 For **whether** [*which*] **is easier, to say, Thy sins be forgiven thee; or to say, Arise, and walk?** [*Any person could say, "Your sins are forgiven," because there is no immediate proof as to whether or not he speaks with authority. But, if a person says, "Arise and walk," there will be immediate evidence as to whether or not he is a fake.*]

6 **But that ye may know that the Son of man** [*the "Son of "Man of Holiness." Man of Holiness is Heavenly Father's name in Adam's language—see Moses 6:57. In other words, Jesus is telling these scribes that He is the Son of God*] **hath power on earth to forgive sins,** (then saith he to the sick of the palsy,) **Arise, take up thy bed, and go unto thine house.**

7 **And he** [*the man healed of palsy*] **arose, and departed to his house.**

JST Matthew 9:5–7

5 For **is it not easier to say**, Thy sins be forgiven thee, than to say, Arise and walk?

6 But **I said this that ye may know that the Son of Man hath power on earth to forgive sins.**

7 Then **Jesus said** unto the sick of the palsy, Arise, take up thy bed, and go unto thy house.

Did you notice that "man" is capitalized in "Son of Man" in JST verse 6, above, whereas it is not capitalized in verse 6 of the Bible? It should be capitalized, because "Son of Man" means "Son of Heavenly Father," as discussed in the note within Bible verse 6 above.

8 But **when the multitudes saw it, they marvelled, and glorified God**, which had given such power unto men.

9 And **as Jesus passed forth from thence, he saw a man, named Matthew**, sitting at the receipt of custom [*Matthew was a tax collector*]: **and he saith unto him, Follow me. And he arose, and followed him.**

10 And it came to pass, **as Jesus sat at meat** [*eating a meal*] in the house, behold, **many publicans** [*Jews who worked for the Romans*

as tax collectors; see Bible Dictionary, under "Publicans"] **and sinners came and sat down with him and his disciples.**

11 **And when the Pharisees** [*religious leaders among the Jews; see Bible Dictionary, under "Pharisees"*] **saw it, they said unto his disciples, Why eateth your Master with publicans and sinners?**

12 But **when Jesus heard that, he said unto them** [*the Pharisees*], **They that be whole need not a physician, but they that are sick.**

13 But **go ye and learn what that meaneth** [*what it means in the scriptures when it says*], **I will have mercy, and not sacrifice** [*quoting Hosea 6:6; the Pharisees were very strict in living the letter of the Law of Moses, including proper animal sacrifice, but did not often show mercy*]: **for I am not come to call the righteous, but sinners to repentance.**

14 **Then came to him the disciples of John** [*followers of John the Baptist, who was in prison by this time and soon to be beheaded by Herod*], **saying, Why do we and the Pharisees fast oft, but thy disciples fast not?**

15 And **Jesus said unto them, Can the children of the bridechamber mourn, as long as the bridegroom is with them?** but **the days will come, when the bridegroom shall be taken** from them, and then shall they fast.

Understanding a bit of Jewish culture will help with the last verse. Wedding imagery is involved. Jesus is the bridegroom, or groom, as we would say it. Faithful followers are the bride. "Bridechamber" would be the place where the wedding feast is held and, symbolically, would be the land of Israel where the Savior was performing His mortal mission. While the groom and the bride are together, much celebrating and feasting—hearing and understanding the Savior's teachings—would take place. It would not make sense to mourn and fast at this time. But, when the Savior is crucified and taken from them, the "children of the bridechamber," the faithful Saints, will mourn and fast.

The JST adds four verses here.

JST Matthew 9:18–21
18 Then said the Pharisees unto him, Why will ye not receive us with our baptism, seeing we keep the whole law?

19 But Jesus said unto them, Ye keep not the law. If ye had kept the law, ye would have received me, for I am he who gave the law.

20 I receive not you with your baptism, because it profiteth you nothing.

21 For when that which is new is come, the old is ready to be put away.

Next, Jesus will teach that people who are set in their ways do not usually accept new ideas, in this case, the true gospel.

16 **No man putteth** [*sews*] **a piece of new cloth** [*the true gospel*] **unto an old garment** [*piece of clothing; symbolic of people set in their ways with false religions and philosophies*], for that which is put in to fill it up taketh from the garment, and the rent [*rip, tear*] is made worse.

New Wine, Old Bottles

17 **Neither do men put new wine** [*symbolic of the newly restored gospel which the Savior was bringing to the people*] **into old bottles** [*symbolic of people who are steeped in tradition*]: else the bottles break, and the wine runneth out, and the bottles perish: but they put new wine into new bottles, and both are preserved.

Healing of Jairus' Daughter

18 While he spake these things unto them, behold, **there came a certain ruler** [*Luke 8:41 tells us his name was Jairus and that he was a ruler in a synagogue*], and worshipped him, **saying, My daughter is even now dead: but come and lay thy hand upon her, and she shall live.**

19 And **Jesus arose, and followed him, and so did his disciples.**

A Woman Touches Christ's Garment

20 And, behold, **a woman,** which was diseased **with an issue of blood** twelve years [*who had been hemorrhaging for twelve years; see Matthew 9:20, footnote a*], **came behind him, and touched the hem of his garment** [*robe*]:

21 **For she said within herself, If I may but touch his garment, I shall be whole** [*healed*].

22 But **Jesus turned him about, and when he saw her, he said, Daughter, be of good comfort; thy faith hath made thee whole.** And the woman was made whole from that hour.

23 And **when Jesus came into the ruler's house,** and saw the minstrels [*musicians*] and the people [*mourners–often paid*] making a noise,

24 **He said** unto them, Give place: for **the maid** [*the ruler's daughter*] **is not dead, but sleepeth. And they laughed him to scorn** [*ridiculed Jesus*].

25 But when the people were put forth [*had been sent out of the house*], **he went in, and took her by the hand, and the maid arose.**

26 And the fame hereof went abroad into all that land.

Two Blind Men Healed

27 And when Jesus departed thence [*from that place*], **two blind men followed him**, crying, and saying, Thou Son of David [*it was widely taught among the Jews that the Messiah would be a descendant of King David; thus, these blind men were acknowledging Jesus as the promised Messiah*], have mercy on us.

28 And when he was come into the house, the blind men came to him: and **Jesus saith unto them, Believe ye that I am able to do this? They said unto him, Yea, Lord.**

29 **Then touched he their eyes, saying, According to your faith be it unto you.**

30 **And their eyes were opened** [*they were healed*]; and **Jesus straitly charged them** [*strictly instructed them*], **saying, See that no man know it.**

31 **But they**, when they were departed, **spread abroad his fame** in all that country.

Man Possessed with a Devil

32 As they went out, behold, **they brought to him a dumb man** [*one who could not speak*] **possessed with a devil** [*an evil spirit*].

33 And **when the devil was cast out**, the dumb spake: and **the multitudes marvelled, saying, It was never so seen in Israel.**

Jesus Is Accused of Healing by Satan's Power

34 **But the Pharisees** [*religious leaders among the Jews*] **said, He casteth out devils through the prince of the devils** [*the Pharisees, who seem good at missing the point, miss it again, and accuse Jesus of working for Satan and using the devil's power to cast out other devils*].

35 And **Jesus went about all the cities and villages, teaching in their synagogues, and preaching the gospel of the kingdom, and healing every sickness and every disease among the people** [*symbolic of the power of the Atonement to cleanse and heal all our spiritual ills*].

36 But **when he saw the multitudes, he was moved with compassion on them**, because they fainted, and were scattered abroad, as sheep having no shepherd [*they didn't really know where they were going*].

37 **Then saith he unto his disciples, The harvest truly is plenteous** [*there are so many people who need the true gospel*], **but the labourers** [*missionaries, etc.*] **are few;**

38 **Pray ye therefore the Lord of the harvest, that he will send forth labourers into his harvest.**

MATTHEW 10

This chapter contains much specific instruction and training for the newly called Apostles. This could be thought of as the first "Handbook of Instructions" for the Twelve.

The Twelve Apostles Are Called and Instructed

1 **And when he had called unto him his twelve disciples** [*the Twelve Apostles; see heading for Matthew chapter 10 in your Bible*], **he gave them power** against unclean spirits, to cast them out, and to heal all manner of sickness and all manner of disease.

2 Now **the names of the twelve apostles** are these; The first, Simon, who is called **Peter**, and **Andrew** his brother; **James** the son of Zebedee, and **John** his brother;

3 **Philip**, and **Bartholomew**; **Thomas**, and **Matthew** the publican [*tax collector*]; **James** the son of Alphaeus, and Lebbaeus, whose surname [*last name; family name*] was **Thaddaeus**;

4 **Simon** the Canaanite, and **Judas Iscariot**, who also betrayed him.

5 **These twelve Jesus sent forth**, and commanded them, **saying, Go not into the way of the Gentiles, and into any city of the Samaritans enter ye not** [*in other words, don't go to the Gentiles yet*]:

6 But **go rather to the lost sheep of the house of Israel.**

7 And as ye go, **preach, saying, The kingdom of heaven is at hand** [*the saving gospel of Jesus Christ is available to you now*].

8 **Heal the sick, cleanse the lepers, raise the dead, cast out devils: freely ye have received, freely give.**

In verses 9–10, next, Jesus instructs His Apostles not to worry about money, food, or clothing as they go forward ministering and preaching. No doubt such worries could become a big distraction and could take them away from the important work (and education) now awaiting them. They are, instead, to go forward with faith that the Lord will, indeed, provide these essentials.

9 **Provide neither gold, nor silver, nor brass in your purses,**

10 **Nor scrip** [*a bag containing food and provisions*] for your journey, **neither two coats**, neither **shoes**, nor yet **staves**: for the workman is worthy of his meat [*the Lord will take care of you*].

11 And **into whatsoever city or town ye shall enter, enquire who in it is worthy; and there abide** till ye go thence [*stay with a worthy person while there*].

12 And **when ye come into an house, salute it** [*Luke 10:5 helps with this; it says "Into whatsoever house ye enter, first say, Peace be to this house"*].

13 And if the house be worthy, let your peace come upon it: but if it be not worthy, let your peace return to you.

14 And **whosoever shall not receive you**, nor hear your words, when ye depart out of that house or city, **shake off the dust of your feet** [*as a witness that they have had an opportunity to accept the gospel*].

JST Matthew 10:12
12 And whosoever shall not receive you, nor hear your words, when ye depart out of that house, or city, shake off the dust of your feet **for a testimony against them**.

15 Verily I say unto you, **It shall be more tolerable for the land of Sodom and Gomorrha** [*Old Testament cities which were destroyed completely because of wickedness*] **in the day of judgment**, than for that city. [*It is a very serious thing to reject the Lord's servants.*]

16 Behold, **I send you forth as sheep in the midst of wolves: be ye therefore wise as serpents** [*use honest cunning and common sense*], **and harmless as doves** [*be without guile*].

JST Matthew 10:14
14 Behold, I **sent** you forth as sheep in the midst of wolves; be ye therefore **wise servants**, and as harmless as doves.

17 **But beware of men** [*worldly and wicked people*]: for they will deliver you up to the councils [*arrest you and turn you over to local courts*], and they will scourge [*flog, whip*] you in their synagogues;

> Did you notice the irony in the last phrase of verse 17, above? It is that the true Apostles of God will be persecuted in the very buildings—the synagogues—that were built for the purpose of worshipping God. It tells you how far astray the religious leaders of the Jews have gone at this point.
>
> Did you also notice that the Savior refers to the synagogues as "their" synagogues, not "His?"

18 And **ye shall be brought before governors and kings for my sake** [*because of Me and My work*], for a testimony against them and the Gentiles.

19 But when they deliver you up [*arrest you*], **take no thought how or what ye shall speak: for it shall be given you** [*by the Spirit*] **in that same hour what ye shall speak**.

20 For **it is not ye that speak, but the Spirit of your Father which speaketh in you**.

> Verses 19–20, above, can be encouraging to our missionaries as well as to us. This marvelous input from the Spirit often helps us when we are teaching classes in church or answering questions others ask us during conversations about the gospel.

The counsel we are reading here is similar to that given in the Doctrine and Covenants:

D&C 100:5–6
5 Therefore, verily I say unto you, lift up your voices unto this people; speak the thoughts that I shall put into your hearts, and you shall not be confounded before men;

6 For it shall be given you in the very hour, yea, in the very moment, what ye shall say.

21 And **the brother shall deliver up the brother** to death, and **the father the child**: and the **children shall rise up against their parents,** and cause them to be put to death [*you will see much wickedness during your missions*].

22 And **ye shall be hated of all men for my name's sake** [*because of the work you do for me*]: **but he that endureth** [*remains faithful*] **to the end** [*can mean "goal" or "purpose," as well as "to the end of mortal life"*] **shall be saved.**

JST Matthew 10:19
19 And ye shall be hated of all **the world** for my name's sake; but he that endureth to the end shall be saved.

23 But **when they persecute you in this city, flee ye into another**: for verily I say unto you, **Ye shall not have gone over the cities of Israel, till the Son of man** [*Christ, Son of Man of Holiness—see Moses 6:57*] **be come** [*there is so much missionary work to be done that it will not all be finished before the Second Coming—see McConkie, Doctrinal New Testament Commentary, Vol. 1, p. 332*].

24 **The disciple is not above his master, nor the servant above his lord** [*just as the Savior will go through much of persecution, so also His servants will go through much*].

25 **It is enough for the disciple that he be** [*become; see Matthew 10:25, footnote a*] **as his master, and the servant as his lord** [*the reward of faithful servants of the Savior is to be joint heirs with Christ, exalted like He will be*]. If they have called the master of the house [*Christ*] Beelzebub [*another name for the devil*], how much more shall they call them of his household [*if they call Me the devil, don't you think you can expect similar treatment*]?

26 **Fear them not therefore** [*they can't take away your exaltation*]: for there is nothing covered [*evil that is hidden, done in secret*], that shall not be revealed; and hid, that shall not be known [*see 2 Nephi 9:14*].

27 What I tell you in darkness [*private*], that speak ye in light [*in public*]: and what ye hear in the ear [*what I whisper to you*], that preach ye upon the housetops [*preach to everybody*].

28 And **fear not them which kill the body, but are not able to kill**

the soul [*don't fear those who may kill you but can't take your salvation from you*]: **but rather fear** [*respect*] **him** [*God, see McConkie, Doctrinal New Testament Commentary, Vol. 1, p. 334*] **which is able to destroy both soul and body in hell.**

The Savior now reminds the Twelve (and us) that the Father is aware of all things and is always aware of our concerns, needs, and desires.

29 Are not two sparrows sold for a farthing? and **one of them shall not fall on the ground without your Father** [*being aware of it*].

JST Matthew 10:26
26 Are not two sparrows sold for a farthing? And one of them shall not fall on the ground without your Father **knoweth it.**

30 But **the very hairs of your head are all numbered** [*the Father literally knows everything about you and can bless you as needed*].

31 **Fear ye not therefore, ye are of more value than many sparrows.**

Did you notice the important doctrinal teaching concerning the relative value of people compared to other forms of life, given in verse 31, above? Some people in our day are badly misguided when it comes to this simple truth given by the Savior Himself. Some even go so far as to claim that other creations of God are more important than people.

Next, in verses 32–33, we see a simple "if—then" type of statement; namely, "if we acknowledge and follow the Savior and His teachings, then He will be our Advocate before the Father." In other words, His Atonement will work for us. (See also D&C 45:3–5.)

32 **Whosoever therefore shall confess me** [*make covenants with Christ; see Matthew 10:32, footnote a*] **before men, him will I confess** [*acknowledge, accept*] **also before my Father which is in heaven.**

33 **But whosoever shall deny me before men, him will I also deny before my Father which is in heaven.**

In the next verses, the Savior tells the Twelve that, on some occasions, the gospel will divide and separate people from others, even from loved ones sometimes.

34 **Think not that I am come to send peace on earth: I came not to send peace, but a sword.**

35 For **I am come to set** a man **at variance** against [*in opposition to*] his father, and the daughter against her mother, and the daughter in law against her mother in law.

36 And **a man's foes shall be they of his own household** [*will be family members*].

37 **He that loveth father or mother more than me is not worthy of me: and he that loveth son or**

daughter more than me is not worthy of me [*we must follow Christ no matter what the cost*].

38 And **he that taketh not his cross** [*whatever sacrifices are necessary to follow Christ*], **and followeth after me, is not worthy of me.**

39 **He that findeth his life** [*follows priorities less important than the gospel*] **shall lose it** [*shall not gain exaltation*]: **and he that loseth his life for my sake** [*prioritizes on the gospel above all else*] **shall find it** [*will gain exaltation*].

JST Matthew 10:34

34 He **who seeketh to save** his life shall lose it; and he **who** loseth his life for my sake shall find it.

40 **He that receiveth you** [*the Apostles*] **receiveth me, and he that receiveth me receiveth him that sent me** [*Heavenly Father*].

41 **He that receiveth a prophet** [*accepts and sustains Church leaders*] **in the name of a prophet shall receive a prophet's reward** [*exaltation*]; **and he that receiveth a righteous man in the name of a righteous man shall receive a righteous man's reward.**

Finally, the Savior reminds His Apostles and us, as His disciples (followers), that charity and service must accompany the above-mentioned attributes, if we want to attain exaltation.

42 And **whosoever shall give to drink unto one of these little ones a cup of cold water** only in the name of a disciple, verily I say unto you, **he shall in no wise lose his reward.**

MATTHEW 11

In this chapter, Matthew informs us that after Jesus finished instructing His Apostles, He departed from that location and began teaching the gospel in various cities and towns in Galilee. At this time, John the Baptist is still in prison, where he hears about the Savior's teaching and ministering, including the miracles that He has been performing. Consequently, John asks two of his faithful followers to go find Jesus and ask Him whether or not He is the prophesied Messiah (the Anointed One or Son of God).

1 And it came to pass, **when Jesus had made an end of commanding his twelve disciples, he departed thence** [*from that place*] **to teach and to preach in their cities.** [*All of the Apostles were from Galilee, in the north, except Judas Iscariot, who was from Judea, in the south.*]

2 **Now when John** [*John the Baptist, who was in prison at this time*] **had heard** in the prison **the works of Christ, he sent two of his disciples** [*John's faithful followers*],

3 And said unto him [*John the Baptist's disciples asked Jesus*], **Art thou he that should come** [*are you the promised Messiah?*], **or do we look for another?**

Matthew 11

4 **Jesus answered** and said unto them, **Go and shew John again those things which ye do hear and see:**

5 The **blind receive their sight, and the lame walk, the lepers are cleansed, and the deaf hear, the dead are raised up, and the poor have the gospel preached to them.** [*John the Baptist will recognize that this is the prophesied Savior, when he hears what He has been doing.*]

6 And **blessed is he, whosoever shall not be offended in me.**

JST Matthew 11:3–6

3 And said unto him, Art thou he **of whom it is written in the prophets** [*in other words, in Old Testament prophecies*] that he should come, or do we look for another?

4 Jesus answered and said unto them, Go and **tell** John again of those things which ye do hear and see;

5 **How** the blind receive their sight, and the lame walk, **and** the lepers are cleansed, and the deaf hear, **and** the dead are raised up, and the poor have the gospel preached **unto** them.

6 And blessed is **John, and** whosoever shall not be offended in me.

7 **And as they** [*John's disciples*] **departed, Jesus began to say unto the multitudes concerning John** [*the Baptist*]**, What went ye out into the wilderness to see? A reed shaken with the wind** [*a man who was timid and afraid of opposition*]?

8 But **what went ye out for to see? A man clothed in soft raiment** [*luxurious clothing; in other words, a man pampered by easy living*]? behold, they that wear soft clothing are in kings' houses.

JST Matthew 11:7–8

7 And as they departed, Jesus began to say unto the multitudes concerning John, What went ye out into the wilderness to see? **Was it** a reed shaken with the wind? **And they answered him, No.**

8 **And he said**, But what went ye out for to see? **Was it** a man clothed in soft raiment? Behold they that wear soft raiment are in king's houses.

9 But **what went ye out for to see? A prophet? yea, I say unto you, and more than a prophet.** [*Jesus has tender feelings for John the Baptist, and bears witness of John's divine calling and mission.*]

10 **For this is he, of whom it is written** [*prophesied*]**, Behold, I send my messenger** [*John the Baptist*] **before thy** [*the Savior*] **face, which shall prepare thy way before thee** [*John is the messenger sent by God to prepare the way before Me*].

11 Verily **I say unto you, Among them that are born of women**

there hath not risen a greater than John the Baptist: notwithstanding he [*Christ*] that is least in the kingdom of heaven [Who is considered by you Jews to *be the least*] is greater than he [*John the Baptist*].

> The clarifying notes in verse 11, above, come from Joseph Smith's teachings. He tells us that John the Baptist is the greatest prophet born of woman, but that He, Christ, who is considered by the Jews to be the least in the kingdom, is above John the Baptist. See *Teachings of the Prophet Joseph Smith*, pp. 275–76.

12 And **from the days of John the Baptist until now the kingdom of heaven suffereth violence**, and the violent take it by force [*violent people have done much to harm the work of the Lord; see Matthew 11:12, footnote a*].

13 For **all the prophets** [*the Old Testament prophets*] **and the law** [*the first five books of the Old Testament*] **prophesied until John** [*prophesied of things leading up to this time*].

14 **And if ye will receive it** [*accept My word about who John is*]**, this is Elias, which was for to come** [*John is the "Elias," the preparer-of-the-way, who was prophesied to prepare the way for the Savior*].

JST Matthew 11:13–15

13 **But the days will come, when the violent shall have no power;** for all the prophets and the law prophesied **that it should be thus** until John.

14 **Yea, as many as have prophesied have foretold of these days.**

15 And if ye will receive it, **verily** [*truly*]**, he was the Elias, who** was for to come **and prepare all things**.

15 **He that hath ears to hear, let him hear** [*he who is in tune with the Spirit will understand what has just been taught*].

16 But **whereunto shall I liken this generation** [*unto what shall I compare the present generation of people*]? It is like unto children sitting in the markets, and calling unto their fellows,

17 And saying, We have piped unto you, and ye have not danced; we have mourned unto you, and ye have not lamented [*the current generation is ignoring the messengers of God*].

> Jesus now tells them that the righteous can never win in the eyes of the wicked. No matter what the righteous do, the wicked still criticize them.

18 For **John** [*the Baptist*] **came neither eating nor drinking** [*came abstaining from wine and certain foods, according to the strict rules of the Nazarite code for living a life dedicated to God; see Numbers 6*]**, and they say, He hath a devil.**

19 **The Son of man** [*the Son of*

God, Christ; see Moses 6:57] **came eating and drinking, and they say, Behold a man gluttonous, and a winebibber** [*a drunkard; see Matthew 11:19, footnote a*]**, a friend of publicans** [*tax collectors*] **and sinners**. But wisdom is justified of her children [*actions, deeds; in other words, wise people will see through this constant criticism*].

Apostle Bruce R. McConkie helps us understand verses 16–19, above, as follows:

"What illustration can I choose to show how petty, peevish, and insincere are you unbelieving Jews? You are like fickle children playing games; when you hold a mock wedding, your playmates refuse to dance; when you change the game to a funeral procession, your playmates refuse to mourn. In like manner you are only playing at religion. As cross and capricious children you reject John because he came with the strictness of the Nazarites, and ye reject me because I display the warm human demeanor that makes for pleasant social intercourse." (McConkie, *Doctrinal New Testament Commentary*, Bookcraft, 1977, Volume 1, page 263)

As mentioned previously, some people ask whether or not the Savior ever did come right out and say that He is the Son of God. As you study Matthew, Mark, Luke, and John, you will find many instances, including at the beginning of verse 19 above, wherein He openly told people that He was the Son of God, the promised Messiah.

Next, in verses 20–26, the Savior scolds the inhabitants of several cities in which He had done many miracles already, because they refuse to repent.

20 **Then began he to upbraid** [*scold*] the cities wherein most of his mighty works were done, **because they repented not:**

21 **Woe unto** thee, **Chorazin** [*about 5 miles north of Capernaum, just northwest of the Sea of Galilee*]! woe unto thee, **Bethsaida** [*on the northeast coast of the Sea of Galilee*]! for if the mighty works, which were done in you, had been done in **Tyre and Sidon** [*major seacoast cities north of Galilee, occupied primarily by Gentiles*], they would have repented long ago in sackcloth and ashes [*"sackcloth and ashes" means in deep humility and mourning for their sins*].

22 But I say unto you, It shall be more tolerable for Tyre and Sidon at the day of judgment, than for you [*because you have the true gospel available and they don't, yet*].

23 And thou, **Capernaum** [*on the northeast coast of the Sea of Galilee*], which art exalted unto heaven [*full of pride*], shalt be brought down to hell: for if the mighty works, which have been done in thee, had been done in Sodom, it would have remained until this day [*would not have been destroyed*].

24 But I say unto you, That it shall be more tolerable for the land of Sodom in the day of judgment, than for thee.

> That Jesus kept in close touch with the Father is evidenced again in these next verses.

25 At that time Jesus answered and said, **I thank thee, O Father,** Lord of heaven and earth, **because thou hast hid these things from the wise and prudent** [*from those who think they are "wise and prudent"; in other words, "old bottles" who won't accept "new wine"*], **and hast revealed them unto babes** [*humble people who are willing to accept truth*].

26 Even so [*let it be so*], Father: **for so it seemed good in thy sight.**

27 **All things are delivered unto me of my Father:** and no man knoweth the Son, but the Father; neither knoweth any man the Father, save the Son, and he to whomsoever the Son will reveal him.

> The Joseph Smith Translation (JST), helps us understand verses 25–27, above:

JST Matthew 11:27–28
27 And at that time, **there came a voice out of heaven, and Jesus answered** and said, I thank thee, O Father, Lord of heaven and earth, because thou hast hid these things from the wise and prudent, and hast revealed them unto babes. Even so, Father, for so it seemed good in thy sight!

28 All things are delivered unto me of my Father; and no man knoweth the Son, but the Father; neither knoweth any man the Father, save the Son, and **they to whom** the Son will reveal **himself; they shall see the Father also**.

28 **Come unto me, all ye that labour and are heavy laden, and I will give you rest.**

29 **Take my yoke upon you** [*make covenants through which you, in effect, bind yourselves to the Savior; in other words, get into the harness with the Savior and do the work with Him*], **and learn of me;** for **I am meek and lowly in heart** [*I am humble and love to help you*]: **and ye shall find rest unto your souls.**

30 For **my yoke is easy, and my burden is light.**

> Above, the Savior teaches us, in effect, that the path to exaltation is actually the easiest way as well as the happiest. The "burdens" one carries as a devout follower of the Master are nothing compared to the burdens of guilt and shame carried by those who choose wickedness as a lifestyle.

MATTHEW 12

This chapter begins with a lesson about the proper use of the Sabbath day. The pharisees were quick to

Matthew 12

criticize the Savior for doing good on the Sabbath. Remember that, over the centuries, the Jewish religious leaders, including those who interpreted the laws and principles given by Moses, had added many tiny, detailed rules and laws, which were detrimental to their worship of God. And the Pharisees tended to watch carefully for infractions of these added rules. For example, under these "forced and unnatural interpretation[s]" of the law of Moses, a Sabbath day's journey was limited to 2,000 cubits. (See Bible Dictionary under "Sabbath Day's Journey.") A cubit is about 18 inches. Watch, now, as these Pharisees attempt to interrupt the Savior's work and how He gives them a lesson on proper understanding of the purposes of the Sabbath.

1 At that time **Jesus went on the sabbath day through the corn** [*grain; perhaps wheat fields*]; **and his disciples were an hungred** [*hungry*]**, and began to pluck the ears of corn** [*the heads of the grain*]**, and to eat.**

2 **But when the Pharisees** [*religious leaders among the Jews*] **saw it, they said** unto him, Behold, **thy disciples do that which is not lawful to do upon the sabbath day.**

3 **But he said unto them, Have ye not read what David did** [*David, the one who killed Goliath and later became king*]**, when he was an hungred, and they that were with him**;

4 How **he entered into the house of God, and did eat the shewbread** [*holy bread used for worship services; see 1 Samuel 21:6*], **which was not lawful for him to eat, neither for them which were with him, but only for the priests?**

5 **Or have ye not read in the law, how that on the sabbath days the priests in the temple profane the sabbath** [*break some of the sabbath rules*]**, and are blameless?** [*In other words, you allow it in some cases, but won't allow My disciples to do it; you are hypocrites.*]

JST Matthew 12:4
4 Or have ye not read in the law, how that on the Sabbath days the priests in the temple profane the Sabbath, and **ye say they are blameless**?

Did you notice in the JST, verse 4, above, that Jesus emphasized that the Pharisees are the ones who say the priests in the temple are blameless ("ye say they are blameless"), implying that they have added false interpretations to the laws given by Moses. This should make them feel a bit uncomfortable.

Next, in verse 6, Jesus again says who He is. In so many words, He basically tells them that He is the Son of God, that they are seeing Him with their own eyes, and that He is thus greater than the Temple because

He is the Old Testament Jehovah to whom the temple was dedicated long ago!

6 But I say unto you, That in this place is one greater than the temple [*implying that you are looking at One greater than the temple; I am here among you and I am greater than the temple because I am the Son of God*].

Next, in verse 7, the Savior continues, teaching these influential Jewish leaders the real purpose of the Sabbath, using an Old Testament scripture they should be familiar with. The point of Hosea 6:6 is that being merciful on the Sabbath is more important than the letter of the law.

7 But if ye had known what this [*the following quote*] **meaneth, I will have mercy, and not sacrifice** [*quoting Hosea 6:6*]**, ye would not have condemned the guiltless.** [*In other words, if you are not merciful to others, all the animal sacrifices you can possibly do are of no value and are just empty ritual. You claim to know the scriptures, but you sure don't understand Hosea 6:6! By the way, "the Guiltless" can be another name for Christ, since He was perfect.*]

The Pharisees and scribes are becoming quite alarmed and puzzled that Jesus knows the Old Testament so well. Of course, as the God of the Old Testament, Christ was the very one who gave the revelations to the Old Testament prophets.

8 For the Son of man [*Son of Man, Son of God; Jesus; see Moses 6:57*] **is Lord even of the sabbath day.** [*I am the one who gave the commandments concerning the Sabbath day.*]

9 And when he was departed thence, **he went into their synagogue:**

Next, in verse 10, the Jewish religious leaders, whose position and status among the people is being threatened by Jesus, especially in their eyes, attempt again to trap Him for violating the Sabbath according to their rules and multitude of laws for living strictly.

10 And, behold, **there was a man which had his hand withered.** And **they** [*the Jewish religious leaders*] **asked him** [*Jesus*], saying, **Is it lawful to heal on the sabbath days?** that they might accuse him [*that they might trap Him and have grounds to have Him arrested*].

As you will see, the Savior is a master at answering questions with questions.

11 **And he said** unto them, **What man shall there be among you, that shall have one sheep, and if it fall into a pit on the sabbath day, will he not lay hold on it, and lift it out?** [*In other words, you yourselves rescue your animals that fall into trouble on the Sabbath.*]

12 **How much then is a man**

better than a sheep [*how much more important are people than sheep*]? **Wherefore** [*therefore*] **it is lawful to do well on the sabbath days.** [*This direct statement, that it is proper to do good on the Sabbath, must have been quite frustrating to these hypocritical religious leaders. To them, it appeared that Jesus was speaking as if He had authority to make the laws, which, of course, He did and does.*]

13 **Then saith he to the man** [*with the withered hand*], **Stretch forth thine hand.** And he stretched it forth; **and it was restored** whole, like as the other. [*The man's hand was healed, and it was done on the Sabbath in front of many witnesses, in defiance of these Pharisees, these Jewish religious leaders.*]

14 **Then the Pharisees went out, and held a council against him, how they might destroy him.**

15 **But when Jesus knew it** [*that they were plotting against Him*], **he withdrew himself from thence: and great multitudes followed him, and he healed them all** [*symbolic of His power to heal all of us spiritually*];

16 **And charged them that they should not make him known** [*He asked them to keep these personal experiences with Him private*]:

JST Matthew 12:13
13 But **Jesus knew when they took counsel, and** he withdrew himself from thence; and great multitudes followed him, and **he healed their** sick, and charged them that they should not make him known;

The next four verses remind us that one of Matthew's main purposes in writing his gospel was to prove that Jesus fulfilled Old Testament prophecies foretelling the coming of the Savior. In other words, Matthew wanted his audience to realize that Jesus was the promised Messiah, indeed the Son of God.

17 **That it might be fulfilled which was spoken by Esaias the prophet**, saying [*quoting Isaiah 42:1–3 in a bit different wording than in the Old Testament*],

Isaiah's Description of the Messiah

18 **Behold my servant** [*Christ*], **whom I have chosen; my beloved, in whom my soul is well pleased: I will put my spirit upon him**, and **he shall shew judgment** [*justice, fairness, mercy*] **to the Gentiles.**

19 **He shall not strive** [*fight, quarrel*], **nor cry** [*shout*]; **neither shall any man hear his voice** [*shouting*] in the streets [*Jesus will be peaceable and low key as He goes forth in His mortal ministry*].

20 **A bruised** [*bent, crushed*] **reed shall he not break** [*He is not here to hurt the weak, the already bruised and broken, but rather to heal and help them and save them if they will*], and **smoking flax** [*literally a tiny spark smoldering in*

a bit of fire starter material] **shall he not quench** [*symbolic of the fact that Christ will come to gently fan the tiny spark of spirituality into a flame, rather than snuffing it out*], **till he send forth judgment unto victory.**

21 And **in his name shall the Gentiles trust** [*a prophecy that many Gentiles will take Christ's name upon them, reminding us that the gospel of Jesus Christ is for all people*].

22 **Then was brought unto him one possessed with a devil, blind, and dumb** [*could not talk*]**: and he healed him**, insomuch that the blind and dumb both spake and saw.

23 And **all the people were amazed**, and said, **Is not this the son of David** [*isn't this the Messiah who was prophesied to come*]?

You can tell, as you read verse 24, next, that the Pharisees are getting desperate by now. They are prime examples of the fact that wickedness does not promote rational thought. The absurdity of their accusation is exposed by Jesus as He responds.

24 **But when the Pharisees** [*corrupt Jewish religious leaders*] **heard it, they said, This fellow doth not cast out devils, but by Beelzebub the prince of the devils** [*Satan—see Bible Dictionary under "Beelzebub;" in other words, the Pharisees claim that Jesus is in partnership with the devil and uses that power to cast out devils*].

25 **And Jesus knew their thoughts, and said** unto them, **Every kingdom divided against itself is brought to desolation** [*destruction*]**; and every city or house divided against itself shall not stand** [*will not survive*]**:**

26 And **if Satan cast out Satan** [*his own underling devils or even himself*]**, he is divided against himself; how shall then his kingdom stand** [*in other words, how can a kingdom divided against itself survive*]?

27 **And if I by Beelzebub** [*using Satan's power*] **cast out devils, by whom do your children cast them out?** therefore they shall be your judges.

28 **But if I cast out devils by the Spirit of God, then the kingdom of God is come unto you** [*then you know that I am the promised Messiah and am making the kingdom of God available to you*].

From JST Matthew 12:22–23, we learn the correct interpretation of verses 27–28, above:

JST Matthew 12:22–23

22 And if I by Beelzebub cast out devils, by whom do your children cast **out devils**? Therefore they shall be your judges.

23 But if I cast out devils by the Spirit of God, then the kingdom of God is come unto you. **For they** [*righteous priesthood holders among the Jews at this time*] **also cast out devils by the Spirit of God, for unto them is**

Matthew 12

given power over devils, that they may cast them out.

From the words in italics, in JST, verse 23, above, we find that there were righteous Jews, obviously baptized and faithful, who were enabled by the Spirit of God to cast out evil spirits. See McConkie, *Doctrinal New Testament Commentary*, Vol. 1, p. 269.

29 **Or else how can one enter into a strong man's house, and spoil** [*plunder, rob*] **his goods, except he first bind the strong man?** and then he will spoil his house [*in other words, one must truly have the power of God over devils in order to cast them out*].

30 **He that is not with me is against me**; and he that gathereth not with me [*does not join with Me*] scattereth abroad [*works against Me*].

Next, starting with verse 31, the Savior explains what it means to deny the Holy Ghost.

31 Wherefore I say unto you, **All manner of sin and blasphemy** [*evil speaking of and evil behavior toward sacred things including God, prophets, scriptures, the sacrament, temples, and so forth*] **shall be forgiven unto men: but the blasphemy against the Holy Ghost** [*denying the Holy Ghost*] **shall not be forgiven unto men.**

JST Matthew 12:26
26 Wherefore I say unto you, All manner of sin and blasphemy shall be forgiven unto men **who receive me and repent**; but the blasphemy against the Holy Ghost, **it** shall not be forgiven unto men.

Simply put, denying the Holy Ghost means knowing full well, by the power of the Holy Ghost, that God exists, that the Church is true, etc., then going completely against that sure knowledge, trying to destroy the Church and knowledge of God. In other words, it means becoming like Satan, thinking like he does and acting like he does. See D&C 76:31–35. See also Teachings of the Prophet Joseph Smith, p. 358.

32 **And whosoever speaketh a word against the Son of man** [*Jesus; Son of Man of Holiness (Heavenly Father); see Moses 6:57*], **it shall be forgiven him: but whosoever speaketh against the Holy Ghost** [*denies the Holy Ghost—see note between verses 31 and 32, above*], **it shall not be forgiven him, neither in this world, neither in the world to come.**

33 **Either make the tree good, and his fruit good; or else make the tree corrupt, and his fruit corrupt: for the tree is known by his fruit.** [*Jesus is rebuking the Pharisees for accusing Him of being evil, yet doing good in the healing of the man in verse 22. He is saying to them to make up their minds. Anybody knows that a bad tree doesn't give good fruit. If I'm doing good, I must be a "good tree."*]

34 **O generation of vipers** [*you*

poisonous serpents! This is exactly what John the Baptist called them in Matthew 3:7], **how can ye, being evil, speak good things? for out of the abundance of the heart the mouth speaketh** [*you can tell what is in your hearts by the evil which comes out of your mouths*].

35 **A good man** out of the good treasure of the heart **bringeth forth good things**: and **an evil man** out of the evil treasure **bringeth forth evil things**.

36 But I say unto you, That **every idle word** [*gossip; unjust criticism, profanity, etc.; see Matthew 12:36, footnotes b and c*] **that men shall speak, they shall give account thereof in the day of judgment.**

37 **For by thy words** [*righteous words*] **thou shalt be justified** [*saved; approved by God on judgment day*], **and by thy words** [*idle words, wicked words*] **thou shalt be condemned** [*stopped; cast out on judgment day*].

38 **Then certain of the scribes** [*lawyers, interpreters of the religious laws among the Jews, usually Pharisees*] **and of the Pharisees** [*religious leaders among the Jews*] **answered** [*responded*], saying, Master, **we would see a sign from thee** [*show us a sign which proves that you are the Messiah, the Christ*].

39 **But he answered** and said unto them, **An evil and adulterous generation seeketh after a sign**; and there shall no sign be given to it, but the sign of the prophet Jonas [*if I do give you a sign, it will not be what you want, as in the case when Jonah was swallowed by the whale*]:

40 **For as Jonas** [*Jonah*] **was three days and three nights in the whale's belly; so shall the Son of man** [*I, Christ; Son of man means Son of Man of Holiness, meaning Son of Heavenly Father—see Moses 6:57*] **be three days and three nights in the heart of the earth** [*I will be in the tomb for three days and three nights*].

41 **The men of Nineveh** [*the city to which Jonah finally went and preached*] **shall rise in judgment with this generation, and shall condemn it: because they repented at the preaching of Jonas** [*Jonah*]; and, behold, **a greater than Jonas is here** [*the Son of God is here among you right now; you have no excuse for not repenting!*].

These scribes and Pharisees do indeed understand that Jesus is telling them that He is the Son of God. The Joseph Smith Translation of the Bible confirms this fact in JST Mark 3:21 as follows: "And then came certain men unto him, accusing him, saying, **Why do ye receive sinners, seeing thou makest thyself the Son of God.**"

42 **The queen of the south** [*the Queen of Sheba, a famous queen who visited Solomon in Jerusalem to learn from him; see 1 Kings 10:1–13*] **shall rise up in the judgment**

with this generation, and shall condemn it: for she came from the uttermost parts of the earth to hear the wisdom of Solomon; and, behold** [*JST "ye behold," i.e., before your very eyes you are seeing*], **a greater than Solomon is here** [*the Son of God is greater than Solomon and you are seeing Me here right now, and if you had the good sense the Queen of Sheba had, you would be seeking My help rather than trying to destroy Me*].

Verses 43–45, which come next, may seem at first to be a bit out of context with the foregoing verses. However, in verses 31 and 32 above, the Savior taught that the sin against the Holy Ghost cannot be forgiven in this life or in the life to come. In verses 33 to 42, Jesus is warning these wicked Jewish leaders that they are seeing things which make them very accountable! They are actually seeing the Savior in person, among them, witnessing His teachings and miracles, perhaps feeling His Spirit, and yet denying it and seeking to destroy Him and His work among them. Next, in verses 43–45, He continues His warning to them by giving an illustration which explains why a person who denies the Holy Ghost can't be forgiven. In effect, a person who denies the Holy Ghost (see the note between verses 31 and 32 above) deliberately invites Satan and his evil spirits into his soul (his "house"), and associates with them until he thinks, acts, and becomes like Satan, having absolutely no desire to be anything other than like the devil, and thus qualifies to live with him and his evil spirits forever as a son of perdition. We will use the JST for clarification, after we have read verses 43–45.

43 **When the unclean spirit is gone out of a man**, he walketh through dry places, seeking rest, and findeth none.

44 Then he saith, I will return into my house from whence I came out; and when he is come, he findeth it empty, swept, and garnished.

45 Then goeth he, and taketh with himself seven other spirits more wicked than himself, and they enter in and dwell there: and the last state of that man is worse than the first. **Even so shall it be also unto this wicked generation**.

As stated previously, we will now use the JST to help us understand verses 43–45, above.

JST Matthew 12:37–39

37 [*Note: This verse is entirely missing from the Bible.*] **Then came some of the scribes** [*Jewish religious leaders who specialized in interpreting the gospel doctrines and laws*] **and said unto him, Master, it is written that, Every sin shall be forgiven; but ye say, Whosoever speaketh against the Holy Ghost shall not be forgiven. And they asked him, saying, How can these things be?** [*In other words, what you,*

Jesus, are teaching contradicts our traditional written doctrines.]

38 And he said unto them, When the unclean spirit is gone out of a man, he [*the evil spirit*] walketh through dry places, seeking rest and findeth none; but when a man speaketh against the Holy Ghost [*when a man reverts back to his evil ways to the extent of denying the Holy Ghost*], then he [*the evil spirit*] saith, I will return into my house [*the man in whom the evil spirit used to reside*] from whence I came out; and when he [*the evil spirit*] is come, he findeth **him** [*the man in whom the evil spirit formerly resided*] empty, swept and garnished [*was cleansed from sin, with a sure testimony given him by the Holy Ghost, but who is now speaking against that testimony*]; **for the good spirit** [*the Holy Ghost*] **leaveth him unto himself**.

39 Then goeth **the evil spirit**, and taketh with himself seven other spirits more wicked than himself; and they enter in and dwell there [*with the man who has denied the Holy Ghost*]; and the last **end** of that man is worse than the first [*the man is worse off now than he was before he gained a sure testimony from the Holy Ghost*]. Even so shall it be also unto this wicked generation.

Elder Bruce R. McConkie helps us understand the above three verses as follows: "JST Matthew 12:37–39. Having already taught that every sin shall be forgiven except the sin against the Holy Ghost, Jesus now illustrates why. In effect he says: 'If you gain a perfect knowledge of me and my mission, it must come by revelation from the Holy Ghost; that Holy Spirit must speak to the spirit within you; and then you shall know, nothing doubting. But to receive this knowledge and revelation, you must cleanse and perfect your own soul; that is, your house must be clean, swept, and garnished. Then if you deny me by speaking against the Holy Ghost who gave you your revelation of the truth, that is if you come out in open rebellion against the perfect light you have received, the Holy Ghost will depart, leaving you to yourself. Your house will now be available for other tenancy, and so the evil spirits and influences you had once conquered will return to plague you. Having completely lost the preserving power of the Spirit, you will then be worse off than if you had never received the truth; and many in this generation shall be so condemned'" (*Doctrinal New Testament Commentary*, Volume 1, p. 276).

46 While he yet talked to the people, behold, his mother and his brethren [*Mary and some family members; see Matthew 12, footnote 46a, in your Bible*] **stood without** [*outside*]**, desiring to speak with him.**

47 Then one [*someone*] **said unto him, Behold** [*look*]**, thy mother and thy brethren stand without, desiring to speak with thee.**

48 But he answered and said unto him that told him, **Who is my mother? and who are my brethren?** [*In other words, who is my family? This is a teaching moment.*]

49 **And he stretched forth his hand toward his disciples** [*followers*]**, and said, Behold** [*you are seeing*] **my mother and my brethren!** [*My followers are my family. This answers the question Christ posed in verse 48. See also the answer in verse 50.*]

50 **For whosoever shall do the will of my Father which is in heaven, the same is my brother, and sister, and mother.**

JST Matthew 12:44
44 **And he gave them charge concerning her** [*asked them to take good care of His mother*], **saying, I go my way, for my Father hath sent me.** And whosoever shall do the will of my Father which is in heaven, the same is my brother, and sister, and mother.

MATTHEW 13

The Savior will now use a number of parables to illustrate his teachings. A parable is a story which is used to teach us about real life situations. The Prophet Joseph Smith said: "I have a key by which I understand the scriptures. I enquire, what was the question which drew out the answer, or caused Jesus to utter the parable?" (*Teachings of the Prophet Joseph Smith*, pp. 276–77).

1 **THE same day went Jesus out of the house, and sat by the sea side.**

2 And **great multitudes** were **gathered** together unto him, **so that he went into a ship, and sat**; and the whole multitude stood on the shore.

The Parable of the Sower

3 **And he spake many things unto them in parables**, saying, Behold, a **sower** [*a farmer*] went forth to sow [*plant seeds*];

4 And when he sowed, **some seeds fell by the way side**, and the fowls [*birds*] came and devoured them up:

5 **Some fell upon stony places** [*where there was only a thin layer of soil; see Matthew 13:5a*], where they had not much earth: and forthwith [*immediately*] they sprung up, because they had no deepness of earth:

JST Matthew 13:5
5 Some fell upon stony places, where they had not much earth; and forthwith they sprung up; **and when the sun was up, they were scorched**, because they had no deepness of earth; **and because they had no root, they withered away**.

6 And when the sun was up, they were scorched; and because they had no root, they withered away [*dried up and died*].

7 And **some fell among thorns**; and the thorns sprung up, and choked them:

8 But **other fell into good ground**, and brought forth fruit, some an hundredfold, [*a hundred times what was planted*] some sixtyfold, some thirtyfold. [*The Savior will explain this parable starting with verse 18.*]

9 **Who hath ears to hear, let him hear** [*those who are spiritually mature and in tune will understand what I am saying*].

Why Parables?

10 And **the disciples came, and said** unto him, **Why speakest thou unto them** [*the multitude in verse 2*] **in parables?**

11 He answered and said unto them, Because it is given unto you to know the mysteries of the kingdom of heaven [*because you want to learn spiritual things*], but to them it is not given [*because they do not want to learn of spiritual things*].

12 For **whosoever hath, to him shall be given**, and he shall have more abundance: **but whosoever hath not, from him shall be taken away even that he hath.**

The JST helps us understand verse 12, above:

JST Matthew 13:10–11
10 For whosoever **receiveth**, to him shall be given, and he shall have more abundance;

11. **But whosoever continueth not to receive**, from him shall be taken away even that he hath.

The point is that these people don't want to understand the Savior's teachings.

13 **Therefore** [*for this reason*] **speak I to them in parables**: because they seeing see not; and hearing they hear not, neither do they understand [*they don't understand spiritual things because they don't want to*].

14 And **in them is fulfilled the prophecy of Esaias** [*Isaiah, in Isaiah 6:9–10*], which saith, By hearing ye shall hear, and shall not understand; and seeing ye shall see, and shall not perceive [*you are so far gone spiritually that you can't understand spiritual things*]:

15 For **this people's heart is waxed gross** [*they have become hard-hearted*], **and their ears are dull of hearing** [*they are deaf to spiritual things*], **and their eyes they have closed** [*they don't want to see spiritual things*]; lest at any time they should see with their eyes, and hear with their ears, and should understand with their heart, and should be converted, and I should heal them [*these people are intentionally avoiding conversion to Christ*].

16 **But blessed are your eyes, for they see: and your ears, for they hear.**

JST Matthew 13:15

15 But blessed are your eyes, for they see; and your ears, for they hear. **And blessed are you because these things are come unto you, that you might understand them.**

17 For verily I say unto you, That **many prophets and righteous men have desired to see those things which ye see, and have not seen them; and to hear those things which ye hear, and have not heard them.**

JST Matthew 13:15

16 And verily, I say unto you, **many righteous prophets** have desired to see **these days** which you see, and have not seen them; and to hear that which **you** hear, and have not heard.

Explanation of Parable of the Sower

18 **Hear ye therefore the parable of the sower** [*I will explain the parable of the sower to you*].

19 **When any one heareth the word of the kingdom** [*the gospel*], **and understandeth it not**, then cometh **the wicked one**, and **catcheth away that which was sown in his heart.** This is he which received seed by the way side.

20 But he that received the seed into **stony places**, the same is he that heareth the word, and anon [*immediately*] with joy receiveth it;

21 Yet hath he not root in himself, but dureth [*lasts*] for a while: for when tribulation or persecution ariseth because of the word [*the gospel*], by and by he is offended.

22 He also that received seed **among the thorns** is he that heareth the word [*the gospel*]; and the care of this world, and the deceitfulness of riches, choke the word, and he becometh unfruitful [*does not remain faithful*].

23 But he that received seed into the **good ground** is he that heareth the word, and understandeth it; [*this takes work and commitment*] which also beareth fruit [*lives the gospel, remains faithful*], and bringeth forth, some an hundredfold, some sixty, some thirty.

Just a reminder, as previously mentioned, the verse numbers in the JST are often different than in the Bible. Among other things, this is because Joseph Smith sometimes added verses that were missing entirely from the Bible. Also, he often combined verses into one verse.

JST Matthew 13:19–21

19 But he that received the seed into **stony places**, the same is he that heareth the word and **readily** with joy receiveth it, yet **he hath** not root in himself, **and endureth but** for a while; for when tribulation or persecution ariseth because of the word, by and by he is offended.

20 He also who received seed

among the thorns, is he that heareth the word; and the care of this world and the deceitfulness of riches, choke the word, and he becometh unfruitful.

21 But he that received seed into the good ground, is he that heareth the word and understandeth **and endureth**; which also beareth fruit, and bringeth forth, some an hundredfold, some sixty, **and** some thirty.

Joseph Smith gives additional insights about the parable of the sower as follows: "But listen to the explanation of the parable of the Sower: 'When any one heareth the word of the Kingdom, and understandeth it not, then cometh the wicked one, and catcheth away that which was sown in his heart.' Now mark the expression—that which was sown in his heart. This is he which receiveth seed by the way side. Men who have no principle of righteousness in themselves, and whose hearts are full of iniquity, and have no desire for the principles of truth, do not understand the word of truth when they hear it. The devil taketh away the word of truth out of their hearts, because there is no desire for righteousness in them. 'But he that receiveth seed in stony places, the same is he that heareth the word, and anon, with joy receiveth it; yet hath he not root in himself, but dureth for a while; for when tribulation or persecution ariseth because of the word, by and by, he is offended. He also that receiveth

seed among the thorns, is he that heareth the word; and the care of this world, and the deceitfulness of riches choke the word, and he becometh unfruitful. But he that received seed into the good ground, is he that heareth the word, and understandeth it, which also beareth fruit, and bringeth forth, some an hundred fold, some sixty, some thirty.' Thus the Savior Himself explains unto His disciples the parable which He put forth, and left no mystery or darkness upon the minds of those who firmly believe on His words.

"We draw the conclusion, then, that the very reason why the multitude, or the world, as they were designated by the Savior, did not receive an explanation upon His parables, was because of unbelief. To you, He says [*speaking to His disciples*] it is given to know the mysteries of the Kingdom of God. And why? Because of the faith and confidence they had in Him" (*Teachings of the Prophet Joseph Smith*, 1976, p. 97).

The Parable of the Wheat and the Tares

24 **Another parable** put he forth unto them, saying, **The kingdom of heaven is likened unto a man** [*Christ, see verse 37*] **which sowed** [*planted*] **good seed** [*faithful followers of Christ, verse 38*] **in his field** [*the world, verse 38*]:

25 But while men slept, his enemy [*the devil, verse 39*] came and sowed tares [*wicked people, verse*

38] among the wheat [*faithful members of the Church*], and went his way.

> A tare is a weed that looks very much like wheat while it is growing. Often, the roots of tares intertwine with the roots of the wheat while both are growing.

26 But when the blade was sprung up, and brought forth fruit, then appeared the tares also.

27 **So the servants of the householder** [*Christ*] **came and said** unto him, Sir, didst not thou sow [*plant*] good seed [*wheat*] in thy field? from whence then hath it tares [*where did the tares come from*]?

28 He said unto them, An enemy hath done this. The servants said unto him, **Wilt thou then that we go and gather them up** [*would you like us to weed out the tares now*]?

29 But **he said, Nay** [*No*]; lest [*for fear that*] while ye gather up the tares, ye root up also the wheat with them.

> There are several messages here in verse 29. One message might be that there are usually insincere and unrighteous members living among the righteous members of wards and branches of the Church. Another message could be that each of us has some "tares" in our own lives and personalities and we would be wise to weed them out as our righteous attributes mature. Jacob 5:65–66 in the Book of Mormon reminds us that as the good in people grows, the bad can gradually be cleared away. See also D&C 86:6.

30 **Let both grow together until the harvest**: and in the time of harvest I will say to the reapers [*harvesters, angels in verse 39*], Gather ye together **first the tares** [*the wicked*], and bind them in bundles to burn them: but gather the wheat [*the righteous*] into my barn [*my kingdom*].

JST 13:29

29 Let both grow together until the harvest, and in the time of harvest, I will say to the reapers, Gather ye together **first the wheat into my barn; and the tares are bound in bundles to be burned**.

Both the JST, quoted above, and D&C 86:7 change the order of the harvesting. The correct order is that the wheat is gathered first. Then the tares are gathered, bundled [*bound*] and burned. This is significant doctrinally, because it indicates that, at the Second Coming, the righteous will be taken up first [*D&C 88:96*], and then the wicked will be burned.

The Parable of the Mustard Seed

31 **Another parable** put he forth unto them, saying, **The kingdom of heaven is like to a grain of mustard seed**, which a man took, and sowed [*planted*] in his field:

32 Which indeed is **the least** [*smallest*] **of all seeds**: but when it is grown, it is the greatest among herbs, and becometh a tree, so that the birds of the air [*symbolic of angels; see* Teachings of the Prophet Joseph Smith, *p. 159*] come and lodge in the branches thereof.

> Joseph Smith explained this parable: "And again, another parable put He forth unto them, having an allusion to the Kingdom that should be set up, just previous to or at the time of the harvest, which reads as follows—'The Kingdom of Heaven is like a grain of mustard seed, which a man took and sowed in his field: which indeed is the least of all seeds: but, when it is grown, it is the greatest among herbs, and becometh a tree, so that the birds of the air come and lodge in the branches thereof.' Now we can discover plainly that this figure is given to represent the Church as it shall come forth in the last days." For more of the Prophet's explanation, see *Teachings of the Prophet Joseph Smith*, pp. 98–99 and p. 159.

The Parable of the Leaven

33 **Another parable** spake he unto them; **The kingdom of heaven is like unto leaven** [*an ingredient such as yeast, which, when mixed into bread dough, causes the whole loaf to rise*], which a woman took, and hid in three measures of meal, till the whole was leavened.

> Joseph Smith explained that the "leaven" in verse 33 could be compared to the true Church as it expands into the whole world. See *Teachings of the Prophet Joseph Smith*, pp. 100–102.

34 **All these things spake Jesus unto the multitude in parables; and without a parable spake he not unto them:**

35 **That it might be fulfilled which was spoken by the prophet**, saying [*in Psalm 78:2*], I will open my mouth in parables; I will utter things which have been kept secret from the foundation of the world.

Parable of Wheat and Tares Explained

36 Then Jesus sent the multitude away, and went into the house: and **his disciples came unto him, saying, Declare** [*explain*] **unto us the parable of the tares of the field** [*verses 24–30*].

37 **He answered** and said unto them, **He that soweth** [*plants*] **the good seed** [*wheat; righteousness*] **is the Son of man** [*Christ; Son of Man of Holiness—see Moses 6:57*];

38 The **field is the world; the good seed are the children of the kingdom** [*faithful members of the Church; the righteous*]; but the **tares are the children of the wicked one** [*the wicked*];

JST Matthew 13:37
37 The field is the world; the good seed are the children of the kingdom; but the tares are the children of the wicked.

Matthew 13

39 The enemy that sowed them is the devil; the **harvest is the end of the world**; and the **reapers** [*harvesters*] **are the angels.**

40 As therefore **the tares** [*the wicked*] **are gathered and burned in the fire; so shall it be in the end of this world** [*the wicked will be burned at the Second Coming*].

> People often ask how the wicked will be burned. D&C 5:19 along with 2 Nephi 12:10, 19, and 21, explain that the wicked will be burned by the brightness of the glory of Christ, who comes in full glory at the time of the Second Coming.

41 The Son of man [*Christ*] **shall send forth his angels, and they shall gather out of his kingdom all things that offend, and them which do iniquity** [*the wicked*];

42 And shall cast them into a furnace of fire: there shall be wailing [*bitter crying*] and gnashing [*grinding*] of teeth.

JST Matthew 13:39–44

39 The harvest is the end of the world, **or the destruction of the wicked**.

40 The reapers are the angels, **or the messengers sent of heaven**.

41 As, therefore, the tares are gathered and burned in the fire, so shall it be in the end of this world, **or the destruction of the wicked**.

42 For in that day, before the Son of man shall come, he shall send forth his angels **and messengers of heaven**.

43 And they shall gather out of his kingdom all things that offend, and them which do iniquity, and **shall cast them out among the wicked**; and there shall be wailing and gnashing of teeth.

44 For the world shall be burned with fire.

43 **Then shall the righteous shine forth as the sun** [*symbolic of celestial glory for the righteous Saints*] **in the kingdom of their Father.** Who hath ears to hear, let him hear [*those who are spiritually in tune will understand what I am saying*].

The Parable of the Treasure Hid in a Field

44 Again [*another parable*], **the kingdom of heaven is like unto treasure hid in a field**; the which when a man hath found, he hideth, and for joy thereof goeth and selleth all that he hath, and buyeth that field. [*It is worth the sacrificing of whatever it takes to join the Church and to remain faithful.*]

JST Matthew 13:46

46 Again, the kingdom of heaven is like unto a treasure hid in a field. **And when a man hath found a treasure which is hid, he secureth it, and, straightway,** for joy thereof, goeth and selleth all that he hath, and buyeth that field.

The Parable of the Pearl of Great Price

45 Again, **the kingdom of heaven is like unto a merchant man, seeking goodly pearls:**

46 Who, when he had found one **pearl of great price** [*this is where the name for the Pearl of Great Price comes from*], went and sold all that he had, and bought it.

The Parable of the Net

47 Again, **the kingdom of heaven is like unto a net,** that was cast into the sea, and gathered of every kind [*the missionary work of the Church gathers all kinds of converts, some sincere who remain faithful, others who are not sincere etc.*]: [*This verse also exemplifies that all people will get a chance to join with the Savior's church, whether in this life or in the spirit world.*]

48 Which, when it was full, they drew to shore, and sat down, and gathered the good into vessels, but cast the bad away.

49 **So shall it be at the end of the world** [*the end of the wicked*]**: the angels shall come forth, and sever the wicked from among the just** [*the righteous*],

50 And **shall cast them** [*the wicked*] **into the furnace of fire** [*the burning of the wicked*]**:** there shall be wailing [*bitter anguish*] and gnashing [*grinding*] of teeth [*symbolic of the extreme suffering of the wicked as they face the consequences of their evil choices*].

JST Matthew 13:50, next, is not found in the Bible. Notice that it defines "the world" in verse 49, above, as "the wicked."

JST Matthew 13:50–51
50 **And the world is the children of the wicked.**

51 The angels shall come forth, and sever the wicked from among the just, **and shall cast them out into the world to be burned**. There shall be wailing and gnashing of teeth.

51 **Jesus saith unto them, Have ye understood all these things?** They say unto him, Yea, Lord.

The Parable of the Scribe Who Is Converted to the Gospel of Christ

52 **Then said he unto them,** Therefore **every scribe** [*scribes were Jewish leaders, generally enemies of Christ; who determined the correct interpretation of the scriptures among their people*] **which is instructed unto the kingdom of heaven** [*who has been converted and become a true follower of Christ, see Matthew 13:52, footnote b*] **is like unto a man that is an householder, which bringeth forth** [*throws out*] **out of his treasure things new and old** [*has to throw out many previously held beliefs; see Sperry Symposium, 1983, p. 101*].

53 And it came to pass, that when

Jesus had **finished these parables,** he departed thence.

The Master Goes to Nazareth

54 And **when he was come into his own country** [*Nazareth*], **he taught them in their synagogue,** insomuch that they were astonished, and said, Whence hath this man this wisdom, and these mighty works?

> From verses 55–56, next, we learn that Joseph and Mary had at least seven children after Mary had Jesus.

55 **Is not this the carpenter's son? is not his mother called Mary?** and his **brethren** [*brothers (actually half-brothers)*], **James,** and **Joses,** and **Simon,** and **Judas**?

56 And his **sisters** [*the Greek form of this word means three or more*], are they not all with us? **Whence then hath this man all these things?** [*Isn't this Joseph and Mary's son? We know the family. How could he possibly be saying and doing such incredible things?*]

57 **And they were offended in him** [*embarrassed and offended by what He was doing*]. **But Jesus said** unto them, **A prophet is not without honour, save** [*except*] **in his own country, and in his own house.**

58 And **he did not many mighty works there because of their unbelief.**

MATTHEW 14

In verse 1, we meet "Herod the tetrarch," also known as Herod Antipas. His father, Herod the Great, was the ruler who commanded that all the infant boys at Bethlehem be killed, in an unsuccessful attempt to kill the Christ child. See Matthew 2:16. Upon the death of Herod the Great, his kingdom was divided among three of his sons, Antipas, Archelaus, and Philip. Herod the tetrarch was the wicked ruler who ordered the death of John the Baptist (about two years ago at this point in Matthew). Herod has heard of Jesus' fame and is afraid that John the Baptist has come back from the dead.

1 AT that time **Herod the tetrarch heard of the fame of Jesus,**

2 **And said unto his servants, This is John the Baptist;** he is risen from the dead [*he has come back from the dead*]; and therefore mighty works do shew forth themselves in him.

Herod Beheads John the Baptist

3 **For Herod had laid hold on** [*arrested*] **John,** and bound him, **and put him in prison** for Herodias' sake [*because of Herodias*], his brother Philip's wife. [*Herod was an immoral man who had married Herodias, his own brother's wife*].

4 **For John** [*the Baptist*] **said unto him** [*Herod the tetrarch*]**, It is not lawful for thee to have her** [*it was wrong for you to marry her*]**.**

5 And **when he** [*Herod*] **would have put him** [*John the Baptist*] **to death, he feared the multitude,** because they counted him as a prophet [*considered John the Baptist to be a prophet*].

6 **But when Herod's birthday was kept** [*when they were celebrating Herod's birthday*]**, the daughter of Herodias** [*the daughter's name was Salome; see Bible Dictionary, under "Salome"*] **danced** before them, **and pleased Herod.**

7 **Whereupon he promised with an oath to give her whatsoever she would ask.**

8 **And she, being before instructed of her mother** [*Salome had already been given instructions by her mother, Herodias, who hated John the Baptist, because he boldly told her she was living in adultery with Herod*]**, said, Give me** here **John Baptist's head in a charger** [*on a platter*]**.**

9 And **the king was sorry: nevertheless** for the oath's sake, and them which sat with him at meat [*because he had promised to her in front of all those at his birthday party*]**, he commanded it** [*John's head*] **to be given her.**

10 And **he sent, and beheaded John in the prison.**

11 And **his head was brought in a charger, and given to the damsel: and she brought it to her mother.**

12 And his disciples [*John's followers*] came, and took up the body, and buried it, and went and told Jesus.

13 **When Jesus heard of it, he departed thence** [*from there*] by ship into a desert place apart: **and** when **the people** had heard thereof, they **followed him** on foot out of the cities.

14 And **Jesus** went forth, and **saw a great multitude,** and was moved with compassion toward them, and he **healed their sick.**

The Feeding of the 5,000

15 And **when it was evening, his disciples came to him, saying,** This is a desert place, and the time is now past; **send the multitude away, that they may** go into the villages, and **buy themselves victuals** [*food*]**.**

Watch now as the Master startles his disciples.

16 But **Jesus said** unto them, **They need not depart; give ye them to eat.**

17 And **they say** unto him, **We have here but five loaves** [*of bread*]**,** and **two fishes.**

18 **He said, Bring them** hither **to me.**

19 And **he commanded the multitude to sit down on the grass,** and

took the five **loaves**, and the two **fishes**, and looking up to heaven, he **blessed**, and **brake**, and **gave the loaves to his disciples, and the disciples to the multitude.**

20 And **they did all eat, and were filled**: and they took up of the fragments that **remained twelve baskets full**.

21 And they that had eaten were about **five thousand men, beside** [*in addition to*] **women and children**.

22 And **straightway Jesus constrained** [*instructed*] **his disciples to get into a ship, and to go before him** [*go on ahead of him*] unto the other side [*of the Sea of Galilee*], while he sent the multitudes away.

23 And when he had sent the multitudes away, **he went up into a mountain** apart [*to be alone*] **to pray**: and when the evening was come, he was there alone.

24 **But the ship was** now in the midst of the sea, **tossed with waves**: for the wind was contrary.

Jesus Walks on the Water

25 And in the fourth watch of the night [*between 3 AM and 6 AM*] **Jesus went unto them, walking on the sea.**

26 And **when the disciples saw him walking on the sea, they were troubled, saying, It is a spirit**; and they cried out for fear [*they thought they were seeing a ghost*].

27 But straightway [*immediately*] **Jesus spake** unto them, saying, **Be of good cheer; it is I; be not afraid.**

Peter Walks on Water

28 And **Peter answered** him and said, Lord, if it be thou, **bid** [*ask*] **me come unto thee on the water.**

29 And he said, Come. And when **Peter** was come down out of the ship, he **walked on the water**, to go to Jesus.

30 **But** when he saw the wind boisterous, **he was afraid; and beginning to sink**, he cried, saying, Lord, save me.

31 And **immediately Jesus stretched forth his hand, and caught him**, and said unto him, O thou of little faith, wherefore [*why*] didst thou doubt?

32 And when they were come into the ship, **the wind ceased.** [*Once again, the Lord's power over the elements is displayed.*]

33 **Then they** that were in the ship came and **worshipped him**, saying, Of a truth [*for sure*] **thou art the Son of God.**

34 And when they were gone over [*had crossed the Sea of Galilee from east to west*], **they came into the land of Gennesaret** [*on the northwestern side of the Sea of Galilee*].

35 And when the men of that place had knowledge of him [*found out*

that it was Jesus], **they** sent out [*spread the word*] into all that country round about, and **brought unto him all that were diseased**;

36 And besought him that they might only touch the hem of his garment: and **as many as touched were made perfectly whole**.

> As mentioned previously, every physical healing performed by the Savior is symbolic of his power and desire to heal us spiritually, in order that we might come to the Father through him and his Atonement.

MATTHEW 15

The Savior began his three-year formal ministry at age 30. With the feeding of the 5000 in chapter 14, we begin our study of the last year of his earthly ministry. By this time, the hatred and jealousy of the Jewish religious leaders had grown to the point that they sent a delegation all the way from Jerusalem to Galilee to challenge Jesus and to try to discredit him. The scribes were the most powerful and influential of these leaders. Perhaps it would be helpful for you at this point to read a description of the scribes, given by a noted Biblical scholar. Here it is:

A Description of the Scribes

"A foremost actor in a New Testament list of characters is the scribe. He is found in Jerusalem, Judea, and Galilee and is not new to Jewish life and culture. Present in Babylon and also throughout the dispersion, he is spokesman of the people; he is the sage; he is the man of wisdom, the rabbi who received his ordination by the laying on of hands. His ability to cross-examine and to question is renowned. Dignified and important, he is an aristocrat among the common people who have no knowledge of the law. Regarding faith and religious practice, he is the authority and the last word; and as a teacher of the law, as a judge in ecclesiastical courts, is the learned one who must be respected, whose judgment is infallible. He travels in the company of the Pharisees, yet he is not necessarily a member of this religious party. He holds office and has status. His worth is beyond that of all the common folk and they must honor him, for he is to be praised by God and by angels in heaven. In fact, so revered are his words regarding law and practice that he must be believed though his statements contradict all common sense, or though he pronounce that the sun does not shine at noon day when in fact it is visible to the naked eye" [Edersheim, *The Life and Times of Jesus the Messiah*, 1:93–94].

1 **THEN came to Jesus scribes and Pharisees** [*wicked religious leaders of the Jews*], **which were of** Jerusalem, **saying,**

2 **Why do thy disciples transgress** [*sin against*] **the tradition**

of the elders [*laws and customs established over the centuries by Jewish religious leaders, not necessarily the laws of God*]? for **they wash not their hands when they eat bread** [*before eating a meal*].

> The Savior will now teach a major lesson, namely, that inner cleanliness of mind and spirit are far more important than outward physical cleanliness.

3 But **he answered** and said unto them, **Why do ye also transgress the commandment of God by your tradition?**

4 For **God commanded**, saying, **Honour thy father and mother**: and, **He that curseth father or mother, let him die the death** [*the penalty, given by Moses for failing to honor one's father and mother, was death*].

> In verses 5 and 6, next, the Savior challenges the wicked practice among the Jews, approved by the Jewish leaders, of dedicating their material means to God, thus gaining freedom from the obligation to take care of their aging parents. This practice was called "Corban" in Mark 7:11. You can read about it in the Bible Dictionary under "Corban." By formally saying, "It is a gift" (verse 5, next), they could basically keep their wealth for themselves.

5 **But ye say, Whosoever shall say to his father or his mother, It is a gift**, by whatsoever thou [*the parents*] **mightest be profited** [*helped*] **by me;**

JST Matthew 15:5
5 But ye say, Whosoever shall say **to father or mother**, By whatsoever thou mightest be profited by me, **it is a gift from me and honor not his father or mother, it is well.**

6 **And honour not his father or his mother, he shall be free** [*of obligation to help his parents*]. **Thus have ye made the commandment of God** [*"Honor thy father and thy mother," Exodus 20:12*] **of none effect by your tradition**.

7 **Ye hypocrites** [*people who want to appear righteous but like to do evil*], **well did Esaias** [*Isaiah*] **prophesy of you, saying** [*in Isaiah 29:13*],

8 **This people draweth nigh unto me with their mouth, and honoureth me with their lips; but their heart is far from me**.

9 But **in vain** [*it does no good*] **they do worship me** [*as illustrated in Isaiah 1:13*], **teaching for doctrines the commandments of men.**

10 And **he called the multitude, and said** unto them, **Hear, and understand:**

11 **Not that which goeth into the mouth defileth a man; but that which cometh out of the mouth, this defileth a man.**

> This is a stinging rebuke to these wicked Jewish leaders. Jesus

said to the multitudes who have gathered around, within the hearing of the scribes and Pharisees, that the teachings which come out of the scribes' mouths and influence daily behavior of their people defile, or, in other words, make filthy. His disciples are worried about his bold scolding of the scribes as evidenced by the next verse.

12 **Then came his disciples, and said** unto him, **Knowest thou that the Pharisees were offended**, after they heard this saying?

13 **But he answered and said, Every plant, which my heavenly Father hath not planted, shall be rooted up** [*everything which is false will ultimately be exposed and destroyed*].

14 **Let them alone: they be blind leaders of the blind. And if the blind lead the blind, both shall fall into the ditch** [*ultimately, they and their followers will get caught up with*].

15 **Then answered** [*responded*] **Peter and said unto him, Declare unto us this parable** [*please explain what You just said*].

16 And **Jesus said, Are ye also yet without understanding?**

17 **Do not ye yet understand, that whatsoever entereth in at the mouth goeth into the belly, and is cast out into the draught** [*eventually leaves the body*]?

18 **But those things which pro-** **ceed out of the mouth come forth from the heart**; and they defile [*make filthy*] the man [*because they show what he is really like*].

19 **For out of the heart proceed evil thoughts**, murders, adulteries, fornications, thefts, false witness, blasphemies:

20 **These are the things which defile a man**: but to eat with unwashen hands [*verse 2*] defileth not a man.

21 **Then Jesus went** thence, and departed **into** the coasts [*borders*] of **Tyre and Sidon** [*a bit north and then west of the Sea of Galilee*].

22 And, behold, **a woman of Canaan** [*a Gentile, non-Israelite, probably a descendant of Ham; see Bible Dictionary, under "Canaan"*] came out of the same coasts [*from the same area*], and **cried unto him, saying, Have mercy on me, O Lord, thou Son of David** [*thou Messiah, who was prophesied to be a descendant of King David*]; **my daughter is grievously vexed** [*is very sick*] **with a devil.**

23 **But he answered her not a word**. And his disciples came and besought him, saying, Send her away; for she crieth after us.

24 But he answered and said, **I am not sent but unto the lost sheep of the house of Israel.**

> As he states here, Jesus' mortal mission was limited to the house of Israel, specifically, the Jews. This limitation will be done away

Matthew 15

with later, as exemplified by Mark 16:15 and Peter's dream in Acts 10:9–48.

25 **Then came she** and worshipped him, **saying, Lord, help me.**

26 But **he answered** and said, **It is not meet** [*appropriate, necessary*] **to take the children's bread** [*the gospel nourishment designated at this time for the Jews—see note above*], **and to cast it to dogs.**

27 And **she said,** Truth, Lord: yet **the dogs eat of the crumbs which fall from their masters' table.**

> The word "dogs" in this context means "little dogs" or household pets (a term of endearment). A Bible scholar named Dummelow explains as follows:
>
> "The rabbis often spoke of the Gentiles as dogs . . . (Jesus) says not 'dogs,' but 'little dogs,' i.e. house-hold, favourite dogs, and the woman cleverly catches at the expression, arguing that if the Gentiles are household dogs, then it is only right that they should be fed with the crumbs that fall from their master's table." (Dummelow, *Commentary*, pp. 678–79)

28 **Then Jesus** answered and **said** unto her, **O woman, great is thy faith: be it unto thee even as thou wilt. And her daughter was made whole** from that very hour.

29 **And Jesus** departed from thence, and **came nigh unto the sea of Galilee; and went up into a mountain, and sat down there.**

30 And **great multitudes came unto him, having with them those that were lame, blind, dumb** [*not able to speak*], **maimed,** and many others, and cast them down at Jesus' feet; **and he healed them:**

31 Insomuch that **the multitude wondered** [*marveled*], when they saw the dumb to speak, the maimed to be whole, the lame to walk, and the blind to see: **and they glorified the God of Israel.**

The Feeding of the 4,000

32 **Then Jesus called his disciples unto him, and said, I have compassion on the multitude, because they continue with me now three days** [*they have been following me for three days*], **and have nothing to eat:** and I will not send them away fasting [*hungry*], lest they faint in the way [*collapse on the way home*].

33 **And his disciples say** unto him, **Whence should we have so much bread** in the wilderness, as **to fill so great a multitude** [*where can we get enough bread to feed such a large group*]?

34 **And Jesus saith** unto them, **How many loaves have ye?** And they said, **Seven, and a few little fishes.**

35 And he commanded the multitude to sit down on the ground.

36 And **he took the seven loaves and the fishes, and gave thanks, and brake them, and gave to his**

disciples, and the disciples to the multitude.

37 **And they did all eat, and were filled**: and they took up of the broken meat [*food*] that was **left seven baskets full.**

38 And they that did eat were **four thousand men, beside** [*plus*] **women and children.**

39 And **he** sent away the multitude, and took ship, and **came into** the coasts [*borders*] of **Magdala** [*near the northwestern shore of the Sea of Galilee*].

MATTHEW 16

The Pharisees and Sadducees, traditionally bitter enemies of each other, have now joined forces to stop Jesus, and have come all the way from Jerusalem to Galilee to confront Him.

1 **THE Pharisees** [*Jewish religious leaders who believed in resurrection*] also **with the Sadducees** [*Jewish religious leaders who did not believe in resurrection*] **came**, and tempting **desired** him that he would shew them **a sign from heaven.**

> The Pharisees and the Sadducees were usually enemies, but here we see them teamed up together against the Savior.

2 **He answered** and said unto them, **When it is evening, ye say, It will be fair weather: for the sky is red.**

3 And **in the morning, It will be foul weather to day: for the sky is** red and lowring [*threatening*], **O ye hypocrites** [*people who want to appear righteous but inwardly like to be evil*], **ye can discern the face of the sky** [*you can predict the weather by looking at the sky*]; **but can ye not discern** [*JST tell*] **the signs of the times** [*the obvious fulfillment of prophecies about Christ's mortal ministry, which, if paid attention to, would present these hypocrites with sure evidence that this Jesus, against whom they were fighting, is the promised Messiah*]?

4 **A wicked and adulterous generation seeketh after a sign**; and there shall no sign be given unto it, but the sign of the prophet Jonas [*just as Jonah spent three days and three nights in the whale's belly, so also will Christ spend three days and three nights in the tomb; see JST Mark 8:12*]. And **he left them, and departed.**

5 And **when his disciples were come to the other side, they had forgotten to take bread.**

6 **Then Jesus said** unto them, Take heed and **beware of the leaven of the Pharisees and of the Sadducees.**

> Here the Master Teacher uses the setting to teach and warn his disciples against the evil doctrines (verse 12) of the Pharisees and Sadducees. He compares these doctrines to leaven (yeast) which is put in bread dough to

make it rise. As the leaven works its way through the entire lump of dough, it influences everything. So also with these hypocritical Jewish leaders, who are influencing everything in Jewish society. At first, the disciples did not understand what Jesus was saying.

7 And **they reasoned among themselves, saying, It is because we have taken no bread.**

8 Which **when Jesus perceived, he said** unto them, **O ye of little faith, why reason ye among yourselves, because ye have brought no bread** [*you are missing the point*]?

JST Matthew 16:9
9 And when they reasoned among themselves, Jesus perceived it; and he said unto them, O ye of little faith! why reason ye among yourselves, because ye have brought no bread?

9 **Do ye not yet understand, neither remember the five loaves of the five thousand, and how many baskets ye took up** [*Matthew 14:20*]?

10 **Neither the seven loaves** of the four thousand, **and how many baskets ye took up** [*Matthew 15:37*]?

11 **How is it that ye do not understand that I spake it** [*what I said about leaven, yeast*] **not to you concerning bread,** [*but, rather*] that ye should **beware of** [*watch out for*] **the leaven** [*influence*] **of the Pharisees and of the Sadducees?**

12 **Then understood they** [*the Apostles*] **how that he bade them** [*warned them*] **not** [*to*] **beware of** the leaven [*yeast*] of bread, but **of the doctrine of the Pharisees and of the Sadducees.**

In other words, just as a little bit of yeast can spread itself throughout the whole lump of bread dough, and thus influence it all, so also can the evil influence of corrupt religious leaders, such as the Pharisees and Sadducees, spread throughout the whole nation.

13 When **Jesus came into** the coasts of [*area around*] **Caesarea Philippi** [*about 15 to 20 miles north of the Sea of Galilee*]**, he asked his disciples,** saying, **Whom do men say that I the Son of man** [*"Son of God," "Son of Man of Holiness;" see Moses 6:57*] **am?**

14 And **they said,** Some say that thou art John the Baptist: some, Elias [*Elijah*]; and others, Jeremias [*Jeremiah*], or one of the prophets.

15 **He saith** unto them, **But whom say ye that I am?**

Peter Bears His Testimony of Christ

16 And Simon **Peter answered** and said, **Thou art the Christ, the Son of the living God.**

17 **And Jesus answered** and said unto him, **Blessed art thou, Simon Bar-jona** [*son of a man named Jona*]**: for flesh and blood** [*man*] **hath not revealed it unto thee,**

but my Father which is in heaven [*you have received your testimony of Me through revelation*].

18 And I say also unto thee, That **thou art Peter, and upon this rock** [*the "rock" of revelation, see TPJS, p. 274; also, Christ is the "rock" upon which the Church is based; see Matthew 16:18, footnote a*] **I will build my church**; and the gates of hell shall not prevail [*win*] against it. [*Satan's kingdom absolutely will not ultimately win against Christ's kingdom, a very comforting fact!*]

19 And **I will give unto thee the keys** [*including the sealing power*] **of the kingdom of heaven** [*Peter is authorized to serve as the president of the Church after the Savior leaves*]: **and whatsoever thou shalt bind** [*seal*] **on earth shall be bound in heaven: and whatsoever thou shalt loose** [*unseal*] **on earth shall be loosed in heaven.**

20 Then charged he his disciples that they should **tell no man that he was Jesus the Christ.**

Apostle Bruce R. McConkie explained verse 20, above, as follows: "For the time being, to avoid persecution and because the available hearers were not prepared to heed their witness, the apostles were restrained from bearing witness of the divine Sonship of their Master" (*Doctrinal New Testament Commentary*, Vol. 1, p. 390).

21 **From that time forth began** Jesus to shew unto his disciples, how that **he must go unto Jerusalem**, and suffer many things of the elders and chief priests and scribes, **and be killed, and be raised again the third day.**

22 Then **Peter took him, and began to rebuke** [*scold*] him, saying, Be it far from thee, Lord: this shall not be unto thee [*this can't happen to You!*].

23 **But he turned, and said unto Peter, Get thee behind me, Satan**: thou art an offence unto me: for thou savourest [*you cherish*] not the things that be of God, but those that be of men. [*You must not try to stop me from following through with the Atonement.*]

24 Then said Jesus unto his disciples, **If any man will come after me, let him deny himself** [*put off worldly concerns*], **and take up his cross** [*sacrifice whatever is necessary*], **and follow me.**

The JST adds a verse after verse 24, above. It is not found in the Bible.

JST Matthew 16:26

26 And now for a man to take up his cross, is to deny himself of all ungodliness, and every worldly lust, and keep my commandments.

25 **For whosoever will save his life shall lose it: and whosoever will lose his life** [*sacrifice his own comforts and desires*] **for my sake shall find it.**

JST Matthew 16:27–28

27 **Break not my commandments for to save your lives**; for whosoever will save his life **in this world**, shall lose it **in the world to come**.

28 And whosoever will lose his **life in this world**, for my sake, shall find it **in the world to come**.

26 **For what is a man profited, if he shall gain the whole world, and lose his own soul?** or what shall a man give in exchange for his soul?

JST Matthew 16:29

29 **Therefore, forsake the world, and save your souls**; for what is a man profited, if he shall gain the whole world, and lose his own soul? Or what shall a man give in exchange for his soul?

27 **For the Son of man shall come in the glory of his Father with his angels** [*the Second Coming—see Matthew 16:27, footnote b*]; and **then he shall reward every man according to his works**. [*Those who sacrifice whatever is necessary to truly follow me will find the reward more than worth it.*]

28 Verily I say unto you, **There be some standing here, which shall not taste of death, till they see the Son of man coming in his kingdom**. [*Some will be translated and will continue living on earth, doing the work of the Lord until He comes again. The Apostle John is the only one of these men whom we know by name as having been translated. See D&C 7. For more information about translated beings, see 3 Nephi 28.*]

MATTHEW 17

It is now near October, and the Savior will be crucified the following April, thus ending His mortal ministry. Three of His Apostles, Peter, James, and John are already taking on the role of First Presidency. They will experience tremendous additional training now as the Master takes them with Him up on the mountain which is referred to as the Mount of Transfiguration. There, they will see Christ transfigured before their eyes, will hear the Father's voice, and will see, among others, the great prophets Moses and Elijah, from whom they will receive additional priesthood keys. From JST Mark 9:3, we learn that John the Baptist was also there.

The Transfiguration of Christ

1 AND after six days **Jesus taketh Peter, James, and John** his brother, and bringeth them up **into an high mountain** apart,

2 **And was transfigured** before them: and his face did shine as the sun, and his raiment [*clothing*] was white as the light.

3 And, behold, **there appeared** unto them Moses and Elias [*Elijah*] talking with him.

4 **Then answered Peter** [*Peter

responded], and said unto Jesus, **Lord, it is good for us to be here**: if thou wilt, let us make here three tabernacles [*small booths, typically used among the Jews for private worship during the annual Feast of Tabernacles*]; one for thee, and one for Moses, and one for Elias [*Elijah*].

5 While he yet spake, behold, **a bright cloud overshadowed them**: and behold **a voice out of the cloud**, which **said, This is my beloved Son, in whom I am well pleased; hear ye him**.

6 **And** when **the disciples** heard it, they **fell on their** face [*a show of humility*], **and were sore** [*very*] **afraid**.

7 And **Jesus came and touched them, and said, Arise, and be not afraid**.

8 **And when they had lifted up their eyes, they saw no man, save** [*except*] **Jesus** only.

> Apostle Bruce R. McConkie summarizes what took place on the Mount of Transfiguration in the following quote: "From the New Testament accounts and from the added light revealed through Joseph Smith it appears evident that:
>
> (1) Jesus singled out Peter, James, and John from the rest of the Twelve; took them upon an unnamed mountain; there He was transfigured before them, and they beheld His glory. Testifying later, John said, "We beheld his glory, the glory as of the only begotten of the Father" (John 1:14); and Peter, speaking of the same event, said they "were eyewitnesses of his majesty" (2 Peter 1:16).
>
> (2) Peter, James, and John, were themselves "transfigured before him" (*Teachings*, p. 158), even as Moses, the Three Nephites, Joseph Smith, and many prophets of all ages have been transfigured, thus enabling them to entertain angels, see visions and comprehend the things of God (*Mormon Doctrine*, pp. 725–26).
>
> (3) Moses and Elijah—two ancient prophets who were translated and taken to heaven without tasting death, so they could return with tangible bodies on this very occasion, an occasion preceding the day of resurrection—appeared on the mountain; and they and Jesus gave the keys of the kingdom to Peter, James, and John (*Teachings*, p. 158).
>
> (4) John the Baptist, previously beheaded by Herod, apparently was also present. It may well be that other unnamed prophets, either coming as translated beings or as spirits from paradise, were also present.
>
> (5) Peter, James, and John saw in vision the transfiguration of the earth, that is, they saw it renewed and returned to its paradisiacal state—an event that is to take place at the Second Coming when the millennial era

Matthew 17

is ushered in (D&C 63:20–21; *Mormon Doctrine,* pp. 718–19).

(6) It appears that Peter, James, and John received their own endowments while on the mountain (*Doctrines of Salvation,* vol. 2, p. 165). Peter says that while there, they "received from God the Father honour and glory," seemingly bearing out this conclusion. It also appears that it was while on the mount that they received the more sure word of prophecy, it then being revealed to them that they were sealed up unto eternal life (2 Peter 1:16–19; D&C 131:5).

(7) Apparently Jesus himself was strengthened and encouraged by Moses and Elijah so as to be prepared for the infinite sufferings and agony ahead of him in connection with working out the infinite and eternal atonement. (*Jesus the Christ,* p. 373.) Similar comfort had been given him by angelic visitants following his forty-day fast and its attendant temptations (Matthew 4:11), and an angel from heaven was yet to strengthen him when he would sweat great drops of blood in the Garden of Gethsemane (Luke 22:42–44).

(8) Certainly the three chosen apostles were taught in plainness "of his death and also his resurrection" (JST Luke 9:31), teachings which would be of inestimable value to them in the trying days ahead.

(9) It should also have been apparent to them that the old dispensations of the past had faded away, that the law (of which Moses was the symbol) and the prophets (of whom Elijah was the typifying representative) were subject to Him whom they were now commanded to hear.

(10) Apparently God the Father, overshadowed and hidden by a cloud, was present on the mountain, although our Lord's three associates, as far as the record stipulates, heard only his voice and did not see his form" (*Doctrinal New Testament Commentary,* Vol. 1, p. 399).

9 And **as they came down from the mountain, Jesus charged** [*instructed*] **them, saying, Tell the vision to no man, until the Son of man be risen again from the dead.**

10 And **his disciples asked** him, saying, **Why then say the scribes that Elias must first come?**

Here, Peter, James, and John seem to be asking the Savior to clear up some doctrinal confusion in their own minds about Elias. They had been taught by their scriptures that Elias would come and prepare the way for the Lord. Yet, they had just seen Elias (Elijah) on the Mount and this was after the Savior had come. In fact, this was near the end of the Master's mortal ministry. It is helpful for us, as we study these scriptures, to be aware that the name "Elias" has many meanings. See Bible Dictionary, p. 663. Thus, here, in this setting as explained by the Savior,

Elias can mean John the Baptist who came before Jesus and prepared the way for Him. It can also mean Elijah who ministered on the Mount of Transfiguration and would yet appear in the Kirtland Temple (D&C 110:13–15). It is also helpful to read JST Matthew 17:10–14 in the back of our Bible, concerning Elias.

11 And **Jesus answered** and said unto them, **Elias truly shall first come, and restore all things.**

12 **But** I say unto you, **That Elias is come already**, and they knew him not, but have done unto him whatsoever they listed. Likewise shall also the Son of man suffer of them.

13 Then the disciples understood that **he spake unto them of John the Baptist.**

JST Matthew 17:10–14

10 And Jesus answered and said unto them, Elias truly shall first come, and restore all things, **as the prophets have written**.

11 And again I say unto you that Elias has come already, **concerning whom it is written, Behold, I will send my messenger, and he shall prepare the way before me**; and they knew him not, and have done unto him, whatsoever they listed.

12 Likewise shall also the Son of man suffer of them.

JST verse 13, next, is not found in the Bible.

13 **But I say unto you, Who is Elias? Behold, this is Elias, whom I send to prepare the way before me.**

14 Then the disciples understood that he spake unto them of John the Baptist, **and also of another** [*Jesus Christ—see JST John 1:27–28*] **who should come and restore all things, as it is written by the prophets.**

The Healing of a Lunatick Son

14 And **when they were come to the multitude, there came to him a certain man, kneeling down to him, and saying,**

15 Lord, have mercy on **my son**: for he **is lunatick**, and sore vexed [*very sick and troubled*]: for ofttimes he falleth into the fire, and oft into the water.

16 And **I brought him to thy disciples, and they could not cure him.**

17 **Then Jesus answered and said, O faithless and perverse generation,** how long shall I be with you? how long shall I suffer you [*put up with you*]? bring him hither to me.

18 And Jesus rebuked the devil; and he departed out of him: and **the child was cured** from that very hour.

This is yet another reminder that Christ has power over Satan and his kingdom. Also, we are reminded here, as elsewhere, that the Savior has power to heal whatever ails us, symbolic of His power to save all who will follow Him.

19 Then came **the disciples** to Jesus apart [*privately*], and **said, Why could not we cast him out?**

20 **And Jesus said** unto them, **Because of your unbelief**: for verily I say unto you, If ye have faith as a grain of mustard seed, ye shall say unto this mountain, Remove hence to yonder place; and it shall remove; and nothing shall be impossible unto you.

21 **Howbeit** [*however*] **this kind goeth not out but by prayer and fasting**.

Jesus Tells His Apostles of His Coming Death and Resurrection

22 And while they abode **in Galilee, Jesus said** unto them, **The Son of man** [*Christ; Son of Man of Holiness; see Moses 6:57*] **shall be betrayed into the hands of men**:

23 And **they shall kill him**, and **the third day he shall be raised again**. And they were exceeding sorry.

Temple Tax Money Miraculously Comes from the Mouth of a Fish

24 And **when they were come to Capernaum** [*Peter's home town on the northern edge of the Sea of Galilee*], **they** [*temple tax collectors*] **that received tribute money** [*annual temple tax of a half shekel, required from every male, twenty years old and older*] **came to Peter, and said, Doth not your master pay tribute** [*the temple tax*]?

25 **He saith, Yes**. And **when he** [*Peter*] **was come into the house, Jesus prevented him** [*spoke to him first, before he had a chance to mention the temple tax to Jesus—see Matthew 17:25, footnote a, in your Bible*], **saying, What thinkest thou, Simon** [*here's a question for you, Peter*]? **of whom** [*from whom*] **do the kings of the earth take custom** [*collect taxes*] **or tribute? of their own children, or of strangers** [*others*]?

26 Peter saith unto him, Of strangers. Jesus saith unto him, Then are the children [*of kings*] free [*exempt*].

There is a subtle play on words at work here. Jesus is the Son of the King (Heavenly Father). He is also the King, the Messiah. He is even the rightful political King of the Jews if the Romans had not been in political power at the time, because Joseph, Mary's husband, was the rightful heir to the political throne of the Jews. Thus, Jesus, as King and as the Son of the King (Elohim) should not have to pay this tax. Approaching it from another angle, since Jesus is a King in many ways, His children (His followers, the apostles, etc.) including Peter, should not have to pay this tribute either.

27 **Notwithstanding** [*nevertheless*], **lest we should offend them**

[*in order to keep the peace*], **go thou to the sea** [*Sea of Galilee, which is probably just a few hundred feet or less away*], and **cast an hook** [*go fishing*], and **take up the fish that first cometh up** [*the first one you catch*]; **and when thou hast opened his mouth, thou shalt find a piece of money** [*a one shekel (four-drachma) coin, the exact amount to pay the temple tax for Christ and Peter; see NIV Bible, Matthew 17:27*]: **that take, and give unto them** [*the temple tax collectors*] **for me and thee.**

MATTHEW 18

In this chapter, you will likely find several verses that are somewhat familiar to you, such as verses 3–4, 6–7, 12–13, 16, 18, 20, 22, and so forth. There is much important counsel about our relationships with others, including being merciful and forgiving.

1 AT the same time came the disciples unto Jesus, saying, **Who is the greatest in the kingdom of heaven?**

2 And **Jesus called a little child unto him, and set him in the midst of them,**

3 And said, Verily I say unto you, **Except ye be converted, and become as little children, ye shall not enter into the kingdom of heaven** [*celestial glory*].

4 **Whosoever therefore shall humble himself as this little child, the same is greatest in the kingdom of heaven.**

5 And **whoso shall receive one such little child in my name receiveth me.**

6 But **whoso shall offend** [*lead astray, cause to commit sin*] **one of these little ones which believe in me, it were better for him that a millstone** [*a large, heavy stone used to grind grain in a flour mill*] **were hanged about his neck, and that he were drowned in the depth of the sea.**

7 Woe unto the world because of offences! for **it must needs be that offences come; but woe to that man by whom the offence cometh!**

> Sometimes people think that, since there needs to be opposition in all things [*2 Nephi 2:11*], they are helping the Lord's plan by being wicked, tempting others to sin, etc. Verse 7, above, shows such thinking to be very wrong!

8 Wherefore **if thy hand** [*friend; see JST explanation after verse 9, below*] **or** thy **foot** [*friend*] **offend thee, cut them off**, and **cast them from thee**: it is better for thee to enter into life halt or maimed, rather than having two hands or two feet to be cast into everlasting fire.

9 And **if thine eye** [*your own family members; see* **offend thee, pluck it out, and cast it from thee** *JST explanation below*]: it is better for thee to enter into life with one

eye, rather than having two eyes to be cast into hell fire.

> JST, verse 9, next (which is not found in the Bible), explains the symbolism of "hand," "foot," and "eye" in verses 8 and 9 above as follows:
>
> **JST Matthew 18:9**
> **9 And a man's hand is his friend, and his foot, also; and a man's eye, are they of his own household.**

10 Take heed that ye **despise not one of these little ones**; for I say unto you, That in heaven their angels do always behold the face of my Father which is in heaven [*they will be saved in the celestial kingdom; see D&C 137:10*].

11 For **the Son of man** [*the Savior*] **is come to save that which was lost.**

> **JST Matthew 18:11**
> 11 For the Son of man is come to save that which was lost, **and to call sinners to repentance; but these little ones have no need of repentance, and I will save them**.

12 **How think ye** [*what do you think*]**? if a man have an hundred sheep, and one of them be gone astray, doth he not leave the ninety and nine, and goeth into the mountains, and seeketh that which is gone astray** [*God does everything he can to bring back the strays (symbolic of sinners)*]?

13 **And if** so be that **he find it**, verily I say unto you, **he rejoiceth** more of that sheep, than of the ninety and nine which went not astray. [*There is much joy when a stray returns to the fold.*]

14 Even so **it is not the will of your Father which is in heaven, that one of these little ones should perish**.

15 Moreover **if thy brother shall trespass against thee**, go and **tell him his fault between thee and him alone** [*keep it private; don't gossip about it; see D&C 20:80*]: if he shall hear thee [*responds positively*], thou hast gained thy brother.

> Gossip (implied in verse 15, above) can actually be a type of emotional terrorism, because it often claims innocent victims.

16 But **if he will not hear thee** [*will not accept your efforts to make peace*], then **take** with thee **one or two** more [*as witnesses that you have tried to work the matter out with him*], that **in the mouth of two or three witnesses every word may be established** [*this is known as the law of witnesses*].

17 And **if he shall neglect to hear them** [*if he won't respond favorably to that effort on your part*], **tell it unto the church** [*go to the authorities of the church*]: but **if he neglect to hear the church, let him be unto thee as an heathen man and a publican** [*go ahead and excommunicate him*].

Remember that the Savior is speaking primarily to His Apostles here whom He called, as recorded in Matthew, chapter 10. In verse 18, next, He instructs them concerning the sealing power of priesthood keys which they will exercise as part of their calling.

Priesthood Keys and Sealing Power

18 Verily I say unto you, **Whatsoever ye** [*the Apostles*] **shall bind on earth shall be bound in heaven: and whatsoever ye shall loose on earth shall be loosed in heaven.**

19 Again I say unto you, That if two of you shall agree on earth as touching any thing that they shall ask, it shall be done for them of my Father which is in heaven.

20 For **where two or three are gathered together in my name, there am I in the midst of them.**

How Often Should We Forgive?

21 Then came Peter to him, and said, Lord, **how oft shall my brother sin against me, and I forgive him?** till seven times?

22 Jesus saith unto him, I say not unto thee, Until seven times: but, **Until seventy times seven.** [*In other words, forgive him every time he repents. See D&C 98:40.*]

This doctrine of forgiving is a most important one for our own salvation. When we forgive others, we free ourselves of the heavy burdens of hatred, grudges, bitterness, pity parties, etc. Nephi is a great example to us in 1 Nephi 7:21 where he "frankly forgave" his brothers. The Savior goes on now to teach Peter and all of us the importance of our forgiving others if we want the Lord to forgive us.

The Parable of the Unmerciful Servant

23 Therefore is **the kingdom of heaven likened unto a certain king**, which would take account of his servants [*see who is in debt to him etc.*].

24 And when he had begun to reckon [*check the accounting records*], **one was brought unto him, which owed him ten thousand talents.**

One calculation of this amount, based on an average day's wage, yields a debt which would require 60,000,000 work days to pay off, which, of course, is an impossible debt to repay. A person who starts full-time work at age 15 and works six days a week for 55 years, would have 17,160 days of work in his or her lifetime.

25 **But forasmuch as he had not to pay, his lord commanded him to be sold, and his wife, and children, and all that he had, and payment to be made.** [*This can be symbolic of the fact that we would lose family and all that counts (see 2 Nephi 9:8–9) without the*

Atonement and its power to free us and cleanse us so that we can enter exaltation and dwell in family units forever.]

26 The servant therefore fell down, and worshipped him, saying, Lord, **have patience with me, and I will pay thee all.**

27 Then **the lord** of that servant **was moved with compassion**, and loosed him, and **forgave him the debt** [*symbolic of the Atonement*].

28 **But the same servant** went out, and **found one of his fellowservants, which owed him an hundred pence** [*an amount equivalent to about 100 days' wages; see Matthew 20:2*]: and **he** laid hands on him, and **took him by the throat, saying, Pay me that thou owest.**

29 And his fellowservant fell down at his feet, and besought him, saying, **Have patience with me, and I will pay thee all** [*the exact words he himself had used as he begged for mercy in verse 26, above*].

30 **And he would not** [*he refused to be merciful to the person who owed him and couldn't pay*]: but went and cast him into prison, till he should pay the debt.

31 So **when his fellowservants saw what was done, they were very sorry, and came and told** unto **their lord** [*the king in verse 23*] **all that was done.**

32 Then his lord, after that he had called him [*the man who refused to forgive the relatively small debt of 100 days' wages*], said unto him, **O thou wicked servant, I forgave thee all that debt, because thou desiredst me:**

33 **Shouldest not thou also have had compassion on thy fellowservant, even as I had pity on thee?**

34 **And his lord** was wroth [*angry; righteous indignation*], and **delivered him to the tormentors, till he should pay all that was due unto him** [*symbolic of the law of justice*].

Symbolically, "tormentors" would represent the punishment of the wicked who are eventually turned over to the buffetings of Satan (D&C 82:21) to pay for their own sins. Even after they have paid the penalty for their own sins, the highest degree of glory they can enter is the Telestial (D&C 76:84–85). Also, this parable teaches the interplay between the Law of Justice and the Law of Mercy. The Law of Mercy allows us to be forgiven of unfathomable debt to God, through obedience to the gospel, including forgiving others. However, if we, through our actions, refuse the Law of Mercy, then the Law of Justice takes over, and we bear the burden of our sins as explained in D&C 19:15–18].

35 **So likewise shall my heavenly Father do also unto you, if ye from your hearts forgive not every one his brother their trespasses.** [*This is fair warning to us*

about forgiving others and quite an answer to Peter's question in verse 21, wherein he asked how often he should forgive others.]

MATTHEW 19

Having recently prophesied to His apostles that He will be arrested, tried, and crucified in Jerusalem and then resurrected three days afterward, the Savior now leaves Galilee and travels toward Jerusalem. Can you imagine how His Apostles felt about this? He continues to instruct them in their duties and teach them how to apply the gospel in their lives. The religious leaders of the Jews continue their attempts to trap Him.

1 AND it came to pass, that when **Jesus** had finished these sayings, he **departed from Galilee, and came into** the coasts [*borders*] of **Judæa** beyond Jordan [*getting close to Jerusalem but still east of the Jordan River*];

2 And **great multitudes followed him; and he healed them there.**

3 **The Pharisees** [*religious leaders of the Jews*] also **came unto him, tempting him** [*trying to trap him so they could arrest Him*], and **saying** unto him, **Is it lawful for a man to put away** [*divorce*] **his wife for every cause?**

4 And **he answered** and said unto them, **Have ye not read**, that he [*Heavenly Father*] which made them at the beginning made them male and female,

5 And said, **For this cause** [*marriage and family*] **shall a man leave father and mother, and shall cleave to** [*stick to; be faithful to*] **his wife: and they twain** [*two*] **shall be one flesh?**

6 **Wherefore they are no more twain** [*two people*], **but one flesh** [*one family unit*]. **What therefore God hath joined together, let not man put asunder** [*take apart*].

> As you can see, they are trying to pit the Master against the great lawgiver and prophet, Moses, who is very highly esteemed among the Jews at this time in the New Testament.

7 **They say** unto him, **Why did Moses then command to give a writing of divorcement** [*a legal certificate of divorce*], **and to put her away** [*divorce her*]?

8 **He saith** unto them, **Moses because of the hardness of your hearts suffered** [*allowed*] **you to put away** [*divorce*] **your wives: but from the beginning it was not so.**

9 And **I say unto you, Whosoever shall put away his wife, except it be for fornication**, and shall marry another, committeth adultery: and whoso marrieth her which is put away doth commit adultery.

> Refer to the note between Matthew, chapter five, verses 31 and 32, in this study guide, for help with verse 9, above.

Matthew 19

10 **His disciples say** unto him, **If the case of the man be so with his wife, it is not good to marry** [*if this is such a serious matter, it would be better not to risk getting married*].

11 But **he said** unto them, **All men cannot receive this saying, save they to whom it is given.**

12 For there are some eunuchs [*men who are physically unable to have children*], which were so born from their mother's womb: and there are some eunuchs, which were made eunuchs of men [*men who have been surgically rendered incapable of having children; see Bible Dictionary, under "Eunuch"*]: and there be eunuchs, which have made themselves eunuchs for the kingdom of heaven's sake. He that is able to receive it, let him receive it.

> Verse 12 above seems incomplete and fragmentary. We don't know what it really means. Concerning this verse, Apostle Bruce R. McConkie said, "Some added background and additional information is needed to understand fully what is meant by this teaching about eunuchs" (*Doctrinal New Testament Commentary*, Vol. 1, p. 549).

13 **Then were there brought unto him little children**, that he should put his hands on them, and pray: **and the disciples rebuked them** [*rebuked those who brought the little children to Jesus*].

14 But Jesus said, **Suffer** [*allow*] **little children, and forbid them not, to come unto me: for of such is the kingdom of heaven.**

15 **And he laid his hands on them**, and departed thence.

16 And, behold, **one** [*the rich young man in verse 22*] **came and said unto him, Good Master** [*"Teacher"; see NIV Bible*], **what good thing shall I do, that I may have eternal life?**

> This rich young man seems to believe that doing one "good thing" will secure his place in heaven. We see this thinking on his part again in verse 18 when he asks which commandment he should keep in order to attain heaven.

17 And **he said** unto him, **Why callest thou me good? there is none good but one, that is, God** [*Jesus wants no glory for Himself, rather, gives all credit and glory to the Father*]: **but if thou wilt enter into life** [*exaltation*], **keep the commandments.**

18 **He saith unto him, Which?** [*The young man still hasn't got the point.*] **Jesus said,** Thou shalt do **no murder,** Thou shalt **not commit adultery,** Thou shalt **not steal,** Thou shalt **not bear false witness,**

19 **Honour thy father and thy mother**: and, Thou shalt **love thy neighbour as thyself.**

20 **The young man saith** unto him, **All these things have I kept from my youth up: what lack I yet?**

From what the Savior says to him next, in verse 21, it seems that the young man lacks true charity. Also, notice that the Master also kindly invites him to come and follow Him, a reminder that qualifying for exaltation is a process, not an event.

21 **Jesus said** unto him, **If thou wilt be perfect, go and sell that thou hast, and give to the poor,** and thou shalt have treasure in heaven: and **come and follow me.**

22 **But** when **the young man** heard that saying, he **went away sorrowful: for he had great possessions** [*was very rich*].

Verse 23, next, reminds us that Jesus is still giving His Apostles some intense training.

23 **Then said Jesus unto his disciples,** Verily [*"Listen carefully, this is an important point."*] I say unto you, **That a rich man shall hardly** [*it is "hard" for him, not "almost impossible"*] **enter into the kingdom of heaven** [*celestial kingdom*].

24 And again I say unto you, **It is easier for a camel to go through the eye of a needle, than for a rich man to enter into the kingdom of God.**

There is a rumor going around that the "eye of a needle" (verse 24, above) was a small gate in the walls of Jerusalem, used for entry into the city by night, after the main gates were closed. The rumor states that it was very difficult for a camel to get down and scrunch through the gate. Bible scholars indicate that this rumor has no truth to it. They indicate that the word "needle," as used in verse 24, refers to an ordinary sewing needle in the original Bible languages. Therefore, what the Savior is doing with this comparison is the use of exaggeration in order to make a point.

25 When **his disciples** heard it, they **were** exceedingly **amazed, saying, Who then can be saved?**

26 But **Jesus** beheld them, and said unto them, **With men this** [*being saved*] **is impossible; but with God** [*with the help of God, through the Atonement*] **all things are possible.**

JST Matthew 19:26
But Jesus beheld **their thoughts,** and said unto them, With men this is impossible; **but if they will forsake all things for my sake**, with God **whatsoever things I speak are possible.**

27 **Then answered Peter** [*this is old English and means that Peter asked a question*] and said unto him, Behold, **we have forsaken all, and followed thee; what shall we have therefore** [*what will our reward be? The answer to Peter's question is given in verses 28 and 29*].

28 And **Jesus said** unto them, Verily [*listen very carefully, this is an important point*] I say unto you, That **ye which have followed me, in the regeneration** [*resurrection*]

when the Son of man [*Christ; Son of Man of Holiness—see Moses 6:57*] **shall sit in the throne of his glory** [*in exaltation*], **ye also shall sit upon twelve thrones** [*you, too, will be exalted*], **judging the twelve tribes of Israel.**

JST Matthew 19:28

28 And Jesus said unto them, Verily I say unto you, that ye **who** have followed me, shall, in the **resurrection**, when the Son of man shall **come sitting on** the throne of his glory, ye shall also shall sit upon twelve thrones, judging the twelve tribes of Israel.

Apostle Bruce R. McConkie explains the judging referred to in verse 28 above in the following quote:

"Christ is the great judge of all the earth. 'The Father judgeth no man, but hath committed all judgment unto the Son' (John 5:22). In due course, every living soul shall stand before his judgment bar, be judged according to his own works, and awarded a place in the mansions that are prepared (Mormon 3:20).

"Under Christ a great hierarchy of judges will operate, each functioning in his assigned sphere. John saw many judges sitting upon thrones (Revelation 20:4). Paul said the Saints would judge both the world and angels (1 Corinthians 6:2–3). The elders are to sit in judgment on those who reject them (D&C 75:21–22; Matthew 10:14–15). Daniel saw that judgment would be given to the Saints (Daniel 7:22). The Nephite Twelve will be judged by the Twelve from Jerusalem and then in turn will judge the Nephite nation (1 Nephi 12:9–10; 3 Nephi 27:27; Mormon 3:19). And the Twelve who served with our Lord in his ministry shall judge the whole house of Israel (D&C 29:12). No doubt there will be many others of many dispensations who will sit in judgment upon the peoples of their days and generations—all judging according to the judgment which Christ shall give them, "which shall be just" (3 Nephi 27:27) (*Doctrinal New Testament Commentary*, Vol. 1, pp. 558–59).

29 [*This is a continuation of the answer to Peter's question in verse 27.*] **And every one that hath forsaken** [*given up*] houses, or brethren, or sisters, or father, or mother, or wife, or children, or lands, **for my name's sake**, shall receive an hundredfold, and **shall inherit everlasting life** [*exaltation*].

30 **But many** that are first [*JST Mark 10:30–31 "who make themselves first"*] **shall be last; and the last** [*those who consider themselves least, and who are humbly obedient*] **shall be first** [*highest up in the celestial kingdom*].

MATTHEW 20

In this chapter, you will first read what is commonly called "The Parable of the Laborers." It is where those who came to work late in the day were paid the same as those who started early in the day. We will talk quite a lot about symbolism as we discuss this parable. In this chapter also, the Savior will prophesy His crucifixion. The mother of James and John will make a request of Jesus that will cause some bad feelings among the rest of the Twelve. Watch how Jesus resolves it. And, finally, two blind men will call loudly to Jesus, asking Him to heal them and thus draw the anger of some in the crowd who want them to be quiet.

The Parable of the Laborers (The Eleventh Hour Parable)

1 FOR **the kingdom of heaven is like unto a man that is an householder**, which **went out early in the morning to hire labourers** into his vineyard.

2 And **when he had agreed with the labourers for a penny a day** [*a day's wages*], **he sent them into his vineyard**.

> When we see the word "penny," we think of a coin of very little worth. This misunderstanding can distract us as we read this parable. The King James Bible [*the version we use*] translators consistently used the word "penny" for "denarius." A denarius is a Roman silver coin (see Bible Dictionary, under "Money"). It was worth a day's wages and thus was a significant amount of money.

3 And **he went out about the third hour, and saw others** standing idle in the marketplace,

4 **And said** unto them; **Go ye also into the vineyard, and whatsoever is right I will give you**. And they went their way.

5 Again he went out about **the sixth and ninth hour**, and did **likewise**.

6 And about **the eleventh hour** he went out, and **found others** standing idle, and saith unto them, Why stand ye here all the day idle?

7 They say unto him, Because no man hath hired us. **He saith unto them, Go ye also into the vineyard**; and whatsoever is right, that shall ye receive.

8 **So when even** [*the end of the day*] **was come, the lord of the vineyard saith unto his steward**, Call the labourers, and **give them their hire** [*wages*], beginning from the last unto the first.

9 **And** when they came that were hired about the eleventh hour, **they received every man a penny** [*a full day's wages*].

10 But when **the first** [*those who began working at the beginning of the day, verse 2*] came, they supposed that they should have received more [*than those who hadn't worked all day*]; and they likewise received every man a penny [*a full day's wages; see note by verse 2 above*].

11 And when they had received it, they **murmured** [*complained*]

against the goodman of the house [*the householder who hired them, verse 1*],

12 Saying, These last have wrought [*worked*] **but one hour, and thou hast made them equal unto us,** which have borne [*had to put up with*] the burden and heat of the day.

13 But **he answered** one of them, and said, **Friend, I do thee no wrong**: didst not thou agree with me for a penny? [*I kept my part of the agreement and gave you full payment as we agreed upon.*]

14 Take that thine is, and go thy way: **I will give unto this last** [*the workers who started at the eleventh hour, verses 6 and 7*], **even as unto thee.**

15 Is it not lawful for me to do what I will with mine own? **Is thine eye evil, because I am good** [*are you jealous because I am generous to others; NIV Bible*]?

16 So **the last shall be first, and the first last**: for many be called, but few chosen [*all are "called" or invited to come to exaltation, but few are chosen to receive it because they don't overcome sins*].

> The Parable of the Laborers, as Matthew 20:1–16 is called, is very rich in symbolism and presents an opportunity for you to improve your skill in recognizing symbolism in the scriptures as you read and study them. We will repeat verses 1–16 here and call your attention to some of the symbolism with notes in parentheses. As is the case with symbolism, there are many ways it can be interpreted, so the following is just one possibility for your consideration:

Matthew 20:1–16 (repeated)

1 FOR the **kingdom of heaven** [*celestial glory*] is like unto **a man** [*Heavenly Father*] that is an householder, which went out early in the morning to hire **labourers** [*faithful Saints who have been active in the Church all their lives*] into his **vineyard** [*the earth*].

2 And when he had agreed with the labourers for **a penny a day** [*full pay for a righteous mortal life; symbolic of exaltation*], he sent them into his **vineyard** [*the earth*].

3 And he went out **about the third hour**, and saw **others standing idle** [*people who had not yet joined the Church or become active*] in the marketplace,

4 And said unto them; **Go ye also into the vineyard** [*"Join the church, get active, go to work."*], and **whatsoever is right I will give you** [*"I will be fair with you."*]. And **they went their way** [*they joined the Church and remained faithful to the end of their lives*].

5 Again he went out **about the sixth and ninth hour**, and did **likewise** [*others joined the Church or became active later in*

their lives and remained faithful in the work].

6 And about **the eleventh hour** [*representing people who find the truth and join the Church or get active near the end of their lives and remain faithful and work hard to the end*] he went out, and found others standing idle, and saith unto them, Why stand ye here all the day idle?

7 They say unto him, Because no man hath hired us. He saith unto them, **Go ye also into the vineyard** [*join the Church and remain faithful*]; and whatsoever is right, that shall ye receive.

8 So when **even** [*"evening," in other words, life is over and judgment day has arrived*] was come, the **lord of the vineyard** [*Heavenly Father*] saith unto **his steward** [*Christ, who is the final judge—see John 5:22*], **Call the labourers, and give them their hire** [*give them their reward*], beginning from the last unto the first.

9 And when they came that were hired about the **eleventh hour, they received every man a penny** [*those who became faithful Saints much later in life—not "deathbed" repentance—were given exaltation*].

Note: In these next verses, lifelong Saints are cautioned not to become jealous or feel unfairly treated since they have "bourne the burden and heat of the day" (verse 12), i.e., sacrificed and worked hard all their lives to be obedient, when they see converts or reactivated Saints get the same reward they have worked longer to achieve.

10 But when **the first** [*those who had been active all their lives*] came, they **supposed that they should have received more**; and they likewise received every man a penny.

11 And when they had received it, **they murmured against the goodman of the house** [*the Father*],

12 **Saying**, These last have wrought [*worked*] but one hour [*haven't worked nearly as long as we have to gain exaltation*], and **thou hast made them equal unto us**, which have borne the burden and heat of the day.

13 But he answered one of them, and said, Friend, I do thee no wrong: didst not thou agree with me for **a penny** [*exaltation*]?

14 **Take that thine is** [*take your exaltation—by the way, the Lord is being very patient with these complainers at this point; if they don't repent of this bad attitude, they will obviously lose their exaltation as indicated in verse 16*], and go thy way: I will give unto this last, even as unto thee.

15 Is it not lawful for me to do what I will with mine own? **Is thine eye evil, because I am good** [*are you jealous and sinning in your heart because I am forgiving and generous*]?

16 So **the last shall be first, and the first last** [*it is possible to lose exaltation because of a bad attitude such as that demonstrated by the workers in verses 10–15*]: for **many be called, but few chosen** [*all are in fact called or invited to become exalted, but not all make it*].

17 And **Jesus going up to Jerusalem took the twelve disciples apart** [*aside where they could be alone*] in the way, **and said** unto them,

18 Behold, **we go up to Jerusalem; and the Son of man** [*Christ, "Son of Man of Holiness" (Heavenly Father)*; see Moses 6:57] **shall be betrayed unto the chief priests and unto the scribes, and they** [*religious leaders of the Jews*] **shall condemn him to death,**

19 And shall **deliver him to the Gentiles** [*the Romans*] to **mock**, and to **scourge**, and to **crucify** him: **and the third day he shall rise again** [*be resurrected*].

20 **Then came to him the mother of Zebedee's children** [*James and John's mother*] **with her sons**, worshipping him, and **desiring a certain thing of him.**

21 And **he said** unto her, **What wilt thou? She saith** unto him, **Grant that these my two sons** [*James and John*] **may sit, the one on thy right hand, and the other on the left, in thy kingdom.**

22 **But Jesus** answered and **said, Ye know not what ye ask.** Are ye able to drink of the cup that I shall drink of, and to be baptized with the baptism that I am baptized with [*can you remain faithful at all costs*]? They [*James and John*] say unto him, We are able.

23 And he saith unto them, **Ye shall drink indeed of my cup**, and be baptized with the baptism that I am baptized with [*in other words, you will go through much persecution also*]: **but to sit on my right hand, and on my left, is not mine to give, but it shall be given to them for whom it is prepared of my Father** [*it is not to be given as a matter of favoritism or mere request, rather it will be given to those who earn it according to the laws established by the Father*].

24 And **when the ten** [*the other ten in the Quorum of Twelve*] **heard it, they were moved with indignation** [*angry*] **against the two** brethren [*the Apostles, James and John*].

> This is a reminder that these Apostles are still learning and maturing in their work and callings, just as each of us is. It is also a view of the Savior's tenderness and patience, as He teaches them yet another lesson.

25 **But Jesus called them unto him**, and said, **Ye know that the princes** [*kings, leaders, etc.*] **of the Gentiles** [*non-Israelites*] **exercise dominion** [*power and authority*] **over them, and they that are great** [*those leaders*] **exercise authority upon them** [*the Gentiles*].

26 **But it shall not be so among you:** but **whosoever will be great among you, let him be your minister;**

27 And **whosoever will be chief among you, let him be your servant:**

28 **Even as the Son of man** [*Christ*] **came not to be ministered unto, but to minister**, and to give his life a ransom for many [*to redeem many*].

29 And **as they departed from Jericho** [*about 25 miles from Jerusalem*], **a great multitude followed him.**

30 And, behold, **two blind men** sitting by the way side, when they heard that Jesus passed by, **cried out**, saying, Have mercy on us, O Lord, thou Son of David [*in other words, You, the Messiah, who are, as prophesied, a descendant of King David*].

31 And **the multitude rebuked** [*scolded*] **them**, because they should hold their peace [*keep quiet*]: **but they cried the more, saying, Have mercy on us**, O Lord, thou Son of David.

32 **And Jesus stood still** [*stopped walking*], **and called them**, and said, **What will ye that I shall do unto you?**

33 They say unto him, Lord, that our eyes may be opened.

34 So **Jesus had compassion** on them, and **touched their eyes**: and immediately their eyes received sight, and **they followed him.**

MATTHEW 21

These next verses lead up to what is known as "the Triumphal Entry," the day when Jesus rode into Jerusalem accompanied by throngs of people shouting "Hosanna to the Son of David." In other words, celebrating and cheering Jesus as the promised Messiah who would save them and free them from their enemies. The Passover was underway and throngs of Jewish pilgrims had arrived in Jerusalem from many lands to join in Passover celebration and worship. This begins the last week of the Savior's mortal life.

The Triumphal Entry

1 AND when **they drew nigh** [*near*] **unto Jerusalem**, and were come to Bethphage [*on the east side of the Mount of Olives*], unto the mount of Olives, **then sent Jesus two disciples,**

2 **Saying** unto them, **Go into the village** over against you [*ahead of you*], and straightway [*immediately*] **ye shall find an ass** [*donkey*] **tied, and a colt** [*a young male donkey*] **with her: loose** [*untie*] **them, and bring them unto me.**

3 And **if any man say ought** unto you [*questions you about what you are doing*], ye shall **say, The Lord hath need of them**; and straightway [*immediately*] **he will send them.**

4 All this was done, that it might be fulfilled which was **spoken by the prophet** [*Zechariah; see Zechariah 9:9*], saying,

5 Tell ye the daughter of Sion, **Behold, thy King cometh unto thee, meek, and sitting upon an ass,** and a colt the foal [*offspring*] of an ass.

> In Hebrew symbolism, a donkey represents humility and submission. Thus, the Savior's riding into Jerusalem on a donkey is symbolic of his humility and submission to the coming suffering and crucifixion.

6 And **the disciples went, and did as Jesus commanded** them,

7 **And brought the ass,** and the colt, and put on them their clothes, **and they set him thereon.**

JST Matthew 21:5
5 And the disciples went, and did as Jesus commanded them; **and brought the colt,** and put **on it their clothes**; **and Jesus took the colt and sat thereon; and they followed him** [*see also Luke 19:30*].

> Have you ever noticed the miracle that just happened here? Luke 19:30 informs us that the colt had never been ridden before. Yet, the Master sat on it with no trouble from the colt, reminding us that Jesus has power over the animal kingdom too.

8 And **a very great multitude spread their garments in the way** [*along the path where Jesus rode*]; **others cut down branches from the trees** [*from palm trees–John 12:13*], **and strawed** [*spread*] **them in the way.**

> In Jewish symbolism, palm branches symbolized triumph and victory. Thus, in cutting palm branches and excitedly waving them and spreading them on the ground in front of the Savior, the crowd was enthusiastically expressing their belief that Jesus would bring them military triumph and victory over their Roman enemies.

9 And **the multitudes** that went before, and that followed, **cried,** saying, **Hosanna to the Son of David: Blessed is he that cometh in the name of the Lord; Hosanna in the highest.**

> The word "Hosanna" means "Lord, save us, now!" (see Bible Dictionary, under "Hosanna") and ties in with the symbolism of palm branches mentioned above.

10 And **when he was come into Jerusalem, all the city was moved** [*everyone in the city was excited about him*], **saying, Who is this?**

11 **And the multitude said, This is Jesus the prophet of Nazareth** of Galilee.

Jesus Cleanses the Temple

12 And Jesus went into the temple of God, and cast out all them that sold and bought in the temple, and overthrew the tables of the moneychangers, and the seats of them that sold doves,

> John tells us (John 2:14–17) that Jesus cleansed the temple at the beginning of his ministry. Now, three years later, Jesus cleanses the temple again. This is the second time. The temple crowd obviously didn't learn their lesson the first time.

13 And said unto them, **It is written** [*in Isaiah 56:7*]**, My house shall be called the house of prayer; but ye have made it a den of thieves.**

14 And the blind and the lame came to him **in the temple**; and he healed them.

> Did you notice that Jesus didn't immediately leave the temple, after having cleansed it? No doubt there was potential danger to him from the authorities. Nevertheless, he remained for a considerable time to heal people who came to him. This must have been extremely frustrating to the Jewish religious leaders who "were sore displeased" (verse 15).

15 And when **the chief priests and scribes** [*Jewish religious leaders*] **saw the wonderful things that he did**, and the **children crying in the temple, and saying, Hosanna** [*"Save now;" see Bible Dictionary, under "Hosanna"*] to the Son of David; **they were sore** [*very*] **displeased,**

JST Matthew 21:13 and part of verse 14 (Bible, verse 16)

13 And when the chief priests and scribes saw the wonderful things that he did, and the children **of the kingdom** [*faithful members of the Church*] crying in the temple, and saying, Hosanna to the Son of David! they were sore displeased, **and said unto him, Hearest thou what these say?**

16 **And said unto him**, Hearest thou what these [*the "children of the kingdom" in verse 15*] say? [*In other words, do you realize how dangerous it is to you for them to be calling you the Messiah?*] **And Jesus saith unto them**, Yea; have ye never read, Out of the mouth of babes and sucklings thou hast perfected praise? [*In other words, among other possible interpretations, Jesus is saying, "You are supposed to know the scriptures. Haven't you ever read that from child-like faithful members come true praises of God?"*]

17 **And he left them, and went** out of the city **into Bethany**; and he **lodged there.**

The Fig Tree Is Cursed and Withers

18 Now **in the morning as he returned into the city** [*Jerusalem*]**, he hungered** [*was hungry*]**.**

19 **And when he saw a fig tree** in

the way [*by the roadside*], **he came to it, and found nothing thereon**, but leaves only, **and said unto it, Let no fruit grow on thee henceforward for ever. And presently** [*immediately*] **the fig tree withered away**.

> The fig tree is symbolic of the hypocritical Jewish religious leaders who pretend to look official but do not produce the fruit of the gospel. It is also symbolic of the Jewish nation, the covenant people, who are "barren" as far as the gospel is concerned. See *Jesus the Christ*, p. 443.

20 And **when the disciples saw it, they marvelled**, saying, How soon is the fig tree withered away!

21 **Jesus answered** [*responded*] **and said unto them, Verily I say unto you, If ye have faith**, and doubt not, **ye shall not only do this** which is done to the fig tree, **but** also **if ye shall say unto this mountain, Be thou removed**, and be thou cast into the sea; **it shall be done**.

22 And **all things, whatsoever ye shall ask in prayer, believing, ye shall receive**. [*See also D&C 46:30, 50:30.*]

23 **And when he was come into the temple, the chief priests and the elders** of the people [*the Jewish religious leaders who are trying to trap Him*] **came** unto him as he was teaching, **and said, By what authority doest thou these things?** and who gave thee this authority?

24 And **Jesus answered** and said unto them, **I also will ask you one thing, which if ye tell me, I in like wise will tell you by what authority I do these things**.

25 **The baptism of John** [*the Baptist*], **whence was it?** from heaven, or of men [*did John the Baptist have authority from heaven, or was he just another man*]? **And they reasoned with themselves, saying, If we shall say, From heaven**; he [*Jesus*] will say unto us, Why did ye not then believe him?

26 **But if we shall say, Of men**; we fear the people; for all hold John as a prophet. [*If we say John the Baptist was just an ordinary man, the people will mob us, because they consider him to be sent from God.*]

27 **And they answered** Jesus, and said, **We cannot tell**. And **he said unto them, Neither tell I you** by what authority I do these things.

> The following parable is known as The Parable of the Two Sons. The second son in the parable represents the hypocritical Jewish religious leaders who claim to agree to do the work of the Lord, but do not do it.

The Parable of the Two Sons

28 **But what think ye?** A certain man had **two sons**; and he came to **the first**, and said, Son, go work to day in my vineyard.

29 He answered and **said, I will not: but afterward he repented, and went**.

30 And he came to **the second**, and said likewise. And he answered and **said, I go, sir: and went not**.

31 **Whether of them twain** [*which of the two*] **did the will of his father?** They say unto him, **The first. Jesus saith** unto them, Verily I say unto you, **That the publicans** [*hated Jewish tax collectors*] **and the harlots** [*prostitutes*] **go into the kingdom of God before you** [*are more likely to get to heaven than you are*].

32 **For John** [*the Baptist*] **came unto you** in the way of righteousness, **and ye believed him not: but the publicans and the harlots** [*sinners*] **believed him** [*repented*]: **and ye**, when ye had seen it, **repented not** afterward [*like the first son in the above parable*], that ye might believe him.

JST Matthew 21:32–34

32 For John came unto you in the way of righteousness, **and bore record of me**, and ye believed him not; but the publicans and the harlots believed him; and **ye, afterward, when ye had seen me, repented not, that ye might believe him.**

33 For he that believed not John concerning me, cannot believe me, except he first repent.

34 And except ye repent, the preaching of John shall condemn you at the day of judgment. And, again, hear another parable; for **unto you that believe not, I speak in parables; that your unrighteousness may be rewarded unto you.**

In this next parable, known as the Parable of the Wicked Husbandmen, the Savior clearly compares the wicked Jewish religious leaders to the wicked husbandmen who kill the owner's son in an attempt to take the kingdom from him. The notes in parentheses in the parable represent one possible interpretation of it.

The Parable of the Wicked Husbandmen

33 Hear another parable: There was **a certain householder** [*Heavenly Father*], which **planted a vineyard** [*had the earth created and put people on it*], and **hedged it round about** [*set up protections for it*], and **digged a winepress in it** [*planned on a good harvest*], and **built a tower** [*so people could watch for enemies*], and **let it out to husbandmen** [*stewards who were supposed to take good care of it*], **and went into a far country** [*heaven*]:

34 And **when the time of the fruit** [*harvest time*] **drew near, he sent his servants** [*prophets*] **to the husbandmen** [*the Jewish religious leaders*], that they might receive the fruits of it.

35 And **the husbandmen took his servants** [*prophets*], **and beat** one, and **killed** another, and **stoned** another.

36 Again, **he sent other servants** [*prophets*] **more than the first: and they** [*the wicked husbandmen*] **did unto them likewise.**

37 But **last of all he sent unto them his son** [*Christ*], saying, They will reverence my son.

38 **But when the husbandmen saw the son, they said among themselves, This is the heir; come, let us kill him, and let us seize on his inheritance.**

39 **And they** caught him, and cast him out of the vineyard, and **slew him** [*crucified Him*].

Now, the question, to which this parable has been leading:

40 **When the lord** [*Christ*] **therefore of the vineyard cometh, what will he do unto those husbandmen?**

The answer:

41 They [*the chief priests and elders in verse 23*] say unto him [*Jesus*], **He will miserably destroy those wicked men, and will let out his vineyard unto other husbandmen** [*righteous religious leaders*], **which shall render him the fruits in their seasons** [*will bring righteous souls to Him at the time of harvest.*

42 **Jesus saith** unto them, **Did ye never read in the scriptures** [*in Psalm 118:22–23*], **The stone** [*Christ*] **which the builders rejected, the same is become the head of the corner** [*the capstone or cornerstone*]: **this is the Lord's doing, and it is marvellous in our eyes**?

43 **Therefore say I unto you** [*Jewish religious leaders*], **The kingdom of God shall be taken from you, and given to a nation** [*Gentiles*] **bringing forth the fruits thereof** [*who will bring the desired harvest of righteous souls to Me*].

44 And **whosoever shall fall on this stone** [*Christ*] **shall be broken: but on whomsoever it shall fall, it will grind him to powder** [*no one can ultimately stop the Lord's work*].

Next, the Jewish religious leaders finally get the message.

45 And when the chief priests and Pharisees had heard his parables, **they perceived that he spake of them.**

"They perceived that he spake of them" in verse 45 above is very important to our understanding of what is going on here. Some people think that the Jewish religious leaders did not really understand who Jesus was. That is not true. They did indeed understand who Jesus was and set out to kill Him. On the cross, when Christ said "Father, forgive them for they know not what they do" (Luke 23:34), He was obviously referring to the Roman soldiers and perhaps others, but not the Jewish religious leaders. This fact is confirmed again in JST Matthew 21:47, quoted after verse 46, below, where it says the same thing, "they perceived that he spake of them."

46 **But when they sought to lay hands on him, they feared the multitude, because they took him for a prophet.** [*They were afraid the people would mob them if they arrested Jesus.*]

The JST contains over two hundred added words of explanation for this parable. They are included here:

JST Matthew 47–56

47 [*Bible, verse 45*] And when the chief priests and Pharisees had heard his parables, they perceived that he spake of them.

48 **And they said among themselves, Shall this man think that he alone can spoil this great kingdom** [*the religious kingdom set up by these Jewish religious leaders for their own advantage*]**? And they were angry with him.**

49 [*Bible, verse 46*] But when they sought to lay hands on him, they feared the multitude, because they **learned that the multitude** took him for a prophet.

50 **And now his disciples came to him, and Jesus said unto them, Marvel ye at the words of the parable which I spake unto them?**

51 **Verily, I say unto you, I am the stone, and those wicked ones reject me.**

52 **I am the head of the corner. These Jews shall fall upon me, and shall be broken.**

53 **And the kingdom of God shall be taken from them, and shall be given to a nation bringing forth the fruits thereof;** [*meaning the Gentiles.*]

54 **Wherefore, on whomsoever this stone shall fall, it shall grind him to powder.**

55 **And when the Lord therefore of the vineyard cometh, he will destroy those miserable, wicked men, and will let again his vineyard unto other husbandmen, even in the last days** [*the restoration through the Prophet Joseph Smith*]**, who shall render him the fruits in their seasons.**

56 **And then understood they the parable which he spake unto them, that the Gentiles** [*the wicked Gentiles in the last days*] **should be destroyed also, when the Lord should descend out of heaven** [*the Second Coming*] **to reign in his vineyard, which is the earth and the inhabitants thereof.**

MATTHEW 22

Jesus will give more parables, but this next one, the Parable of the Marriage of the King's Son, will be the last one directed specifically at the Jewish religious leaders and rulers who have been aggressively trying to trap Him all day (see chapter

21 above). The parable is a direct warning to the murderous Jewish rulers who have killed past prophets and now seek to arrest and kill Jesus. Notes in brackets provide one possible interpretation of the parable.

The Parable of the Marriage of the King's Son

1 AND **Jesus** answered and **spake unto them again by parables**, and said,

2 **The kingdom of heaven is like** unto **a certain king** [*Heavenly Father*], which **made a marriage** [*marriage symbolizes an opportunity to make covenants; the "bride" for this marriage would be those who are willing to become righteous Saints by making and keeping covenants*] **for his son** [*Christ*],

3 And **sent forth his servants** [*prophets, missionaries, members, etc.*] **to call them** that were bidden [*invited; Israelites*] **to the wedding**: and **they would not come**.

4 Again, **he sent forth other servants** [*prophets*], saying, Tell them which are bidden, Behold, **I have prepared my dinner** [*gospel feast*]: my oxen and my **fatlings** [*the very best; symbolic of the gospel of Jesus Christ*] are killed, and all things are ready: **come unto the marriage**. [*In other words, I have a great gospel feast prepared for you. Come make covenants with Me in order to partake.*]

5 **But they made light of it** [*made fun of it, ridiculed it*], **and went their ways**, one to his farm, another to his merchandise: [*Some ignored the invitation.*]

6 **And the remnant** [*the wicked Jewish religious leaders and rulers in Matthew 21:23*] **took his servants, and entreated them spitefully** [*treated them cruelly*], **and slew them.** [*Some violently opposed the Lord's servants who brought the invitation to come to the feast.*]

7 **But when the king heard thereof, he was wroth** [*angry*]: **and he sent forth his armies, and destroyed those murderers, and burned up their city.** [*This was partially fulfilled when the Roman armies devastated the Jews, especially about 70 to A.D. 73.*]

8 **Then saith he to his servants, The wedding** [*the gospel, the true Church*] **is ready, but they which were bidden** [*the covenant people who were in a state of wickedness and apostasy at the time of Christ*] **were not worthy.**

9 **Go ye therefore into the highways**, and **as many as ye shall find, bid to the marriage.** [*Go to all the world and invite everyone.*]

10 **So those servants** went out into the highways, and **gathered** together all **as many as they found, both bad and good** [*note that in this gathering, some unrighteous join the Church, along with the righteous converts*]:

and the wedding was furnished with guests.

11 And **when the king came** in to see the guests, **he saw there a man which had not on a wedding garment** [*"robes of righteousness"—see N. T. student manual, Rel. 211, p. 146; symbolic of one who had had time and opportunity to properly prepare for meeting the Savior, but had not*]:

12 **And he saith** unto him, Friend, **how camest thou in hither not having a wedding garment** [*not having made and kept covenants; personal righteousness—see Revelation 19:8*]? **And he was speechless** [*was without excuse—see 2 Nephi 9:14*].

13 **Then said the king** to the servants, **Bind** him hand and foot, and take him away, and **cast him into outer darkness** [*in this context, "outer darkness" would mean the spirit prison—see Alma 40:13—and also could mean telestial glory—see D&C 76:103*]; there shall be weeping and gnashing of teeth. [*The wicked cannot remain in the presence of God and must be punished for their sins.*]

14 **For many are called** [*to make and keep covenants with God*], **but few are chosen** [*to receive exaltation*]. [*In fact, all are "called" to come unto Christ, but few are "chosen" to remain with him forever, because they do not make themselves worthy.*]

JST Matthew 22:14

14 For many are called, but few chosen; **wherefore all do not have on the wedding garment** [*symbolic of having made and kept covenants with God*].

The "few" in verse 14, above, must be considered in context of the wicked Jewish kingdom at this time in the history of the world. Few of them will be ultimately chosen for exaltation because they deliberately reject the Savior.

Elsewhere in the scriptures, we find that there will ultimately be "innumerable" who will make it to exaltation (see D&C 76:67, Revelation 7:9). Also, taking into account that "all children who die before they arrive at the years of accountability are saved in the celestial kingdom of heaven" (D&C 137:10), and recognizing that statistics show that between 50% and 80% of all children born have died in infancy throughout the history of the world, we come to the conclusion that well over half of the people ever born will inherit celestial glory. Furthermore, President Joseph F. Smith taught that these children not only gain celestial glory, but they "will inherit their exaltation" (*Gospel Doctrine*, pp. 453–55).

As we continue, we see that the leaders of the Jews are now getting desperate.

15 **Then went the Pharisees** [*Jewish religious leaders*], **and**

took counsel how they might entangle [*trap*] **him in his talk.**

16 **And they sent out unto him** [*Christ*] **their disciples** [*their loyal, wicked followers*] **with the Herodians** [*a political party among the Jews (see Bible Dictionary, under "Herodians") who normally opposed the Pharisees, but now joined with them in opposing Christ*], **saying, Master, we know that thou art true, and teachest the way of God in truth, neither carest thou for any man: for thou regardest not the person of men.**

> Verse 16, above, is dripping with sarcasm and false flattery. These men are going to try to get Jesus to say something against the Roman government so they can get him arrested and executed for treason. Watch as they attempt to lure Him into their trap, in verse 17, next.

Paying Taxes

17 Tell us therefore, **What thinkest thou? Is it lawful to give tribute** [*pay taxes*] **unto Cæsar** [*the Roman emperor*], **or not?**

18 **But Jesus perceived their wickedness, and said, Why tempt ye me, ye hypocrites?**

19 **Shew** [*pronounced "show"*] **me the tribute money. And they brought unto him a penny** [*a Roman denarius, about the equivalent of a day's pay*].

20 And he saith unto them, **Whose is this image** [*picture*] **and superscription** [*the writing on the coin*]?

21 **They say** unto him, **Cæsar's.** **Then saith he** unto them, **Render** [*give*] **therefore unto Cæsar the things which are Cæsar's; and unto God the things that are God's.**

22 **When they had heard these words, they marvelled** [*were amazed*], and left him, **and went their way.**

23 **The same day came to him the Sadducees**, which say that there is no resurrection [*who do not believe in the resurrection*], **and asked him**,

> The Sadducees were another influential group of religious leaders among the Jews. They did not believe in the resurrection, and were normally enemies of the Pharisees who did believe in resurrection. The Sadducees have now joined forces with the Pharisees in attempting to do away with Jesus.

24 Saying, **Master, Moses said, If a man die, having no children, his brother shall marry his wife, and raise up seed unto his brother** [*have children for his dead brother; plural marriage was in practice at this time in the Old and New Testament*].

One Wife, Seven Brothers

25 Now **there were with us seven brethren** [*brothers*]: **and the first, when he had married a wife, deceased** [*died*], **and, having no issue** [*children*], **left his wife unto his brother** [*as required by the Law of Moses—see Deuteronomy 25:5*]:

26 **Likewise the second also, and the third, unto the seventh.** [*Each of the six brothers likewise married her, but died, without her having any children.*]

27 And **last of all the woman died also.**

And now, the question designed by the Sadducees to entrap the Master.

28 **Therefore in the resurrection whose wife shall she be of the seven? for they all had her** [*had her as a wife*].

Eternal Marriage Is Preached Here in These Verses.

Here is a major doctrinal point. Many religions use these next two verses to prove that there is no such thing as eternal marriage and family in the next life. On the contrary, the simple fact that the Sadducees asked the Savior (in verse 28) whose wife she will be when they are all resurrected is proof that the Savior had indeed preached marriage in the resurrection, in other words, eternal marriage. Otherwise, their question would not make any sense at all!

29 **Jesus answered** and said unto them, **Ye do err, not knowing the scriptures,** nor the power of God.

30 For **in the resurrection they neither marry, nor are given in marriage, but are as the angels of God in heaven** [*refers to those who do not qualify for eternal marriage either in this life or in the postmortal spirit world or during the Millennium—see D&C 132:15–17*].

Here again, correct doctrine needs to be understood. After everyone from this earth is resurrected, there will be no more eternal marriages performed for them, because such marriages have to be done by mortals for themselves, or by mortals who serve as proxies for those who have died—see D&C 128:15 & 18. Brigham Young said: "And **when the Millennium is over, ...all the sons and daughters of Adam and Eve**, down to the last of their posterity (bold added for emphasis), **who come within the reach of the clemency of the Gospel, [will] have been redeemed in hundreds of temples through the administration of their children as proxies for them.**" *Discourses of Brigham Young*, p. 395. Since there will be no mortals left on earth after the resurrection is completed, there would be no one left to serve as proxies for eternal marriages.

31 **But as touching the resurrection of the dead, have ye not read** that which was spoken unto you by God, saying,

32 I am the God of Abraham, and the God of Isaac, and the God of Jacob [*quoting Exodus 3:6*]? **God is not the God of the dead, but of the living.** [*In other words, you Sadducees should believe in resurrection.*]

33 And **when the multitude heard this, they were astonished at his doctrine.**

34 But **when the Pharisees had heard that he had put the Sadducees to silence, they were gathered together.** [*The Pharisees now take over again, since the Sadducees were unsuccessful.*]

35 Then **one of them, which was a lawyer, asked him a question**, tempting him [*trying to trap Jesus*], and saying,

36 **Master, which is the great commandment in the law?** [*"The law," as used here, means the Law of Moses, in other words, the first five books of the Old Testament: Genesis, Exodus, Leviticus, Numbers, Deuteronomy.*]

37 **Jesus said** unto him, **Thou shalt love the Lord thy God with all thy heart, and with all thy soul, and with all thy mind** [*Deuteronomy 6:5*].

38 **This is the first and great commandment.**

39 And **the second is like unto it, Thou shalt love thy neighbour as thyself** [*Leviticus 19:18*].

40 **On these two commandments hang all the law and the prophets.** [*All the other commandments are based on these two commandments. As stated above, the "law" meant Genesis, Exodus, Leviticus, Numbers, and Deuteronomy. The "prophets" meant writings of Old Testament prophets such as Isaiah, Jeremiah, etc.*]

41 While the Pharisees were gathered together, **Jesus asked them,**

42 Saying, **What think ye of Christ? whose son is he? They say unto him, The Son of David** [*a descendant of King David*].

43 **He saith** unto them, **How then doth David in spirit call him Lord** [*why would David, speaking under inspiration, refer to Him as "Lord?"*], **saying,**

44 **The LORD** [*Heavenly Father*] **said unto my Lord** [*Christ*], **Sit thou on my right hand, till I make thine enemies thy footstool?** [*See Hebrews 1:3 for the interpretations given in brackets above; also see Bruce R. McConkie, Doctrinal New Testament Commentary, Vol. 1, p. 612.*]

45 **If David then call him Lord, how is he his son?**

46 And **no man was able to answer** him a word, **neither durst** [*dared*] **any man from that day forth ask him any more questions.** [*It was getting pretty embarrassing trying to trap Jesus with questions because He outsmarted them every time!*]

MATTHEW 23

In this chapter, the scribes and Pharisees get a scathing rebuke from the Savior because of their wickedness and hypocrisy. Perhaps you have noticed that hypocrites were the only category of people who incurred such scathing righteous indignation of the Savior. It is obviously wise to avoid hypocrisy, since it is one of the most spiritually debilitating sins.

Imagine the rapt attention given to the Master as He delivered the following words to the scribes and Pharisees within the hearing of the multitudes as well as His loyal followers.

1 **THEN spake Jesus to the multitude, and to his disciples,**

2 Saying, **The scribes and the Pharisees sit in Moses' seat** [*have offices of high authority among you*]:

3 **All therefore whatsoever they bid you observe, that observe and do** [*go ahead and do everything they ask you to do; in other words, respect the office they hold*]; **but do not ye after their works** [*don't behave like they do*]: **for they say, and do not** [*they are hypocrites*].

4 For **they bind heavy burdens and grievous to be borne, and lay them on men's shoulders** [*they give you all kinds of very difficult tasks to accomplish*]; **but they themselves will not move them with one of their fingers** [*but they won't lift a finger to help*].

5 **But all their works they do for to be seen of men** [*everything they do is for show*]: **they make broad their phylacteries, and enlarge the borders of their garments,**

Phylacteries were small leather boxes, beautifully crafted, which faithful Jews tied to their forehead ("forehead" was symbolic of loyalty to God in their culture) and left arm (to be near the heart). Inside these small leather boxes were four tiny scrolls containing Exodus 13:2–10, Exodus 13:11–17, Deuteronomy 6:4–9, and Deuteronomy 11:13–21. The scribes and Pharisees had made their phylacteries larger than normal so people could see how "righteous" they were. Likewise, they had enlarged the blue fringes on their clothing (see Numbers 15:38–39) which symbolized keeping the commandments of God.

6 **And love the uppermost rooms at feasts** [*want to be seen and recognized publicly as very important people*], **and the chief seats in the synagogues** [*Jewish church buildings*],

7 **And greetings in the markets, and to be called of** [*by*] **men, Rabbi, Rabbi** [*"my master"— see Bible Dictionary, under "Rabbi"*].

8 **But be not ye** [*Jesus is addressing the multitude and His disciples— see verse 1*] **called Rabbi: for one**

is your Master, even Christ; and all ye are brethren [*you should not consider yourselves better than each other*].

9 And **call no man your father upon the earth**: for one is your Father, which is in heaven.

JST Matthew 23:6

6 And call no **one your creator** upon the earth, **or your heavenly Father; for one is your creator and heavenly Father, even he who** is in heaven.

10 **Neither be ye called masters: for one is your Master, even Christ.**

JST Matthew 23:7

7 Neither be ye called masters; for one is your master, **even he whom your heavenly Father sent, which is Christ; for he hath sent him among you that ye might have life**.

11 But **he that is greatest among you shall be your servant.** [*This is a major message that Christ is teaching the multitude and His disciples.*]

12 **And whosoever shall exalt himself** [*pridefully set himself up as an example*] **shall be abased** [*humbled, put down*]; **and he that shall humble himself shall be exalted.**

JST Matthew 23:9

9 And whosoever shall exalt himself shall be abased **of him**; and he that shall humble himself shall be exalted **of him**.

13 **But woe unto you, scribes and Pharisees, hypocrites! for ye shut up the kingdom of heaven against men** [*you make so many nitpicky rules that nobody could get into heaven*]: **for ye neither go in yourselves** [*you won't get to heaven yourselves*], **neither suffer** [*allow*] **ye them that are entering to go in** [*and you won't let anyone else in either!*].

14 **Woe unto you, scribes and Pharisees, hypocrites! for ye devour widows' houses** [*foreclose on widows' mortgages and take their houses from them via technicalities of the law*], **and for a pretence** [*for show*] **make long prayer: therefore ye shall receive the greater damnation.**

15 **Woe unto you, scribes and Pharisees, hypocrites! for ye compass sea and land to make one proselyte** [*you travel far and wide to get one convert*], **and when he is made** [*when he joins your church*], **ye make him twofold more the child of hell than yourselves.**

JST Matthew 23:12

12 Woe unto you, scribes and Pharisees, hypocrites! For ye compass sea and land to make one proselyte; and when he is made, ye make him **twofold more the child of hell than he was before, like unto yourselves**.

In verses 16–24, next, Jesus

points out several examples of the hypocritical, nitpicky, laden-with-details rules which these religious leaders have forced upon their people. They have made so many rules that nobody can figure them out and follow them all properly, which puts these leaders in a position of constant power over the people.

16 **Woe unto you, ye blind guides, which say, Whosoever shall swear** [*make vows, promises, covenants*] **by the temple, it is nothing; but whosoever shall swear by the gold of the temple, he is a debtor!**

17 **Ye fools and blind: for whether is greater** [*which is more important*], **the gold, or the temple that sanctifieth the gold** [*makes the gold holy*]?

18 **And** [*according to the rules you have made*], **Whosoever shall swear by the altar, it is nothing; but whosoever sweareth by the gift that is upon it, he is guilty** [*of sin*].

19 **Ye fools and blind: for whether is greater** [*which is more important*], **the gift, or the altar that sanctifieth the gift?**

20 **Whoso therefore shall swear by the altar, sweareth by it, and by all things thereon.**

21 **And whoso shall swear by the temple, sweareth by it, and by him that dwelleth therein.**

22 **And he that shall swear by heaven, sweareth by the throne of God, and by him that sitteth thereon.** [*More of their impossible rules.*]

23 **Woe unto you, scribes and Pharisees, hypocrites! for ye pay tithe of mint and anise** [*dill*] **and cummin** [*you weigh out the tiniest amounts of seeds and spices with exactness to see how much tithing you should pay on them*], **and have omitted** the weightier [*more important*] **matters of the law, judgment** [*fairness; integrity*], **mercy,** and **faith: these ought ye to have done, and not to leave the other undone.**

24 **Ye blind guides, which strain at a gnat** [*Greek: "strain out a gnat"*], **and swallow a camel.**

JST Matthew 23:21
21 Ye blind guides, who strain at a gnat, and swallow a camel; **who make yourselves appear unto men that ye would not commit the least sin, and yet ye yourselves, transgress the whole law.**

The Savior's use of gnats and camels in verse 24, above, carries an extra dimension of meaning for these hypocrites, since both gnats (Leviticus 11:23) and camels (Leviticus 11:4) were "unclean" and thus forbidden as food for the Jews.

25 **Woe unto you, scribes and Pharisees, hypocrites! for ye make clean the outside of the cup and of the platter, but within they are full of extortion** [*greed*] **and excess** [*self-indulgence—see*

Matthew 23:25, footnotes a and b].

26 Thou blind Pharisee, **cleanse first that which is within the cup and platter, that the outside of them may be clean also.**

27 **Woe unto you, scribes and Pharisees, hypocrites!** for ye are like unto whited sepulchres [*whitewashed graves, tombs*], which indeed appear beautiful outward, but are within [*inside*] full of dead men's bones, and of all uncleanness.

28 Even so **ye also outwardly appear righteous unto men, but within ye are full of hypocrisy and iniquity** [*wickedness*].

29 **Woe unto you, scribes and Pharisees, hypocrites!** because **ye build the tombs of the prophets, and garnish** [*decorate*] **the sepulchres** [*graves, tombs*] **of the righteous** [*you appear to honor ancient prophets, such as Abraham, Moses, Isaiah, Jeremiah, etc.*],

30 **And say, If we had been** [*lived*] **in the days of our fathers** [*ancestors*], **we would not have been partakers with them in the blood of the prophets** [*we wouldn't have killed prophets like they did*].

31 Wherefore **ye be witnesses unto yourselves**, that ye are the children of them which killed the prophets. [*You are just like your ancestors!*]

JST Matthew 23:28
28 Wherefore, **ye are witnesses unto yourselves of your own wickedness**, and ye are the children of them who killed the prophets;

32 **Fill ye up then the measure of your fathers** [*go ahead and fill your lives with sin just like your ancestors did*].

JST Matthew 23:29
29 **And will fill up the measure then of your fathers** [*will become as wicked as your ancestors*]; **for ye, yourselves, kill the prophets like unto your fathers**.

33 **Ye serpents** [*you are like Satan—see Revelation 12:9*], **ye generation of vipers** [*poisonous snakes*], **how can ye escape the damnation of hell?**

Some people claim that Jesus never did come right out and claim that He was the promised Messiah, the Son of God or the God of the Old Testament. Such is clearly not the case, as evidenced in verse 34, next.

34 Wherefore, **behold, I send unto you prophets, and wise men, and scribes:** and some of them ye shall kill and crucify; and some of them shall ye scourge [*whip, beat*] in your synagogues [*churches*], and persecute them from city to city:

35 **That upon you may come all the righteous blood shed upon the earth** [*you have murderous hearts and deserve to be punished with others who have likewise persecuted and killed the righteous in the past*], from the blood of righteous **Abel** unto the blood

of **Zacharias** [*John the Baptist's father*] son of Barachias, **whom ye slew between the temple and the altar.**

> Zacharias was the father of John the Baptist. Joseph Smith tells us that when King Herod ordered all the babies two years old and younger killed in Bethlehem and surrounding area (see Matthew 2:16), Zacharias sent Elizabeth and John "into the mountains" to hide. "When his father refused to disclose his hiding place (he) was slain by Herod's order, between the porch and the altar." of the temple. See *Teachings of the Prophet Joseph Smith*, p. 261. Apparently, from what Jesus is saying to the scribes and Pharisees in verse 35, these evil leaders must have had a hand in getting Zacharias killed.

36 Verily I say unto you, **All these things shall come upon this generation.**

> The JST adds three verses here:

JST Matthew 23:34–36

34 Ye bear testimony against your fathers, when ye, yourselves, are partakers of the same wickedness.

35 Behold your fathers did it through ignorance, but ye do not; wherefore, their sins shall be upon your heads.

36 Then Jesus began to weep over Jerusalem, saying,

37 **O Jerusalem, Jerusalem, thou that killest the prophets, and stonest them which are sent unto thee, how often would I have gathered thy children together, even as a hen gathereth her chickens under her wings, and ye would not!** [*You wouldn't let Me gather and protect you.*]

38 Behold, **your house is left unto you desolate** [*your nation will be destroyed and scattered*].

39 For **I say unto you, Ye shall not see me henceforth, till ye shall say, Blessed is he that cometh in the name of the Lord.** [*You won't see me until the Second Coming.*]

JST Matthew 23:39–41

39 For I say unto you, that ye shall not see me henceforth, **and know that I am he of whom it is written by the prophets,** until ye shall say,

40 Blessed is he who cometh in the name of the Lord, **in the clouds of heaven, and all the holy angels with him** [*the Second Coming*].

41 **Then understood his disciples that he should come again on the earth, after that he was glorified and crowned on the right hand of God.**

MATTHEW 24

At this point in history, it is still the third day of the last week of the Savior's mortal life (see the New Testament student manual, Religion 211, pp. 136 and 150). The most common thinking is

Matthew 24

that this is Tuesday. He will be crucified on Friday. After His severe scolding of the hypocritical Jewish leaders in chapter 23, Jesus has left the temple. He will not teach the public any more, rather He will spend the rest of the last week of His mortal life teaching the Twelve. They will approach Him now and look back at the temple, and He will teach them many things that will occur before His Second Coming.

Matthew 24 is very well known among Christians because it contains so many prophecies which will be fulfilled before the Second Coming. These prophecies are known as "the signs of the times." Many of them are being fulfilled in our day and bear witness to us that the gospel is true and that the Second Coming is near. However, since we do not know how close it is, we should plan on living a full lifetime and keeping our lives in order, so that when we meet the Savior, whether at our death, or at His coming, we will be prepared.

Because Joseph Smith added about 450 words to this chapter, as well as rearranged the verse order in some cases in JS—Matthew in the Pearl of Great Price, we will include it in this study guide after we have gone through Matthew 24 as it stands in our Bible.

1 AND **Jesus went out, and departed from the temple** [*in Jerusalem*]: **and his disciples came to him for to shew** [*show*] **him the buildings of the temple**.

2 **And Jesus said** unto them, See ye not all these things? verily I say unto you, **There shall not be left here one stone upon another, that shall not be thrown down.** [*The temple will be destroyed. The Romans destroyed much, culminating with the final conquering of Jerusalem about A.D. 70.*]

3 And **as he sat upon the mount of Olives** [*located just outside of Jerusalem*], **the disciples came unto him privately, saying, Tell us, when shall these things be** [*the things Jesus had just prophesied*]? and **what shall be the sign of thy coming, and of the end of the world?**

JST Matthew 24:1–4

1 And Jesus went out, and departed from the temple; and his disciples came to him for to **hear him, saying, Master, show us concerning** the buildings of the temple; **as thou hast said; They shall be thrown down and left unto you desolate.**

2 And Jesus said unto them, See ye not all these things? **And do ye not understand them? Verily I say unto you,** There shall not be left **here upon this temple**, one stone upon another, that shall not be thrown down.

3 **And Jesus left them and went upon the mount of Olives.**

4 And as he sat upon the mount of Olives, the disciples came

unto him privately, saying, Tell us, when shall these things be **which thou hast said concerning the destruction of the temple, and the Jews;** and what is the sign of thy coming; and of the end of the world? **(or the destruction of the wicked, which is the end of the world.)**

In verse 3, above, the disciples asked Jesus two questions: (1) "When shall these things be?" (meaning the things that will happen to Jerusalem, the Jews, and the early Christians following the crucifixion), and (2) "What shall be the sign of thy coming, and of the end of the world?" (meaning the "signs of the times" preceding His Second Coming).

4 And **Jesus answered** and said unto them, **Take heed** [*be careful*] **that no man deceive you.**

5 For **many shall come in my name**, saying, I am Christ; and **shall deceive many.**

6 And ye shall hear of **wars and rumours of wars**: see that ye be not troubled [*don't let the signs of the times cause undue fear or panic in you*]: for all these things must come to pass, but the end is not yet.

7 For **nation shall rise against nation**, and kingdom against kingdom: and there shall be **famines**, and **pestilences**, and **earthquakes**, in divers [*various*] places.

8 All these are the beginning of sorrows.

9 **Then shall they deliver you up to be afflicted**, and shall **kill you**: and **ye shall be hated of all nations for my name's sake.**

10 And then shall **many** be **offended** [*many will leave the Church*], and shall **betray one another**, and shall **hate one another.**

11 And many **false prophets** shall rise, and shall deceive many.

> Many people, when they read "false prophets," think only of false ministers and preachers of false doctrines and philosophies. They would be wise not to limit their understanding to these types, rather to include any famous, influential individuals and groups who gather followers and lead them astray. This can include politicians, movie stars, singers, gang leaders, and so forth.

12 And because **iniquity** [*wickedness*] **shall abound** [*will be everywhere*], the **love of many shall wax** [*grow*] **cold.**

13 **But he that shall endure unto the end, the same shall be saved.**

14 And **this gospel of the kingdom shall be preached in all the world for a witness unto all nations** [*one of the last major signs which will happen before the Savior's Second Coming*]; **and then shall the end** [*of wickedness*] **come.** [*The Millennium will then begin*].

15 When ye therefore shall see **the abomination of desolation**, spoken of by Daniel the prophet

[*in Dan. 11:31; 12:11*], **stand in the holy place**, (whoso readeth, let him understand):

"Abomination of desolation" means terrible things which will cause much destruction and misery. The abomination of desolation spoken of by Daniel was to have two fulfillments. The first occurred in A.D. 70 when Titus, with his Roman legions, surrounded Jerusalem and laid siege to conquer the Jews. This siege resulted in much destruction and terrible human misery and loss of life. In the last days, the abomination of desolation will occur again (see Joseph Smith–Matthew 1:31–32), meaning that Jerusalem will again be under siege. (See also Bible Dictionary, under "Abomination of Desolation).

16 **Then let them which be in Judæa flee into the mountains**: [*Many faithful Saints heeded this warning and fled to Pella, east of Samaria, and thus escaped the Romans.*]

17 **Let him which is on the housetop not come down to take any thing out of his house:**

18 **Neither let him which is in the field return back to take his clothes.**

19 And **woe unto them that are with child, and to them that give suck in those days!**

20 But **pray ye that your flight be not in the winter, neither on the sabbath day** [*when city gates are closed*]:

21 For then shall be **great tribulation**, such as was not since the beginning of the world to this time, no, nor ever shall be.

22 And **except those days should be shortened, there should no flesh be saved**: but for the elect's sake those days shall be shortened [*the Lord will stop the destructions in time so that some covenant people will remain*].

23 [*Now, Jesus answers their second question—see note, verse 4.*] **Then if any man shall say unto you, Lo, here is Christ, or there; believe it not.**

24 For there shall arise **false Christs, and false prophets**, and shall shew [*show*] great signs and wonders; insomuch that, **if it were possible, they shall deceive the very elect** [*meaning those who have made covenants with God—see Joseph Smith–Matthew 1:22, in the Pearl of Great Price*].

25 **Behold, I have told you before**.

26 Wherefore **if they** [*false prophets, "gatherers," teachers, leaders, etc.*] **shall say unto you, Behold, he** [*Christ*] **is in the desert; go not forth** [*don't go to see him*]: **behold, he is in the secret chambers; believe it not.**

27 For **as the lightning** [*"lightning" is a mistake in the translation of the Bible, since lightning can come in any direction; it should be "as the light of the morning cometh out of the east"; see Joseph Smith–Matthew 1:26*] **cometh out of the**

east, and shineth even unto the west; so shall also the coming of the Son of man be. [*In other words, when He comes for the actual Second Coming, everyone will see Him. It will not be a low-key, quiet, secret coming as some false gatherers will suggest—see verse 26.*]

28 For wheresoever the carcase [*carcass*] **is, there will the eagles be gathered together.**

This is an unusual use of the word "carcase." Symbolically, in this context, it means "the body of the Church." In other words, the true Church with the true gospel. The "eagles" are converts, faithful members of the Church who will be gathered to the Church for nourishment in all parts of the world. See JS–Matthew 1:27. In short, this verse prophecies of the gathering of Israel in the last days prior to the Second Coming. See also *Doctrinal New Testament Commentary*, Vol. 1, pp. 648–49.

29 Immediately after the tribulation of those days shall the **sun** be **darkened**, and the **moon shall not give her light** [*can refer to spiritual darkness as well as actual things in nature*], and the **stars shall fall from heaven**, and the **powers of the heavens shall be shaken:**

30 And **then shall appear the sign of the Son of man in heaven** [*we don't yet know what this means*]: and **then shall all the tribes of the earth mourn** [*the wicked will mourn, but the righteous will rejoice—see 2 Nephi 9:14, D&C 88:96*]**, and they shall see the Son of man coming in the clouds of heaven with power and great glory.**

Even those who caused the Savior's crucifixion will see Him at this time. See Revelation 1:7.

31 [*As you can see, these verses are not all in chronological order.*] And he shall send his angels with a great sound of a trumpet, and **they shall gather together his elect from the four winds, from one end of heaven to the other.** [*This is the final gathering of the righteous.*]

The Parable of the Fig Tree

32 Now learn a parable of the fig tree; **When his branch is yet tender, and putteth forth leaves, ye know that summer is nigh** [*when a fruit tree starts putting on leaves, you know that summer is near*]:

33 **So likewise ye, when ye shall see all these things** [*signs of the times being fulfilled*]**, know that it** [*the Second Coming*] **is near, even at the doors.**

34 Verily I say unto you, **This generation** [*"generation" can sometimes mean "dispensation"*] **shall not pass, till all these things be fulfilled.**

35 **Heaven and earth shall pass away, but my words shall not pass away** [*you can rely on My words completely!*]**.**

36 But of that day and hour knoweth no man, no, not the angels of heaven, but my Father only.

> On occasion we hear of people who claim to know when the Second Coming will be. Sometimes they gather others around them to await the exact day they have predicted He will come. Some say they don't know the hour and day, but they do know the month and year. Some say that the Brethren know but are not allowed to tell us. Elder M. Russell Ballard, of the Quorum of the Twelve, taught the following:
>
> "I do not know when He is going to come again. As far as I know, none of my brethren in the Council of the Twelve or even in the First Presidency knows. And I would humbly suggest to you, my young brothers and sisters, that if we do not know, then nobody knows" (Talk given March 12, 1996 at a BYU Devotional).

37 But as the days of Noe [*Noah*] **were, so shall also the coming of the Son of man** [*Jesus*] **be.** [*Just as the wicked in the days of Noah did not believe the Flood would come, so also the wicked in the last days will not believe the Savior will come and thus will be caught unprepared.*]

38 For as **in the days** that were **before the flood** they were **eating** and **drinking, marrying** and giving in marriage, **until the day that Noe** [*Noah*] **entered into the ark,**

39 And knew not until **the flood came, and took them all away** [*destroyed them*]; **so shall also the coming of the Son of man** [*Jesus*] **be.**

40 Then shall two be in the field; the **one shall be taken, and the other left.** [*One who is worthy will be taken up to meet Christ (see D&C 88:96), and the other who is not worthy will be left on earth to be destroyed at His coming.*]

41 Two women shall be grinding at the mill; the **one shall be taken, and the other left.**

42 Watch therefore: for ye know not what hour your Lord doth come.

43 But **know this,** that **if the goodman** [*symbolic of people who will be caught off guard by the Second Coming*] **of the house had known in what watch** [*the Jews divided the night into "watches" of about four hours each; see Bible Dictionary, under "Watches"*] **the thief would come, he would have watched** [*would have been ready*], and would not have suffered [*allowed*] his house to be broken up.

44 Therefore be ye also **ready: for in such an hour as ye think not the Son of man cometh.**

> In the next verses, the Savior, in effect, asks the disciples who they think the people are who will be saved at the Second Coming. He answers His own question and basically says that it will be those who are faithful to the gospel and who, as servants

in the gospel, serve others with kindness and wisdom.

45 Who then is a faithful and wise servant, whom his lord hath made ruler over his household, **to give them** [*people under his jurisdiction*] **meat** [*food, nourishment*] **in due season** [*according to their needs*]?

46 Blessed is that servant, whom his lord when he cometh shall find so doing.

47 Verily I say unto you, That **he shall make him ruler over all his goods.** [*They will be exalted and will become gods. See D&C 84:38, D&C 132:20.*]

48 But and **if that evil servant** [*symbolic of the wicked in the last days*] **shall say in his heart, My lord** [*Christ*] **delayeth his coming** [*similar to the wicked in 3 Nephi 1*];

49 And shall begin to smite his fellowservants [*be mean and cruel to others*], **and to eat and drink with the drunken** [*participate in riotous living*];

50 The lord [*Christ*] **of that servant shall come in a day when he looketh not for him**, and in an hour that he is not aware of,

51 And shall cut him asunder [*destroy him*], **and appoint him his portion** [*put him in hell*] **with the hypocrites** [*people who want to appear righteous but like to do evil*]: there shall be weeping and gnashing of teeth [*grinding of teeth together in agony and misery*].

As stated in the notes at the beginning of Matthew 24, in this study guide, the Prophet Joseph Smith added about 450 words to the Bible version of Matthew 24, and rearranged the order of some verses. Thus, we are in a much better position to understand this chapter. The Prophet's revision of this chapter appears as Joseph Smith–Matthew in the Pearl of Great Price. It is included next in this book in a parallel column format so that you can compare at-a-glance the inspired contributions of the Prophet Joseph Smith with Matthew, chapter 24, as it stands in the King James version of the Bible.

JOSEPH SMITH—MATTHEW AND MATTHEW 24
PARALLEL COLUMN COMPARISON

Prepared by David J. Ridges—October 2006

Joseph Smith—Matthew	King James Version
(With Joseph Smith's changes in **bold**)	Matthew 24

Joseph Smith—Matthew

1 For I say unto you, that ye shall not see me henceforth **and know that I am he of whom it is written by the prophets,** until ye shall say: Blessed is he who cometh in the name of the Lord, **in the clouds of heaven, and all the holy angels with him. Then understood his disciples that he should come again on the earth, after that he was glorified and crowned on the right hand of God**.

2 And Jesus went out, and departed from the temple; and his disciples came to him, for to **hear him, saying: Master,** show **us concerning** the buildings of the temple, **as thou hast said—They shall be thrown down, and left unto you desolate.**

3 And Jesus said unto them: See ye not all these things, **and do ye not understand them?** Verily I say unto you, there shall not be left here, **upon this temple,** one stone upon another that shall not be thrown down.

King James Version

Matthew 23:39 For I say unto you, Ye shall not see me henceforth, till ye shall say, Blessed *is* he that cometh in the name of the Lord.

1 And Jesus went out, and departed from the temple: and his disciples came to *him* for to shew him the buildings of the temple.

2 And Jesus said unto them, See ye not all these things? verily I say unto you, There shall not be left here one stone upon another, that shall not be thrown down.

Joseph Smith—Matthew

4 **And Jesus left them, and went upon the Mount of Olives.** And as he sat upon the Mount of Olives, the disciples came unto him privately, saying: Tell us when shall these things be **which thou hast said concerning the destruction of the temple, and the Jews;** and what is the sign of thy coming, and of the end of the world, **or the destruction of the wicked, which is the end of the world?**

5 And Jesus answered, and said unto them: Take heed that no man deceive you;

6 For many shall come in my name, saying—I am Christ—and shall deceive many;

7 Then shall they deliver you up to be afflicted, and shall kill you, and ye shall be hated of all nations, for my name's sake;

8 And then shall many be offended, and shall betray one another, and shall hate one another;

9 And many false prophets shall arise, and shall deceive many;

10 And because iniquity shall abound, the love of many shall wax cold;

11 But he that **remaineth steadfast and is not overcome,** the same shall be saved.

Matthew 24

3 And as he sat upon the mount of Olives, the disciples came unto him privately, saying, Tell us, when shall these things be? and what *shall be* the sign of thy coming, and of the end of the world?

4 And Jesus answered and said unto them, Take heed that no man deceive you.

5 For many shall come in my name, saying, I am Christ; and shall deceive many.

9 Then shall they deliver you up to be afflicted, and shall kill you: and ye shall be hated of all nations for my name's sake.

10 And then shall many be offended, and shall betray one another, and shall hate one another.

11 And many false prophets shall rise, and shall deceive many.

12 And because iniquity shall abound, the love of many shall wax cold.

13 But he that shall endure unto the end, the same shall be saved.

14 And this gospel of the kingdom shall be preached in all the world for a witness unto all nations; and then shall the end come.

Joseph Smith—Matthew	Matthew 24
12 When you, therefore, shall see the abomination of desolation, spoken of by Daniel the prophet, **concerning the destruction of Jerusalem, then** you shall stand in the holy place; whoso readeth let him understand.	15 When ye therefore shall see the abomination of desolation, spoken of by Daniel the prophet, stand in the holy place, (whoso readeth, let him understand:)
13 Then let them **who are** in Judea flee into the mountains;	16 Then let them which be in Judæa flee into the mountains:
14 Let him who is on the housetop **flee, and not return** to take anything out of his house;	17 Let him which is on the housetop not come down to take any thing out of his house:
15 Neither let him **who** is in the field return back to take his clothes;	18 Neither let him which is in the field return back to take his clothes.
16 And wo unto them that are with child, and unto them that give suck in those days;	19 And woe unto them that are with child, and to them that give suck in those days!
17 **Therefore,** pray ye **the Lord** that your flight be not in the winter, neither on the Sabbath day;	20 But pray ye that your flight be not in the winter, neither on the sabbath day:
18 For then, **in those days,** shall be great tribulation **on the Jews, and upon the inhabitants of Jerusalem,** such as was not **before sent upon Israel, of God,** since the beginning of **their kingdom until this time;** no, nor ever shall be **sent again upon Israel.**	21 For then shall be great tribulation, such as was not since the beginning of the world to this time, no, nor ever shall be.
19 **All things which have befallen them** are **only** the beginning of **the** sorrows **which shall come upon them.**	8 All these *are* the beginning of sorrows.
20 And except those days should be shortened, there should none of their flesh be saved; but for the elect's sake, **according to the covenant,** those days shall be shortened.	22 And except those days should be shortened, there should no flesh be saved: but for the elect's sake those days shall be shortened.

Joseph Smith—Matthew

21 Behold, these things I have spoken unto you concerning the Jews; and again, after the tribulation of those days which shall come upon Jerusalem, if any man shall say unto you, Lo, here is Christ, or there, believe him not;

22 For **in those days** there shall **also** arise false Christs, and false prophets, and shall show great signs and wonders, insomuch, that, if possible, they shall deceive the very elect, **who are the elect according to the covenant.**

23 **Behold, I speak these things unto you for the elect's sake;** and **you also** shall hear of wars, and rumors of wars; see that ye be not troubled, for all **I have told you** must come to pass; but the end is not yet.

24 Behold, I have told you before;

25 Wherefore, if they shall say unto you: Behold, he is in the desert; go not forth: Behold, he is in the secret chambers; believe it not;

26 For as the **light of the morning** cometh out of the east, and shineth even unto the west, **and covereth the whole earth,** so shall also the coming of the Son of Man be.

27 **And now I show unto you a parable. Behold,** wheresoever the carcass is, there will the eagles be gathered together; **so likewise shall mine elect be gathered from the four quarters of the earth.**

Matthew 24

23 Then if any man shall say unto you, Lo, here is Christ, or there; believe *it* not.

24 For there shall arise false Christs, and false prophets, and shall shew great signs and wonders; insomuch that, if it *were* possible, they shall deceive the very elect.

6 And ye shall hear of wars and rumours of wars: see that ye be not troubled: for all *these things* must come to pass, but the end is not yet.

25 Behold, I have told you before.

26 Wherefore if they shall say unto you, Behold, he is in the desert; go not forth: behold, *he* is in the secret chambers; believe *it* not.

27 For as the lightning cometh out of the east, and shineth even unto the west; so shall also the coming of the Son of man be.

28 For wheresoever the carcase is, there will the eagles be gathered together.

Joseph Smith—Matthew	Matthew 24
28 **And they shall hear of wars and rumors of wars.**	
29 **Behold I speak for mine elect's sake;** for nation shall rise against nation, and kingdom against kingdom; there shall be famines, and pestilences, and earthquakes, in divers places.	7 For nation shall rise against nation, and kingdom against kingdom: and there shall be famines, and pestilences, and earthquakes, in divers places.
30 **And again, because iniquity shall abound, the love of men shall wax cold; but he that shall not be overcome, the same shall be saved.**	
31 And **again,** this Gospel of the Kingdom shall be preached in all the world, for a witness unto all nations, and then shall the end come, **or the destruction of the wicked;**	14 And this gospel of the kingdom shall be preached in all the world for a witness unto all nations; and then shall the end come.
32 **(This is <u>not</u> the same as verse 15 in Matthew 24.) And again shall the abomination of desolation, spoken of by Daniel the prophet, be fulfilled.**	
33 **And** immediately after the tribulation of those days, **the sun shall be darkened,** and the moon shall not give her light, and the stars shall fall from heaven, and the powers of heaven shall be shaken.	29 Immediately after the tribulation of those days shall the sun be darkened, and the moon shall not give her light, and the stars shall fall from heaven, and the powers of the heavens shall be shaken:
34 Verily, I say unto you, this generation, **in which these things shall be shown forth,** shall not pass **away until** all **I have told you shall** be fulfilled.	34 Verily I say unto you, This generation shall not pass, till all these things be fulfilled.

| Joseph Smith—Matthew | Matthew 24 |

Joseph Smith—Matthew

35 **Although, the days will come, that** heaven and earth shall pass away; yet my words shall not pass away, **but all shall be fulfilled.**

36 And, **as I said before, after the tribulation of those days, and the powers of the heavens shall be shaken,** then shall appear the sign of the Son of Man in heaven, and then shall all the tribes of the earth mourn; and they shall see the Son of Man coming in the clouds of heaven, with power and great glory;

37 **And whoso treasureth up my word, shall not be deceived, for the Son of Man shall come,** and he shall send his angels **before him** with **the** great sound of a trumpet, and they shall gather together **the remainder of** his elect **from the four winds,** from one end of heaven to the other.

38 Now learn a parable of the fig-tree—When **its** branch**es are** yet tender, and **it begins to** put forth leaves, **you** know that summer is nigh **at hand;**

39 So likewise, **mine elect**, when **they** shall see all these things, **they** shall know that **he** is near, even at the doors;

40 But of that day, and hour, no **one** knoweth; no, not the angels of **God in** heaven, but my Father only.

Matthew 24

35 Heaven and earth shall pass away, but my words shall not pass away.

30 And then shall appear the sign of the Son of man in heaven: and then shall all the tribes of the earth mourn, and they shall see the Son of man coming in the clouds of heaven with power and great glory.

31 And he shall send his angels with a great sound of a trumpet, and they shall gather together his elect from the four winds, from one end of heaven to the other.

32 Now learn a parable of the fig tree; When his branch is yet tender, and putteth forth leaves, ye know that summer *is* nigh:

33 So likewise ye, when ye shall see all these things, know that it is near, *even* at the doors

36 But of that day and hour knoweth no *man*, no, not the angels of heaven, but my Father only.

Joseph Smith—Matthew & Matthew 24 Comparison

Joseph Smith—Matthew	Matthew 24
41 But as **it was in** the days of Noah, so **it** shall **be** also **at** the coming of the Son of Man;	37 But as the days of Noe *were*, so shall also the coming of the Son of man be.
42 For **it shall be with them,** as **it was** in the days **which** were before the flood; **for until the day that Noah entered into the ark** they were eating and drinking, marrying and giving in marriage;	38 For as in the days that were before the flood they were eating and drinking, marrying and giving in marriage, until the day that Noe entered into the ark,
43 And knew not until the flood came, and took them all away; so shall also the coming of the Son of Man be.	39 And knew not until the flood came, and took them all away; so shall also the coming of the Son of man be.
44 Then **shall be fulfilled that which is written, that in the last days,** two shall be in the field, the one shall be taken, and the other left;	40 Then shall two be in the field; the one shall be taken, and the other left.
45 Two shall be grinding at the mill, the one shall be taken, and the other left;	41 Two *women shall* be grinding at the mill; the one shall be taken, and the other left
46 **And what I say unto one, I say unto all men;** watch, therefore, for **you** know not at what hour your Lord doth come.	42 Watch therefore: for ye know not what hour your Lord doth come.
47 But know this, if the good man of the house had known in what watch the thief would come, he would have watched, and would not have suffered his house to have been broken up, **but would have been ready.**	43 But know this, that if the goodman of the house had known in what watch the thief would come, he would have watched, and would not have suffered his house to be broken up.
48 Therefore be ye also ready, for in such an hour as ye think not, the Son of Man cometh.	44 Therefore be ye also ready: for in such an hour as ye think not the Son of man cometh.

Joseph Smith—Matthew

49 Who, then, is a faithful and wise servant, whom his lord hath made ruler over his household, to give them meat in due season?

50 Blessed is that servant whom his lord, when he cometh, shall find so doing; **and** verily I say unto you, he shall make him ruler over all his goods.

51 But if that evil servant shall say in his heart: My lord delayeth his coming,

52 And shall begin to smite his fellow-servants, and to eat and drink with the drunken,

53 The lord of that servant shall come in a day when he looketh not for him, and in an hour that he is not aware of,

54 And shall cut him asunder, and **shall** appoint him his portion with the hypocrites; there shall be weeping and gnashing of teeth.

55 And thus cometh the end of the wicked, according to the prophecy of Moses, saying: They shall be cut off from among the people; but the end of the earth is not yet, but by and by.

Matthew 24

45 Who then is a faithful and wise servant, whom his lord hath made ruler over his household, to give them meat in due season?

46 Blessed *is* that servant, whom his lord when he cometh shall find so doing.

47 Verily I say unto you, That he shall make him ruler over all his goods.

48 But and if that evil servant shall say in his heart, My lord delayeth his coming;

49 And shall begin to smite *his* fellowservants, and to eat and drink with the drunken;

50 The lord of that servant shall come in a day when he looketh not for *him*, and in an hour that he is not aware of,

51 And shall cut him asunder, and appoint *him* his portion with the hypocrites: there shall be weeping and gnashing of teeth.

MATTHEW 25

In chapter 24, many prophecies were given which will be fulfilled as the time of the Second Coming approaches, and counsel was given to be prepared by living faithfully and serving others. Chapter 25 continues with instructions on how to prepare personally for the Second Coming. The Savior uses the parable of the ten virgins to teach us how to prepare.

The Parable of the Ten Virgins

1 **THEN** [*the last days leading up to the time of the Second Coming*] **shall the kingdom of heaven be likened unto ten virgins** [*symbolic of members of the Church; see McConkie,* Doctrinal New Testament Commentary, *Vol. 1, pp. 684–85*], **which took their lamps, and went forth to meet the bridegroom** [*"groom;" symbolic of Christ—see Talmage,* Jesus the Christ, *p. 578*].

JST Matthew 25:1
1 And then, **at that day, before the Son of man comes, the kingdom of heaven shall be likened** unto ten virgins, **who** took their lamps, and went forth to meet the bridegroom.

2 And **five** of them were **wise**, and **five** were **foolish**.

3 They that were **foolish** took their lamps, and **took no oil with them:**

4 But the **wise took oil in their vessels with their lamps.**

Did you notice that all ten virgins had lamps with oil in them to begin with? But the five wise virgins carried flasks with extra oil and thus were able to "endure to the end" until the bridegroom [*groom*] finally arrived.

5 **While the bridegroom tarried, they all slumbered and slept.**

6 And **at midnight** [*ties in with the "eleventh hour" parable, in Matthew 20:6 (verses 1–16)*] there was a cry made, Behold, **the bridegroom cometh** [*symbolic of the Second Coming*]; go ye out to meet him.

7 Then **all those virgins arose, and trimmed their lamps.**

8 And **the foolish said unto the wise, Give us of your oil; for our lamps are gone out.**

9 But **the wise answered**, saying, **Not so; lest there be not enough for us and you**: but **go ye rather to them that sell, and buy for yourselves.**

To some, it may seem that the five wise virgins were not living the gospel because they would not share their supplies of oil with the five foolish virgins. The point is that their extra oil is symbolic of personal worthiness and preparedness which the righteous cannot share or give to others, such as personal righteousness, church attendance, tithe paying, moral cleanliness, Sabbath observance, keeping the commandments, and so forth.

10 **And while they** [*the foolish virgins*] **went to buy, the bridegroom came** [*sadly, they were unprepared and unworthy, and could not get ready in time*]; and **they that were ready went in with him to the marriage** [*"marriage" generally symbolizes making and keeping covenants with God; here, the marriage represents the Second Coming, see Talmage, Jesus the Christ, p. 578*]: **and the door was shut.**

11 **Afterward came also the other virgins, saying, Lord, Lord, open to us.**

12 But he answered and said, Verily I say unto you, **I know you not.** [*"I know you not" is another way of saying "You do not know me." Or, "You have not made covenants with Me." See Talmage, Jesus the Christ, p. 579. See also JST quoted next.*]

JST Matthew 25:11
11 But he answered and said, Verily I say unto you, **Ye know me not**.

13 **Watch** therefore, **for ye know neither the day nor the hour wherein the Son of man** [*Christ*] **cometh.**

As the Savior continues to teach His Apostles, we are given additional advice as to how to prepare ourselves for the Second Coming.

The Parable of the Talents

14 For **the kingdom of heaven is as a man** [*symbolic of Christ (who will be crucified within three days)*] travelling into a far country [*symbolic of heaven*], who called his own servants [*disciples, apostles*], and delivered unto them his goods.

15 And unto one he gave five talents, to another two, and to another one; to every man according to his several ability [*in other words, each is an individual and is given a stewardship according to personal capacities, talents and abilities*]; and straightway took his journey.

Some biblical scholars suggest that a talent was a substantial sum of money in New Testament times. See Bible Dictionary, under "Money," wherein it says a talent is a sum of money.

16 Then **he that had received the five** talents went and traded with the same, and **made them other five talents.** [*He developed and increased his God-given talents.*]

17 And likewise **he that had received two**, he also **gained other two.** [*He developed and increased his talents.*]

18 **But he that had received one** went and digged in the earth, and **hid his lord's money.** [*He did not develop and increase his talent.*]

19 After a long time **the lord** [*symbolic of Christ*] of those servants **cometh, and reckoneth with them** [*had them account for how they had used that which He gave them; symbolic of Judgment Day*].

20 And so **he that had received five** talents came and **brought**

other five talents, saying, Lord, thou deliveredst unto me five talents: behold, I have gained beside them five talents more.

21 **His lord said** unto him, **Well done, thou good and faithful servant: thou hast been faithful over a few things, I will make thee ruler over many things** [*symbolic of exaltation*]: **enter thou into the joy of thy lord.**

22 **He** also **that had received two talents** came and said, Lord, thou deliveredst unto me two talents: behold, I have **gained two other talents** beside them.

23 **His lord said** unto him, **Well done, good and faithful servant; thou hast been faithful over a few things, I will make thee ruler over many things** [*symbolic of exaltation*]: **enter thou into the joy of thy lord.**

> Did you notice that the reward for both the servant who had received five talents and the servant who was given two talents, was exactly the same? Note wording of the rewards in verses 21 and 23. It is comforting that those with fewer talents and abilities, who do their best, will receive the same reward, exaltation, as those who currently have higher abilities.

24 **Then he which had received the one talent came and said** [*made excuses for his lack of performance*], **Lord, I knew thee that thou art an hard man** [*that You expect a lot from Your employees*], reaping [*harvesting*] where thou hast not sown [*planted*], and gathering [*harvesting*] where thou hast not strawed [*thrown or scattered seeds*]:

25 And **I was afraid**, and went and hid thy talent in the earth: **lo, there thou hast that is thine.**

26 **His lord answered** and said unto him, **Thou wicked and slothful** [*lazy*] **servant**, thou knewest that I reap [*harvest*] where I sowed [*planted*] not, and gather [*harvest*] where I have not strawed [*planted; in other words, you knew that you would someday have to account to Me*]:

27 **Thou oughtest therefore to have put my money to the exchangers, and then at my coming I should have received mine own with usury** [*interest*].

28 **Take therefore the talent from him, and give it unto him which hath ten talents.**

> Next, the Master explains the important message He had in mind for us as He gave the parable of the talents.

29 For **unto every one that hath** [*symbolizing those who have done the best they can with what they were given*] **shall be given, and he shall have abundance** [*symbolic of exaltation*]: **but from him that hath not** [*symbolizing those who have not done their best with what the Lord gave them*] **shall be taken away even that which he hath.**

30 And **cast ye the unprofitable servant** [*symbolic of the wicked*] **into outer darkness** [*see Alma 40:13*]: **there shall be weeping and gnashing of teeth** [*among other things, symbolic of the fact that the wicked will have to suffer for their own sins since they were unwilling to repent and take advantage of the Atonement; see D&C 19:15–16*].

31 **When the Son of man** [*Jesus*] **shall come in his glory** [*the Second Coming*], and all the holy angels with him, **then shall he sit upon the throne of his glory** [*He will be our King during the Millennium*]:

The Parable of the Sheep and the Goats

32 And before him shall be gathered all nations: **and he shall separate** them one from another, as a shepherd divideth his **sheep from the goats:**

33 And **he shall set the sheep on his right hand, but the goats on the left.**

> Here, in this context, sheep symbolize the righteous and goats symbolize the wicked. The right hand, in Jewish symbolism, is the covenant hand. Thus, being on the Lord's right hand symbolizes those who have made and kept covenants.

34 **Then shall the King say unto them on his right hand,** Come, ye blessed of my Father, inherit the kingdom [*celestial kingdom*] prepared for you from the foundation of the world [*as planned in the premortal council*]:

In the next verses, the Savior will beautifully detail more ways to be righteous and prepared for the Second Coming, as was the case with the five wise virgins. In other words, He is showing us how to have extra oil for our lamps.

35 For **I was an hungred** [*hungry*], **and ye gave me meat** [*food*]: **I was thirsty, and ye gave me drink:** I was **a stranger, and ye took me in**:

36 **Naked, and ye clothed me**: I was **sick, and ye visited me**: I was **in prison, and ye came unto me.**

37 Then shall the righteous answer him, saying, **Lord, when saw we thee** an **hungred**, and fed thee? or **thirsty**, and gave thee drink?

38 When saw we thee **a stranger**, and took thee in? **or naked**, and clothed thee?

39 Or when saw we thee **sick**, or in **prison**, and came unto thee?

40 **And the King** [*Christ*] **shall answer** and say unto them, **Verily** [*listen carefully, this is the main point*] **I say unto you, Inasmuch as ye have done it unto one of the least of these my brethren, ye have done it unto me.** [*King Benjamin talked about this kind of service to others in Mosiah 2:17.*]

41 **Then shall he say also unto them on the left hand** [*in this context, being on the left hand of God symbolizes the wicked*], **Depart from me,** ye cursed, into everlasting fire [*hell*], prepared for the devil and his angels:

42 For I was an hungred, and **ye gave me no meat** [*food*]: I was thirsty, and ye gave me **no drink**:

43 I was a stranger, and **ye took me not in**: naked, and ye **clothed me not**: sick, and in prison, and ye **visited me not**.

44 **Then shall they also answer him, saying, Lord, when saw we thee** an hungred, or athirst, or a stranger, or naked, or sick, or in prison, and did not minister unto thee [*take care of your needs*]?

45 **Then shall he answer** them, saying, Verily [*when He says "verily," it means "listen very carefully because this is the point I am trying to teach you."*] I say unto you, **Inasmuch as ye did it not to one of the least of these, ye did it not to me.**

46 And **these shall go away into everlasting punishment: but the righteous into life eternal** [*celestial glory and exaltation*].

MATTHEW 26

In this chapter, the Savior will again prophesy of His coming crucifixion. As the Jewish religious leaders continue to plot His death, He will institute the sacrament, then go to Gethsemane, be betrayed by Judas, be arrested, and be subjected to an illegal trial. Peter will deny that he knows Jesus three times.

1 AND it came to pass, **when Jesus had finished all these sayings, he said unto his disciples,**

2 Ye know that **after two days is the feast of the passover, and the Son of man is betrayed to be crucified**.

The Feast of the Passover was celebrated in the springtime at about the same time as we celebrate Easter. It commemorated the time when the destroying angel passed over the houses of the children of Israel in Egypt, when the firstborn of the Egyptians were killed. The Israelites in Egypt at the time were instructed by Moses to sacrifice a lamb without blemish and to put blood from the lamb which was sacrificed on the doorposts of their houses. See Bible Dictionary, under "Feasts." Thus, through the blood of a lamb, the Israelites were protected from the anguish and punishment brought to the Egyptians by the destroying angel. The symbolism is clear. It is by the "blood of the Lamb" (the sacrifice of the Savior) that we are saved, after all we can do (2 Nephi 25:23). Now, at the time of Passover in Jerusalem, the "Lamb of God," Christ, will present Himself to be sacrificed, that we might be saved. The Feast of the Passover brought large numbers of Jews from near and far to Jerusalem to join in the worship and celebration.

As we continue, verse 3 informs us that the Jewish leaders have gathered together to plot the death of Jesus.

3 **Then assembled together the chief priests**, and the **scribes**, and the **elders** of the people [*the Jewish*

religious leaders], **unto the palace of the high priest,** who was called Caiaphas,

4 And consulted that they might take Jesus by subtilty, and kill him. [*In other words, they plotted how they might arrest Jesus as quietly as possible so that they would not stir up the people and perhaps get mobbed themselves.*]

5 But they said, Not on the feast day, [*not on Thursday, the day of Passover*] **lest there be an uproar** among the people.

6 Now when **Jesus was in Bethany** [*about two or three miles east and south of Jerusalem*], in the house of Simon the leper,

> In verses 7–13, a woman (Mary—see John 12:3) anoints Jesus with costly ointment. Jesus is the Messiah. "Messiah" means "the Anointed One" (Bible Dictionary, under "Messiah"). It would seem that this woman understood what the disciples did not yet fully understand, and symbolically "anointed" the Savior in preparation for His Atoning sacrifice. This sheds light on the divine nature and spiritual sensitivity of women.

7 There came unto him a woman having an alabaster box of **very precious ointment,** and **poured it on his head,** as he sat at meat [*at dinner*].

8 But when his disciples saw it, they had indignation, saying, To what purpose is this waste [*why are you wasting this expensive ointment*]?

9 For **this ointment might have been sold for much, and given to the poor.**

10 When **Jesus** understood it, he said unto them, **Why trouble ye the woman? for she hath wrought** [*done*] **a good work upon me.**

11 For **ye have the poor always with you; but me ye have not always.** [*You need to keep things in perspective.*]

12 For in that she hath poured this ointment on my body, **she did it for my burial.** [*In other words, she understands that I will be crucified and buried now.*]

> Next, the Master gives a prophecy about what this woman did.

13 Verily I say unto you, **Wheresoever this gospel shall be preached** in the whole world, there **shall also this, that this woman hath done, be told for a memorial of her.**

The Betrayal by Judas Iscariot

14 **Then** one of the twelve, called **Judas Iscariot, went unto the chief priests** [*the Jewish religious leaders, Christ's enemies*],

15 **And said** unto them, **What will ye give me, and I will deliver him unto you?** And they covenanted with him for **thirty pieces of silver.**

> Thirty pieces of silver was an insult to Judas and demeaned Jesus, since it was the going price for a common slave.

16 **And from that time he** [*Judas*]

sought opportunity to betray him [*Christ*].

17 Now **the first day** [*Thursday*] of the feast of unleavened bread [*part of the Passover*] **the disciples came to Jesus**, saying unto him, **Where wilt thou that we prepare for thee to eat the passover?**

18 And **he said, Go into the city to such a man, and say unto him, The Master saith, My time is at hand** [*it is time for Me to be sacrificed*]; **I will keep the passover at thy house** with my disciples.

19 And **the disciples** did as Jesus had appointed them; and they **made ready the Passover** [*the Passover meal*].

20 Now **when the even** [*evening*] **was come, he sat down with the twelve**.

21 And as they did eat, he said, Verily I say unto you, that **one of you shall betray me**.

22 And they were exceeding sorrowful, and began every one of them to say unto him, **Lord, is it I?**

23 And he answered and said, **He that dippeth his hand with me in the dish**, the same shall betray me.

24 **The Son of man goeth as it is written of him** [*I will perform the Atonement and be crucified as prophesied in the scriptures*]: **but woe unto that man by whom the Son of man is betrayed!** it had been good for that man if he had not been born. [*It would have been better for Judas Iscariot not to have been born.*]

25 **Then Judas**, which betrayed him, **answered** [*responded*] and said, **Master, is it I? He said** unto him, **Thou hast said.**

Many versions of the Bible give "Thou hast said" as "Yes." in one form or another, which fits with JST Mark 14:30 which says, "And he said unto Judas Iscariot, What thou doest, do quickly; but beware of innocent blood." It is likely that this was a whispered conversation between Jesus and Judas because Matthew, Mark, Luke, and John do not indicate that the other Apostles were aware of it.

In the next verses, Jesus introduces the sacrament to His Apostles. This is known as the "Last Supper."

The Savior Introduces the Sacrament

26 And as they were eating, **Jesus took bread, and blessed it, and brake it, and gave it to the disciples**, and said, **Take, eat; this is my body** [*this bread is symbolic of the Savior's body; when we partake of the sacrament bread, we are symbolically "internalizing" His gospel and making it a part of us*].

27 And **he took the cup** [*representing the blood which the Savior shed for our sins*], **and gave thanks, and gave it to them, saying, Drink ye all of it** [*not "part" of it, rather,*

"all" of it, symbolizing that we must fully accept Christ and His gospel and apply it in our lives];

28 For **this is my blood** of the new testament [*"testament" means "covenant;" in other words, the new covenants associated with the full gospel which Christ had restored*], **which is shed for many for the remission of sins.**

<u>**JST Matthew 26:24–25**</u>
24 For this is **in remembrance of** my blood of the new testament, which is shed for **as many as shall believe on my name, for the remission of their sins.**

25 And I give unto you a commandment, that ye shall observe to do the things which ye have seen me do, and bear record of me even unto the end.

JST, verse 25, above, is not found in the Bible.

29 But I say unto you, **I will not drink henceforth of this fruit of the vine, until that day when I drink it new with you in my Father's kingdom.** [*This is the last time the Master will partake of the sacrament with His disciples during His mortal life.*]

30 And when **they** had **sung an hymn,** they **went out into the mount of Olives** [*just a few minutes walk from the city wall of Jerusalem*].

31 Then saith Jesus unto them, **All ye shall be offended because of me this night** [*meaning they will desert Him—see verses 33–34, 56*]: for it is written [*in Zechariah 13:7*], I will smite the shepherd [*Christ*], and the sheep of the flock [*disciples*] shall be scattered abroad.

32 **But after I am risen** again [*resurrected*], **I will go before you** [*ahead of you*] **into Galilee.**

33 **Peter** answered and **said** unto him, **Though all men shall be offended because of thee, yet will I never be offended.**

34 **Jesus said** unto him, **Verily I say unto thee, That this night, before the cock crow** [*before the rooster crows in the early morning*], **thou shalt deny me thrice** [*three times*].

Verse 34 presents a difficult dilemma to the student of the scriptures with respect to Peter. We need clarification on this situation and until we get it from a reliable source, we are left to wonder about his denying knowing the Savior three times. Some think he denied his testimony and thus denied the Holy Ghost, which is an unpardonable sin. He did not. He denied knowing the Savior. It is out of character for Peter to be afraid of people and what they think. In fact, before this most difficult night is over, he will draw a sword and cut off an ear of one of those who arrested Christ (see verse 51). Perhaps the Savior was prophetically commanding Peter to deny knowing Him on the three upcoming occasions during the night when it will be claimed that he is an associate of Jesus, in order to prevent Peter's death at this time. Perhaps it is to remind Peter that he is not as strong and committed as he thinks he is. Whatever the case, we need more information before we draw any final conclusion on this matter.

35 **Peter said** unto him, **Though I should die with thee, yet will I not deny thee. Likewise also said all the disciples.**

The Garden of Gethsemane

36 **Then cometh Jesus with them unto a place called Gethsemane** [*the Garden of Gethsemane, just a few minutes walk from Jerusalem*], **and saith** unto the disciples, **Sit ye here, while I go and pray yonder.**

"Gethsemane" means "oil press." There is significant symbolism here. The Jews put olives into bags made of mesh fabric and placed them in a press to squeeze olive oil out of them. The first pressings yielded pure olive oil which was prized for many uses, including healing and giving light in lanterns. In fact, we consecrate it and use it to administer to the sick. The last pressing of the olives, under the tremendous pressure of additional weights added to the press, yielded a bitter, red liquid which can remind us of blood and the "bitter cup" which the Savior partook of. Symbolically, the Savior is going into the "oil press" (Gethsemane) to submit to the "pressure" of all our sins which will "squeeze" His blood out in order that we might have the healing "oil" of the Atonement to heal us from our sins.

37 And **he took** with him **Peter and the two sons of Zebedee** [*James and John*], and **began to be sorrowful and very heavy.**

38 Then saith he unto them, **My soul is exceeding sorrowful, even unto death**: tarry [*wait*] ye here, and watch with me.

39 And he went a little further, and fell on his face [*showing submission and humility, in Jewish culture*], and prayed, saying, **O my Father, if it be possible, let this cup pass from me: nevertheless not as I will, but as thou wilt.**

40 And **he cometh unto the disciples, and findeth them asleep**, and saith unto Peter, What, could ye not watch with me one hour?

41 **Watch and pray, that ye enter not into temptation: the spirit indeed is willing, but the flesh is weak.**

42 He went away again the second time, and prayed, saying, **O my Father, if this cup may not pass away from me, except I drink it, thy will be done.**

43 And he came and **found them asleep again**: for their eyes were heavy [*they were very sleepy; it had been a very difficult and sleepless week for the Apostles, worrying about the Savior's safety*].

44 And he left them, and went away again, and **prayed the third**

time, saying the same words.

45 Then cometh he to his disciples, and saith unto them, Sleep on now, and take your rest: behold, **the hour is at hand** [*the time has come*], **and the Son of man** [*Christ; in other words, "Son of Man of Holiness" (Heavenly Father), see Moses 6:57*] **is betrayed into the hands of sinners.**

46 Rise, let us be going: behold, he [*Judas*] is at hand that doth betray me.

47 And while he yet spake, lo, **Judas**, one of the twelve, **came**, and **with** him **a great multitude with swords and staves** [*NIV "clubs"*], from the chief priests and elders of the people [*the religious leaders of the Jews*].

48 **Now he** [*Judas*] **that betrayed him gave them** [*the soldiers*] **a sign, saying, Whomsoever I shall kiss, that same is he: hold him fast.** [*I will kiss Jesus so you know which one He is, then arrest Him and hold on to Him securely.*]

49 And forthwith **he came to Jesus, and said, Hail, master; and kissed him.**

50 And Jesus said unto him, Friend, wherefore [*why*] art thou come? **Then came they, and laid hands on Jesus, and took him.**

51 And, behold, **one of them** [*Peter*] which were with Jesus stretched out his hand, and **drew his sword, and struck a servant of the high priest's, and smote off his ear.** [*Jesus healed this man's ear; see Luke 22:51.*]

52 **Then said Jesus unto** him, **Put up** again **thy sword** into his place: for all they that take the sword shall perish with the sword.

53 **Thinkest thou that I cannot now pray to my Father, and he shall presently** [*immediately*] **give me more than twelve legions** [*a "legion" was about 6,000 infantry plus some cavalry—see Bible Dictionary, under "Legion"*] **of angels?** [*In other words, don't you realize that if I wanted to stop this, I could?*]

54 But how then shall the scriptures be fulfilled, that **thus it must be**? [*I must be crucified.*]

55 In that same hour said Jesus to the multitudes, **Are ye come out as against a thief** with swords and staves for to take me? **I sat daily with you teaching in the temple, and ye laid no hold on me.**

56 But all this was done, that the scriptures of the prophets might be fulfilled. **Then all the disciples forsook him, and fled** [*as prophesied in verse 31*].

57 And **they** that had laid hold on [*arrested*] Jesus **led him away to Caiaphas the high priest**, where the scribes and the elders were assembled.

> This trial during the night time was completely illegal according to the Jews' own laws.

58 But **Peter followed him** afar off

unto the high priest's palace, and went in, and sat with the servants, to see the end.

59 Now **the chief priests, and elders, and all the council, sought false witness against Jesus**, to put him to death;

60 **But found none**: yea, though many false witnesses came, yet found they none [*whose false witness would work for their purposes*]. **At the last came two false witnesses**,

61 **And said**, This fellow said, I am able to destroy the temple of God, and to build it in three days.

62 And **the high priest arose, and said unto him** [*Jesus*], **Answerest thou nothing** [*why don't you say something*]? what is it which these witness against thee?

63 **But Jesus held his peace** [*said nothing*]. And **the high priest** answered and **said** unto him, I adjure thee [*I place you under oath*] by the living God, that thou **tell us whether thou be the Christ, the Son of God**.

64 **Jesus saith unto him, Thou hast said** [*NIV "Yes, it is as you say." In other words, Jesus is saying that He is God's Son*]: nevertheless I say unto you, **Hereafter shall ye see the Son of man** [*Me*] **sitting on the right hand of power** [*God*], **and coming in the clouds of heaven** [*you will see Me at My second coming*].

In addition to what the Savior told these men, in verse 64, above, Revelation 1:7 also informs us that those who crucified Christ will indeed see His Second Coming.

65 **Then the high priest rent his clothes** [*tore his clothes, a sign of extreme emotion*], **saying, He hath spoken blasphemy** [*great disrespect for God and our religious beliefs; blasphemy was punishable by death*]; **what further need have we of witnesses? behold, now ye have heard his blasphemy.**

66 **What think ye?** They answered and said, **He is guilty of death.**

JST Matthew 26:67
67 They answered and said, He is guilty, and worthy of death.

67 Then did **they spit in his face, and buffeted** [*hit*] **him**; and others smote [*hit*] him with the palms of their hands,

68 **Saying, Prophesy unto us, thou Christ, Who is he that smote thee?** [*Luke 22:54 tells us that they had put a blindfold on Him before hitting Him; thus they were mocking Him and asking Him to use His "great powers" to tell them which of them were hitting Him.*]

69 Now **Peter sat without** [*outside of the trial room*] in the palace: **and a damsel** [*young lady*] **came unto him, saying, Thou also wast with Jesus of Galilee.**

70 **But he denied** before them all, saying, I know not what thou sayest.

71 And when he was gone out into

the porch, **another maid saw him**, and said unto them that were there, **This fellow was also with Jesus of Nazareth.**

72 And **again he denied** with an oath [*strongly*], I do not know the man [*Christ*].

73 And **after a while came unto him they that stood by, and said** to Peter, **Surely thou also art one of them** [*one of Christ's followers*]; for thy speech bewrayeth thee [*your Galilean accent gives you away*].

74 Then began he to curse and to swear, saying, **I know not the man** [*Jesus*]. And **immediately the cock crew** [*the rooster crowed*].

75 **And Peter remembered the word of Jesus** [*in verse 34*], which said unto him, Before the cock crow, thou shalt deny me thrice. **And he went out, and wept bitterly.**

> As mentioned previously (after verse 34, above), we will someday know more about Peter's denial of knowing Christ, at the time of His trial. One thing is certain. He did not "deny" Christ in the sense of denying that He was the Christ. Rather, he denied knowing Him. Apostle James E. Talmage taught the following about this scene:
>
> "When Jesus was taken into custody in the Garden of Gethsemane, all the Eleven forsook Him and fled. This is not to be accounted as certain evidence of cowardice, for the Lord had indicated that they should go. Peter and at least one other disciple followed afar off; and, after the armed guard had entered the palace of the high priest with their Prisoner, Peter "went in, and sat with the servants to see the end." He was assisted in securing admittance by the unnamed disciple, who was on terms of acquaintanceship with the high priest. That other disciple was in all probability John, as may be inferred from the fact that he is mentioned only in the fourth Gospel, the author of which characteristically refers to himself anonymously.
>
> "While Jesus was before the Sanhedrists, Peter remained below with the servants. The attendant at the door was a young woman; her feminine suspicions had been aroused when she admitted Peter, and as he sat with a crowd in the palace court she came up, and having intently observed him, said: 'Thou also wast with Jesus of Galilee.' But Peter denied, averring he did not know Jesus. Peter was restless; his conscience and the fear of identification as one of the Lord's disciples troubled him. He left the crowd and sought partial seclusion in the porch; but there another maid spied him out, and said to those nearby: 'This fellow was also with Jesus of Nazareth'; to which accusation Peter replied with an oath: "I do not know the man."
>
> "The April night was chilly, and an open fire had been made in the hall or court of the palace.

Peter sat with others at the fire, thinking, perhaps, that brazen openness was better than skulking caution as a possible safeguard against detection. About an hour after his former denials, some of the men around the fire charged him with being a disciple of Jesus, and referred to his Galilean dialect as evidence that he was at least a fellow countryman with the high priest's Prisoner; but, most threatening of all, a kinsman of Malthus [Malchus—see John 18:10], whose ear Peter had slashed with the sword, asked peremptorily: 'Did not I see thee in the garden with him?' Then Peter went so far in the course of falsehood upon which he had entered as to curse and swear, and to vehemently declare for the third time, 'I know not the man.' As the last profane falsehood left his lips, the clear notes of a crowing cock broke upon his ears, and the remembrance of his Lord's prediction welled up in his mind. Trembling in wretched realization of his perfidious cowardice, he turned from the crowd and met the gaze of the suffering Christ, who from the midst of the insolent mob looked into the face of His boastful, yet loving but weak apostle. Hastening from the palace, Peter went out into the night, weeping bitterly. As his later life attests, his tears were those of real contrition and true repentance." (*Jesus the Christ*, pp. 629–31)

MATTHEW 27

This is the day of the Savior's crucifixion. The Roman governor, Pontius Pilate, will yield to the cunning plot of the Jewish religious leaders and the illegal clamor of the masses to crucify Jesus, and will wash his hands of the whole thing. The Master will be mocked, crucified, and hastily placed in a new tomb donated by Joseph of Arimathaea.

1 **WHEN** the **morning was come** [*Friday morning, the day of the Savior's crucifixion*], all the **chief priests** and **elders** of the people **took counsel** [*plotted*] **against Jesus to put him to death:**

2 And when they had **bound him**, they **led him away**, and delivered him **to Pontius Pilate** the governor [*the Roman governor over that part of the Holy Land*].

3 **Then Judas**, which had betrayed him, when he saw that he was condemned, **repented himself** [*changed his mind*], **and brought again** [*returned*] **the thirty pieces of silver** [*which he had been paid to betray Jesus*] **to the chief priests and elders,**

4 **Saying**, I have sinned in that **I have betrayed the innocent blood.** And **they said, What is that to us? see thou to that** [*that is your problem!*].

JST Matthew 27:5

5 And they said **unto him,** What is that to us? See thou to **it; thy sins be upon thee.**

5 And he cast down [*threw down*] the pieces of silver in the temple, and departed, and went and **hanged himself**.

JST Matthew 27:6

6 And he cast down the pieces of silver in the temple, and departed, and went, and hanged himself **on a tree. And straightway he fell down, and his bowels gushed out, and he died**.

6 And **the chief priests took the silver** pieces, and said, It is not lawful [*legal*] for to put them into the treasury, because it is the price of blood [*it is blood money, the price paid to have someone killed*].

7 And they took counsel [*talked it over*], **and bought** with them [*the thirty pieces of silver*] **the potter's field, to bury strangers** [*foreigners*] **in**.

8 Wherefore that field was called, **The field of blood**, unto this day.

9 **Then was fulfilled that which was spoken by Jeremy** [*Jeremiah—we don't have this quote from Jeremiah in our Bible; it is apparently one of the missing scriptures—but we do have a related quote in Zechariah 11:12–13*] the prophet, saying, And **they took the thirty pieces of silver, the price of him that was valued, whom they of the children of Israel did value;**

10 **And gave them for the potter's field**, as the Lord appointed me.

JST Matthew 27:10

10 **And therefore they took the pieces of silver,** and gave them for the potter's field, as the Lord appointed **by the mouth of Jeremy** [*Jeremiah—see note in Bible verse 9, above*].

The Trial before Pontius Pilate

11 And **Jesus stood before the governor** [*Pontius Pilate*]: and **the governor asked** him, saying, **Art thou the King of the Jews? And Jesus said** unto him, **Thou sayest** [*in other words, it is as you say, yes, I am; see John 18:37*].

We learn more about Pontius Pilate from our Bible Dictionary: "Roman procurator in Judaea, A.D. 26–36 (Luke 3:1). His headquarters were at Caesarea, but he was generally present in Jerusalem at feast time. He had a great contempt for the Jewish people and for their religion. During his term of office there was much disorder, mainly in consequence of an attempt he made to introduce into the city silver busts of the emperor on the Roman ensigns. In Luke 13:1 there is a reference to an outbreak during one of the feasts, when Pilate sent soldiers into the temple courts and certain Galileans were slain. He is prominent in the story of our Lord's Passion (Matthew 27:2–26; 27:58–66; Mark 15:1–15, 42–47; Luke 23:1–25, 50–53; John 18:28—19:22, 31, 38). As the Sanhedrin had no power to carry out their sentence of death, Pilate's consent had to be obtained. The Lord was therefore charged before him

MATTHEW 27

with stirring up sedition, making himself a king, and forbidding to give tribute to Caesar. Pilate saw that there was no evidence to support the charge, and, having received a warning from his wife, he wished to dismiss the case. He also tried to avoid all responsibility in the matter by sending our Lord for trial to Herod Antipas, tetrarch of Galilee, but Herod sent him back without any formal decision on the case. It was not until the Jews threatened to send a report to the Emperor Tiberius, whose suspicious nature Pilate well knew, that he passed a death sentence, knowing it to be unjust. The sentence was carried out under his directions by Roman soldiers. Pilate was removed from office a few years later in consequence of a disturbance in Samaria."

12 And **when he was accused of the chief priests and elders** [*when the leaders of the Jews accused him in front of Pilate*]**, he answered nothing**.

13 **Then said Pilate** unto him, **Hearest thou not how many things they witness against thee** [*don't you hear what they are accusing you of*]?

14 And **he answered him** to **never a word** [*Jesus did not reply*]; insomuch that the governor marvelled greatly [*was very surprised*].

15 Now **at that feast the governor was wont to release** [*was accustomed to releasing*] unto the people **a prisoner**, whom they would. [*It was a tradition for the governor to release a prisoner of the people's choice each year during the feast of the Passover.*]

16 And **they had then a notable** [*famous*] **prisoner, called Barabbas.**

The name "Barabbas" means "son of the father" (see Bible Dictionary, under "Barabbas"). This may be symbolic in that the "imposter," Satan, stirred up the multitude to demand the release of an "imposter," Barabbas, while the true "Son of the Father" is punished for crimes which He did not commit.

17 Therefore when they were gathered together, Pilate said unto them [*the multitude which had gathered*], **Whom will ye that I release unto you? Barabbas, or Jesus** which is called Christ?

18 For **he knew that for envy** [*because of hatred*] **they had delivered him** [*turned Christ over to Pilot*].

19 When he [*Pilate*] was set down on the judgment seat, **his wife sent unto him, saying, Have thou nothing to do with that just** [*NIV "innocent"*] **man** [*Jesus*]: for I have suffered many things this day in a dream because of him. [*Pilate's wife had been warned in a dream that her husband should not allow any injustice to happen to Jesus.*]

20 But the **chief priests and elders persuaded the multitude that they should ask** [*ask for*] **Barabbas, and destroy Jesus.**

21 **The governor** answered and **said** unto them [*the multitude*], **Whether of the twain** [*which of the two*] **will ye that I release unto you? They said, Barabbas.**

22 Pilate saith unto them, **What shall I do** then **with Jesus** which is called Christ? **They all say unto him, Let him be crucified.**

23 And the governor said, **Why, what evil hath he done?** But they cried out the more [*all the louder*], saying, **Let him be crucified.**

24 When **Pilate** saw that he could prevail nothing [*that he could not get the multitude to change their minds*], but that rather a tumult was made [*an uprising was in the making*], he took water, and **washed his hands** before the multitude, **saying, I am innocent of the blood of this just** [*innocent*] **person**: see ye to it [*it is on your heads now*].

25 **Then answered all the people, and said, His blood be on us, and on our children.** [*We and our children will take responsibility for killing Jesus.*]

26 Then **released** he **Barabbas** unto them: and when he had **scourged** [*whipped*] **Jesus,** he **delivered him to be crucified.**

> "Scourging" was a very severe punishment and many prisoners did not live through it. It consisted of being whipped with a whip which was composed of leather thongs with bits of metal, bone, etc., secured to the ends of the thongs.

The Soldiers Mock Jesus

27 **Then the soldiers** of the governor **took Jesus** into the common hall [*the governor's house*], and gathered unto him the whole band of soldiers. [*The soldiers brought Jesus in front of all the soldiers to mock him.*]

28 And they **stripped him, and put on him a scarlet** [*JST: purple*] **robe** [*symbolic of royalty, mocking him for his claim to be king of the Jews*].

29 And when they had platted [*made, woven*] **a crown of thorns,** they put it upon his head, and **a reed** [*a stick, in mockery of a king's scepter*] in his right hand: and they bowed the knee before him, and **mocked him,** saying, Hail, King of the Jews!

30 And they **spit upon him,** and took the reed, and **smote** [*hit*] **him on the head.**

The Crucifixion

31 And **after that they** had mocked him, they took the robe off from him, and put his own raiment [*clothing*] on him, and **led him away to crucify him.**

32 And as they came out, they found a man of Cyrene [*a city in northern Africa*], **Simon** by name: him they **compelled** [*forced*] **to bear his cross.** [*Jesus was too weak to carry His cross because of His suffering in the Garden of Gethsemane as well as the scourging.*]

33 And **when they were come unto** a place called **Golgotha**, that is to say, a place of a skull,

JST Matthew 27:35
And when they were come unto a place called Golgotha **(that is to say, a place of burial)**,

34 **They gave him vinegar to drink mingled with gall** [*designed to drug the victim of crucifixion to lessen the pain somewhat—see Jesus the Christ, pp. 654–55*]: and when he had tasted thereof, **he would not drink.**

35 And **they crucified him**, and parted his garments [*divided his clothing up among themselves*], casting lots: that it might be fulfilled which was spoken by the prophet [*Psalm 22:18*], They parted my garments among them, and upon my vesture [*clothing*] did they cast lots.

36 And sitting down they watched him there;

37 And set up over his head his accusation written [*they placed a sign over his head which said*], **THIS IS JESUS THE KING OF THE JEWS.**

JST Matthew 27:39–42
39 And Pilate wrote a title, and put it on the cross, and the writing was,

40 JESUS OF NAZARETH, THE KING OF THE JEWS, **in letters of Greek, and Latin, and Hebrew.**

41 And the chief priests said unto Pilate, It should be written and set up over his head, his accusation, This is he that said he was Jesus, the King of the Jews.

42 But Pilate answered and said, What I have written, I have written; let it alone.

JST verses 41–42, above, are not found in Matthew in the Bible.

38 Then were there **two thieves** crucified with him, one on the right hand, and another on the left.

39 And **they that passed by reviled** [*made fun of Him*] **him**, wagging their heads [*shaking their heads*],

40 And saying, Thou that destroyest the temple, and buildest it in three days, save thyself. **If thou be the Son of God, come down from the cross.**

These people obviously misunderstood what Jesus said regarding the temple. What he said is in John 2:19–21. He said that if they destroyed His body (the "temple of His body"), He would raise it up in three days (be resurrected in three days). By the time Jesus is on the cross, His statement has been misquoted and spread so that the mockers claim that He said He would destroy their massive temple in Jerusalem and rebuild it in three days.

41 Likewise **also the chief priests mocking him, with the scribes and elders**, said,

42 He saved others; himself he cannot save. **If he be the King of Israel, let him now come down from the cross, and we will believe him.**

43 He trusted in God; let him deliver him now, if he will have him: for he said, I am the Son of God.

44 The thieves also, which were crucified with him, **cast the same in his teeth** [*threw similar statements at Him*].

> The JST informs us that only one of the thieves railed against the Master.

<u>**JST Matthew 27:47–48**</u>
47 **One of the thieves** also, which were crucified with him, cast the same in his teeth. **But the other rebuked him, saying, Dost thou not fear God, seeing thou art under the same condemnation; and this man is just, and hath not sinned; and he cried unto the Lord that he would save him.**

48 And the Lord said unto him, This day thou shalt be with me in Paradise.

45 Now **from the sixth hour** [*about noon*] there was **darkness over all the land** unto the ninth hour.

> In the Jewish time system, the "sixth hour" would be about noon, the "ninth hour" would be about 3 P.M. in our time system. We understand that Jesus was nailed onto the cross at the "third hour" which would be about 9 A.M.

46 And **about the ninth hour Jesus cried with a loud voice**, saying, Eli, Eli, lama sabachthani? that is to say, **My God, my God, why hast thou forsaken me?**

> This was a very difficult time for the Savior, incomprehensibly difficult for us to understand. Apparently, as part of the Atonement, Jesus had to experience what sinners do when they sin so much that the Spirit leaves them. At this point on the cross, we understand that all available help from the Father withdrew in order that the Savior might experience all things, including the withdrawal of the Spirit which sinners experience.

Statements from the Cross

There are seven recorded statements made by the Savior from the cross. The refer-ences for these statements and the statements themselves follow, and are in chronological order:

1. Luke 23:34 "Father, forgive them; for they know not what they do."

2. Luke 23:43 "Today shalt thou be with me in paradise."

3. John 19:26–27 "Woman, behold thy son!" Behold thy mother!"

4. Matthew 27:46 "My God, my God, why hast thou forsaken me?"

5. John 19:28 "I thirst."

6. John 19:30 "It is finished."

Matthew 27

7. Luke 23:46 "Father, into thy hands I commend my spirit."

47 **Some** of them that stood there, when they heard that, **said, This man calleth for Elias** [*Elijah—see footnote 47a, in your Bible*].

48 And **straightway** [*immediately*] **one** of them ran, and **took a spunge, and filled it with vinegar, and put it on a reed, and gave him to drink**.

49 **The rest said, Let be, let us see whether Elias** [*Elijah*] **will come to save him** [*don't help him; let's see if Elijah comes to help Him*].

50 **Jesus, when he had cried again with a loud voice, yielded up the ghost** [*left His body, died*].

JST Matthew 27:54
54 Jesus when he had cried again with a loud voice, **saying, Father, it is finished, thy will is done**, yielded up the ghost.

It startled some of the onlookers that Jesus had so much strength that He could speak so loudly. It was to them as if He had power to leave His body when He so chose, which indeed He did! We see this doctrine taught in John:

John 10:17–18
17 Therefore doth my Father love me, because **I lay down my life, that I might take it again**. This commandment have I received of my Father.

51 And, behold, **the veil of the temple** [*in Jerusalem*] **was rent in twain** [*torn in two*] from the top to the bottom; and **the earth did quake**, and the rocks rent [*were torn apart*];

52 And **the graves were opened**; and **many** bodies of the **saints** [*those worthy of celestial glory*] **which slept** [*were dead*] **arose** [*were resurrected (three days later when Jesus was resurrected)*],

53 **And came out of the graves after his resurrection**, and went into the holy city [*Jerusalem*], **and appeared unto many**.

Verses 52 and 53 are out of chronological order. The resurrection of these Saints did not occur until Christ's resurrection. The resurrection of the Saints referred to here is mentioned in D&C 133:54–55. We understand this first resurrection to have included all those worthy of celestial resurrection from Adam and Eve up to the time of Christ's resurrection. This would include John the Baptist. Nobody worthy of terrestrial or telestial resurrection has yet been resurrected. The next major resurrection will be at the beginning of the Millennium when those who have died since Christ's resurrection and who are worthy of celestial glory will be resurrected at the Second Coming (see D&C 88:97–98). This is often referred to as "the morning of the first resurrection."

18 **No man taketh it from me**, but **I lay it down of myself. I have power to lay it down, and I have power to take it**

54 Now when **the centurion, and they that were with him**, watching Jesus, saw the earthquake, and those things that were done, they **feared greatly, saying, Truly this was the Son of God.**

55 And **many women were there** beholding [*watching*] afar off, which followed Jesus from Galilee, ministering unto him:

56 Among which was **Mary Magdalene**, and **Mary the mother of James and Joses** [*possibly the Savior's mother—see Mark 6:3*], **and the mother** [*named Salome, Mark 15:40*] **of Zebedee's children** [*James and John—see Mark 1:19*].

Joseph of Arimathaea Provides a Tomb for the Savior

57 When the even [*evening*] was come, there came **a rich man of Arimathæa, named Joseph**, who also himself was Jesus' disciple [*follower*]:

58 He **went to Pilate** [*the Roman governor of the area*], and **begged** [*requested*] **the body of Jesus.** Then Pilate commanded the body to be delivered [*given to Joseph of Arimathaea*].

59 And when Joseph had taken the body, **he wrapped it in a clean linen cloth,**

We understand from John 19:38–40 that Nicodemus assisted Joseph of Arimathaea and in fact brought a very costly "hundredweight" of spices for anointing the Savior's body.

60 **And laid it in his own new tomb**, which he had hewn out in the rock: and he **rolled a great** [*large*] **stone to the door of the sepulchre** [*tomb*], and departed.

There was an urgency to quickly get Christ's body in the tomb and close the tomb, because it was evening and the Jewish Sabbath [*Saturday*] was about to begin.

61 And there was **Mary Magdalene, and the other Mary, sitting over against** [*in front of*] **the sepulchre** [*tomb*].

Because of the approaching Sabbath, which began in the evening in the Jewish system of days, there was no time for these women to do their part in the customary preparation of a body for final burial. Luke 23:55–56 tells us that they watched as the Savior's body was laid in the tomb and then left to prepare spices for Sunday morning (Sunday was the first day of the week among the Jews; Saturday was their Sabbath) when they would return to the tomb to finish anointing the body—see Luke 24:1.

62 Now **the next day** [*Saturday, the Jewish Sabbath*], that followed the day of the preparation [*part of Passover*], **the chief priests and Pharisees came** together **unto Pilate,**

63 **Saying, Sir,** we remember that **that deceiver** [*imposter, referring to Jesus, who they claimed was a deceiver*] **said, while he was yet alive, After three days I will rise**

again [*in John 2:19–21, Jesus said that if they destroyed His body, He would raise it up again in three days*].

64 **Command therefore that the sepulchre** [*tomb*] **be made sure** [*secure*] **until the third day, lest his disciples** [*followers*] **come by night, and steal him away, and say unto the people, He is risen from the dead**: so the last error [*attempted deception*] shall be worse than the first. [*In other words, these wicked Jewish leaders feared that if Christ's disciples were to succeed in stealing the body and pretending that Jesus had resurrected, it would be harder for them to deal with than Christ's claim to come back to life if they killed him (John 2:19).*]

65 **Pilate said** unto them, **Ye have a watch** [*a group of soldiers of your own*]: **go your way, make it as sure as ye can** [*take your own soldiers and guard the tomb*].

66 **So they went, and made the sepulchre** [*tomb*] **sure, sealing the stone, and setting a watch.** [*They put a wax seal between the stone door and the wall of the tomb so they could tell if someone moved the stone, plus they set guards to watch the tomb for three days.*]

MATTHEW 28

The most glorious of all mornings is recorded by Matthew in this chapter. The Savior has been resurrected! In sorrow the faithful women come to finish the preparation of the Master's crucified body, since there was not enough time for them to complete their tender ministering and preparing of the Lord's mortal remains after His body was removed from the cross on Friday. Picture them as their deep sorrow gradually turns to joy as first the angels (two witnesses) announce the Lord's resurrection, and then the Savior Himself personally meets them (verse 9) as they hurry to tell the disciples.

Imagine also the Joy in the Savior's heart as He appears to them, and later to others, having finished the Atonement and sharing His joy with them. Isaiah prophesied of this joy when he wrote, "He shall see of the travail of his soul, and shall be satisfied" (Isaiah 53:11).

The Resurrection of Christ

1 **IN the end of the sabbath** [*after the Sabbath was over*], **as it began to dawn** toward the **first day of the week** [*Sunday*], **came Mary Magdalene and the other Mary to see the sepulchre** [*tomb*].

> Up to now, Saturday was the Sabbath or holy day for the Jews. But Acts 20:7 shows us that, among the followers of Christ (the Christians), Sunday became the holy day or Sabbath, after the resurrection of the Savior.

2 And, behold, there was **a great earthquake**: for **the angel** of the Lord descended from heaven, and came and **rolled back the stone** from the door [*from the opening into the tomb*], and sat upon it.

JST Matthew 28:2

2 And behold, there **had been** a great earthquake; for **two angels** of the Lord descended from heaven, and came and rolled back the stone from the door, and sat upon it.

3 **His countenance** [*face*] was like lightning, and **his raiment** [*clothing*] white as snow:

4 And for fear of **him** the keepers [*guards*] did shake, and became **as dead men**.

5 And the **angel** answered and **said** unto the women, Fear not ye: for **I know that ye seek Jesus, which was crucified.**

JST Matthew 28:3–4

3 And **their countenance** was like lightning, and **their raiment** white as snow; and for fear of **them** the keepers did shake, and became **as though they were dead**.

4 And the **angels** answered and **said** unto the women, Fear not ye; for **we** know that ye seek Jesus **who** was crucified.

6 **He is not here: for he is risen** [*resurrected*], as he said. **Come, see the place where the Lord lay.**

7 And **go quickly, and tell his disciples that he is risen from the dead**; and, behold, **he goeth** before you [*ahead of you*] **into Galilee; there shall ye see him**: lo, I have told you.

Jesus told his disciples He would meet them in Galilee after His crucifixion—see Matthew 26:32. A description of His meeting them there is found in John, chapter 21.

8 And **they** [*the women in verse one*] **departed quickly** from the sepulchre [*tomb*] **with fear and great joy; and did run to bring his disciples word.**

9 And **as they went** to tell his disciples, behold, **Jesus met them**, saying, All hail [*a greeting*]. **And they came and held him by the feet, and worshipped him.**

10 **Then said Jesus** unto them, Be not afraid: **go tell my brethren** [*the Apostles*] **that they** [*should*] **go into Galilee** [*as Jesus told them in Matthew 26:32*], and **there shall they see me.**

The next verses describe the dilemma faced by the soldiers who had been on duty when the angels rolled back the stone from the entrance to the tomb, revealing that the body of the Savior was no longer there. Watch what the chief priests and elders conspire to do to attempt to cover up the resurrection of Christ.

11 **Now when they were going** [*while the women were going to tell the Apostles*], behold, **some of the watch** [*soldiers who had been assigned to guard the tomb*] came into the city, and **shewed**

[*told*] **unto the chief priests all the things that were done.**

12 **And when they** [*the chief priests*] **were assembled with the elders, and had taken counsel** [*had plotted together*], **they gave large money** [*bribes*] **unto the soldiers,**

13 **Saying, Say ye, His disciples came by night, and stole him away while we slept.** [*In other words, lie about what happened.*]

14 **And if this** [*news of Jesus' body being gone from the tomb and angels saying that he is resurrected*] **come to the governor's ears, we will persuade him** [*we will handle him*], **and secure you** [*protect you from being executed for sleeping on guard duty*].

15 **So they** [*the soldiers*] **took the money** [*the bribes*], **and did as they were taught**: and this saying [*story*] is commonly reported among the Jews until this day.

The Remaining Eleven Apostles Go to Galilee as Instructed

16 **Then the eleven disciples** [*Apostles*] **went away into Galilee,** into a mountain where Jesus had appointed them.

17 **And when they saw him,** they **worshipped him**: but some doubted.

The statement "but some doubted" in verse 17, above, undoubtedly refers to people other than these Apostles who met the Savior as described in verses 18–20 and detailed in John 21. Some might think that this could refer to Thomas who is sometimes referred to as "doubting Thomas," but his doubt was done away with (see John 20:27–28) before they went to Galilee. Thus, "some doubted" is most likely a general comment of Matthew, contrasting the witness of the Apostles who "worshipped him" (verse 17) as opposed to some members who still doubted that He had been resurrected.

As you will recall, up to now, the Savior had limited His mortal ministry to the Jews. Now, though, He instructs His Apostles to take the gospel to all nations. Not only is this a major change in policy, but it is a strong statement that all must have the opportunity to hear and understand the gospel of Jesus Christ.

Remember that the Jews considered themselves to be superior in status to all other people, in the sight of God, because they were direct descendants of Abraham (Matthew 3:9). What Jesus now instructs is a clear reminder to these Apostles that their cultural background must be discarded in favor of the true doctrine that all souls are of equal worth in the sight of God (D&C 18:10).

18 And **Jesus came** and spake unto them, **saying, All power is given unto me in heaven and in earth.**

19 **Go** ye therefore, **and teach all nations, baptizing them in the name of the Father, and of the Son, and of the Holy Ghost:**

20 **Teaching them to observe all things whatsoever I have commanded you**: and, lo, I am with you alway [*always*], even unto the end of the world. Amen.

THE GOSPEL ACCORDING TO
ST MARK

The JST (Joseph Smith Translation of the Bible) calls this book "The Testimony of St Mark." The Gospel of Mark was written by John Mark, a missionary companion of the Apostle Paul (see Acts 12:25). Tradition has it that Mark also associated much with Peter, the Apostle, and that Mark got most of his material from Peter and wrote the book of Mark from Rome. His main emphasis, as he bears witness of the Savior, seems to be the miracles performed by Jesus. Mark is the shortest of the "Four Gospels" (Matthew, Mark, Luke and John) and has many of the same things as Matthew and Luke.

MARK 1

First, Mark introduces his readers to the coming of John the Baptist, who, according to the prophecies, was to come and prepare the way for the Messiah's mortal mission. As you can see in verses 2 and 3, Mark wants his readers to know that John the Baptist indeed fulfilled the prophecy in Isaiah 40:3.

The Coming of John the Baptist

1 **THE beginning of the gospel of Jesus Christ, the Son of God;**

2 **As it is written in the prophets** [*the Old Testament, including Isaiah 40:3*], **Behold, I send my messenger before thy face, which shall prepare thy way before thee.** [*Old Testament prophets prophesied that John the Baptist would come and prepare the way for Christ's earthly ministry.*]

3 **The voice of one** [*John the Baptist*] **crying** [*preaching*] **in the wilderness, Prepare ye the way of the Lord**, make his paths straight [*clear the way; symbolizing making a straight path into your heart for the Savior*].

4 **John** [*the Baptist*] **did baptize** in the wilderness, **and preach the baptism of repentance for the remission of sins.**

5 And **there went out unto him all** the land **of Judea, and** they

of **Jerusalem** [*many people came out to listen to John the Baptist, including people from Jerusalem*], and **were all baptized of him** in the river of Jordan, confessing their sins.

As you can see, in the JST quoted next, the Prophet Joseph Smith made a correction for verse 5, above. Instead of everyone being baptized, the correct rendering of this verse is that "many" were baptized.

JST Mark 1:4

4 And there went out unto him all the land of Judea, and they of Jerusalem, and **many were baptized of him** in the river Jordan, confessing their sins.

The fact that they came all the way out to the Jordan River which was several miles from major population centers, is a reminder that baptism was performed by immersion. In fact the word "baptize" means "to immerse." See Bible Dictionary, under "Baptism."

6 And **John was clothed with camel's hair** [*wore clothing made from camel's hair*], and **with a girdle of a skin about his loins** [*wore a leather belt around his waist*]; and he did eat locusts and wild honey;

Perhaps this rough desert clothing worn by John the Baptist might have reminded people of Elijah the Prophet in the Old Testament who wore similar clothing (see 2 Kings 1:8).

As you can see, in verses 7–8, next, John is very careful to prevent people from thinking that he, himself, might be the Messiah. He humbly proclaims the difference between him and the coming Savior.

7 And **preached,** saying, **There cometh one** [*Christ*] **mightier than I after me, the latchet of whose shoes I am not worthy to stoop down and unloose** [*I am not even worthy to take off His shoes for Him*].

8 **I** indeed **have baptized you with water: but he** [*Christ*] **shall baptize you with the Holy Ghost.**

JST Mark 1:6

6 I indeed have baptized you with water; but **he shall not only baptize you with water, but with fire, and the Holy Ghost**.

The Baptism of Jesus

9 And it came to pass in those days, that **Jesus came from Nazareth** of Galilee, **and was baptized of** [*by*] **John** in Jordan [*in the Jordan River, about 25 miles from Jerusalem*].

The Holy Ghost Bears Witness

10 And straightway [*immediately*] coming up out of the water, **he** [*John*] **saw the heavens opened, and the Spirit** [*the Holy Ghost*] like a dove **descending upon him** [*the Savior*]:

Joseph Smith explained that the Holy Ghost does not turn into a dove and further explained that the Holy Ghost was present to testify to John of the truthfulness of what he was doing for the Savior (*Teachings of the Prophet Joseph Smith*, pp. 275–76).

The Father Bears Witness of the Son

11 And **there came a voice** [*the Father's voice*] **from heaven, saying, Thou art my beloved Son, in whom I am well pleased.**

12 And immediately **the Spirit driveth him into the wilderness.**

13 And he was there in the wilderness forty days, **tempted of Satan** [*see JST quoted below for clarification*]; and was with the wild beasts; and the angels ministered unto him.

JST Matthew 4:1

1 Then Jesus was led up of the Spirit, into the wilderness, **to be with God.**

JST Mark 1:10–11

10 And immediately the Spirit **took** him into the wilderness.

11 And he was there in the wilderness forty days, **Satan seeking to tempt him**; and was with the wild beasts; and the angels ministered unto him.

John the Baptist Is Put in Prison

14 Now **after** that **John was put in prison** [*for criticizing Herod's marriage to Herodias—see Mark 6:16–29*], **Jesus came into Galilee,** preaching the gospel of the kingdom of God,

15 And **saying,** The time is fulfilled, and **the kingdom of God is at hand** [*is now being made available to you*]: **repent ye, and believe the gospel.**

The Calling of Peter, Andrew, James, and John

16 Now **as he walked by the sea of Galilee, he saw Simon** [*Peter*] **and Andrew** his brother casting a net into the sea: for they were fishers [*they fished for a living*].

17 And **Jesus said** unto them, **Come ye after me**, and I will make you to become fishers of men.

18 And **straightway** [*immediately*] **they** forsook [*left*] their nets, and **followed him.** [*They immediately gave up their professional fishing business and followed Jesus.*]

19 And **when he had gone a little further** thence, **he saw James** the son of Zebedee, **and John** his brother, who also were in the ship mending their nets.

20 And straightway [*immediately*] **he called them: and they** left their father Zebedee in the ship with the hired servants, and **went after him** [*followed Jesus*].

The Master Teaches in a Synagogue on the Jewish Sabbath (Saturday)

21 And **they went into Capernaum** [*a city on the north end of*

the Sea of Galilee]; **and** straightway [*first thing*] **on the sabbath day he entered into the synagogue** [*Jewish church building*]**, and taught.**

22 And **they were astonished at his doctrine: for he taught them as one that had authority**, and not as the scribes [*religious leaders and teachers who interpreted the gospel for the Jews*].

Jesus Casts Out an Evil Spirit

23 And **there was in their synagogue a man with an unclean spirit** [*possessed by an evil spirit*]**; and he** [*the evil spirit*] **cried out,**

> From the wording in verses 23 and 24 here, it appears that this evil spirit is speaking for several of his colleague evil spirits as he questions Christ about what He is doing.

24 Saying, **Let us alone; what have we to do with thee** [*what business is it of Yours what we do?*]**, thou Jesus** of Nazareth? **art thou come to destroy us** [*to ruin our opportunity to possess people*]**? I know thee who thou art, the Holy One of God.**

> Here we learn an important thing, namely that evil spirits (the one third who were cast out of heaven—see Revelation 12:4—and are here on earth tempting us) do not have the veil over their memory of premortal life. Thus, they recognize Christ and know what He is doing.

25 And **Jesus rebuked him, saying, Hold thy peace** [*Jesus doesn't want evil spirits bearing witness of Him*]**, and come out of him.**

26 And **when the unclean spirit had torn him** [*severely shaken him*]**, and cried with a loud voice, he came out** of him.

27 And **they were all amazed**, insomuch that they questioned among themselves, saying, What thing is this? what new doctrine is this? for with authority commandeth he even the unclean spirits, and they do obey him.

28 And immediately **his fame spread** abroad throughout all the region round about Galilee.

29 And forthwith [*immediately*], when they were come out of the synagogue [*church*], **they entered into the house of Simon and Andrew**, with James and John [*the newly-called disciples—see verses 16–20*].

Jesus Heals Peter's Mother-in-law

30 But **Simon's wife's mother** [*Peter's mother-in-law*] **lay sick** of a fever, and anon [*immediately*] they tell him [*Christ*] of her.

> This verse (30), which mentions Peter's wife's mother, is a good reminder that the early Apostles were married and that celibacy (deliberately remaining single as a sign of loyalty to God) was not part of the gospel taught by Jesus.

31 And **he came and took her by the hand, and lifted her up**; and

immediately **the fever left her,** and she ministered unto them [*served them, probably including giving them something to eat*].

Many Are Healed

32 And at even [*evening*], when the sun did set, **they brought unto him all that were diseased, and** them that were **possessed with devils.**

> There is beautiful symbolism in the Savior's healing of the people. While Christ's miracles of healing all kinds of sickness were literal, the symbolism is that Jesus can heal all kinds of spiritual illness, through his Atonement. Therefore, each time you read of a healing performed by the Savior, you can consider it to be a reminder that he can heal us spiritually also, through the cleansing and healing power of the Atonement.

33 And all the city was gathered together at the door.

34 And **he healed many** that were sick of divers [*various*] diseases, and cast out many devils; and suffered not [*did not allow*] the devils to speak, because they knew him [*did not allow the evil spirits to acknowledge Him in public*].

> Perhaps the Savior's not allowing evil spirits to bear witness of Him (see also verse 25) involves a principle similar to that seen when Satan commanded Cain to offer sacrifice to the Lord (Moses 5:18). Righteous testimony, accompanied by the witness of the Holy Ghost, cannot come from an unrighteous source.

35 And **in the morning**, rising up **a great while before day, he** [*Jesus*] went out, and **departed into a solitary place** [*a place where He could be alone*], **and** there **prayed.**

36 And **Simon** [*Peter*] **and they that were with him followed after him.**

37 And when they had found him, they said unto him, **All men seek for thee** [*everyone is looking for you*].

38 And he said unto them, Let us go into the next towns, that I may preach there also: for **therefore came I forth** [*that is the reason I came*].

39 And **he preached** in their synagogues [*Jewish churches*] **throughout all Galilee, and cast out devils.**

Healing of a Leper

40 And **there came a leper** [*a man with leprosy, a very painful and serious disease which caused the ends of fingers, toes, ears, nose, etc., to rot away; see note by Matthew 8:2 in this study guide*] to him, beseeching him, and kneeling down to him, and saying unto him, **If thou wilt** [*if it is Thy will*], **thou canst make me clean** [*heal me*].

41 And **Jesus, moved with compassion,** put forth his hand, and **touched him, and saith unto him, I will; be thou clean.**

42 And as soon as he had spoken, **immediately the leprosy departed from him**, and he was cleansed.

> Here, again, is beautiful Atonement symbolism. The symbolism is that Christ can heal us from very serious sin and make us whole. See additional help with symbolism and leprosy in the note accompanying Matthew 5:17 in this study guide.

43 And **he straitly charged him** [*very firmly told him not to tell anyone but the priest—see verse 44*], and forthwith [*immediately*] **sent him away**;

44 And saith unto him, See thou **say nothing to any man: but go thy way, shew thyself to the priest**, and offer for thy cleansing those things which Moses commanded [*see Leviticus, chapter 14*], for a testimony unto them.

45 But he [*the leper*] **went out, and began to publish it much, and to blaze abroad the matter** [*the leper went out and told everyone he could about his being healed*], insomuch that **Jesus could no more openly enter into the city** [*because so many people were crowding to see Him*], **but was without** [*outside of the city*] **in desert places: and they came to him from every quarter.**

MARK 2

As this chapter begins, Mark tells us that after some time, Jesus came back to Capernaum, where Peter and Andrew lived—see chapter 1, verses 21 and 29. Jesus made Capernaum (on the northwestern edge of the northern coast of the Sea of Galilee) His home base for the majority of His Galilean ministry.

1 AND again **he entered into Capernaum after some days**; and it was noised [*made known*] that he was in the house.

2 And **straightway** [*immediately*] **many** were **gathered** together, insomuch that there was **no room to receive them**, no, not so much as about the door: and he preached the word unto them.

The Palsied Man Is Healed

3 And **they come unto him, bringing one sick of the palsy**, which was borne of four [*carried by four people*].

4 And when they could not come nigh [*near*] unto him for the press [*because of the crowd*], **they uncovered the roof** [*climbed up onto the housetop and took part of the roof off*] where he [*Jesus*] was: and when they had broken it [*the roof*] up, they **let down** [*lowered*] **the bed wherein the sick of the palsy lay.**

Jesus Forgives Sins

5 When Jesus saw their faith, **he said** unto the sick of the palsy, **Son, thy sins be forgiven thee** [*a reminder to all of us that it is through the Atonement of Christ that our sins are forgiven, through repentance*].

6 But there were certain of the **scribes** [*Jewish religious leaders whose position was threatened by Christ's popularity*] **sitting there**, and reasoning in their hearts,

7 **Why doth this man** [*Jesus*] **thus speak blasphemies** [*disrespectful speaking of God; mocking sacred things*]? **who can forgive sins but God only?** [*Only God can forgive sins, so why is Jesus pretending to forgive sins? This is terrible!*]

8 And immediately when **Jesus perceived in his spirit that they so reasoned within themselves** [*when Jesus read their minds*], he **said** unto them, **Why reason ye these things in your hearts** [*why are you thinking such thoughts*]?

9 **Whether is** it **easier to say** [*which is easier to say*] to the sick of the palsy, **Thy sins be forgiven thee; or** to say, **Arise, and take up thy bed, and walk?** [*In other words, which would be safer for a fake, which you think I am, to say, without being exposed as an imposter: "Your sins are forgiven." or "Be healed, pick up your bed and walk away."?*]

10 **But that ye may know that the Son of man** [*Christ; see Moses 6:57 where we see that "Son of Man of Holiness" (Heavenly Father) is another name for Jesus*] **hath power on earth to forgive sins,** (he saith to the sick of the palsy,)

11 I say unto thee, **Arise, and take up thy bed, and go thy way into thine house.**

12 And **immediately he arose, took up the bed**, and went forth before [*in front of*] them all; insomuch that they were all amazed, and glorified God, saying, We never saw it on this fashion [*we've never seen anything like this before!*].

13 And **he went forth again by the sea side** [*the Sea of Galilee*]; **and all the multitude resorted** [*came*] **unto him, and he taught them.**

Matthew (Levi) Is Called

14 And as he passed by, **he saw Levi** [*Matthew, who will become an Apostle*] the son of Alphæus sitting at the receipt of custom [*collecting taxes—Matthew worked as a tax collector*], **and said unto him, Follow me. And he arose and followed him.**

> Have you noticed how quickly these great men, who are being called to follow the Savior, obey? Certainly, there is a lesson for us in this. The simple faith which enabled them to follow the Master so completely is the key also to our exaltation.

15 And it came to pass, that, **as Jesus sat at meat** [*at dinner*] **in his house** [*Levi's house*], **many publicans** [*much-hated and despised tax collectors—see Bible Dictionary, under "Publicans"*] **and sinners sat** also together **with Jesus and his disciples**: for there were many, and they followed him [*Jesus*].

> If you read the reference in the Bible Dictionary, under "Publicans," you will see that Matthew (Levi) had no doubt been excommunicated from the Jewish

religion because he was a tax collector. Such was the case with all Jews who chose to work for the Roman government as tax collectors. This is helpful background for verses 16–17, next.

16 And **when the scribes and Pharisees** [*Jewish religious leaders*] **saw him eat with publicans and sinners, they said** unto his disciples, **How is it** [*why is it*] **that he** [*Jesus*] **eateth and drinketh with publicans and sinners** [*something the scribes and Pharisees would never lower themselves to do*]?

The Whole Need No Physician

17 When Jesus heard it, he saith unto them, **They that are whole** [*are well, not sick*] **have no need of the physician, but they that are sick**: I came not to call the righteous, but sinners to repentance. [*In other words, how can I help those who need My help if I refuse to associate with them?*]

Mark gives us a bit of background in the first part of verse 18, next, which helps us understand the question asked by the scribes and Pharisees in the last part.

18 And **the disciples** [*followers*] **of John** [*the Baptist*] **and of the Pharisees used to fast** [*go without food and drink for religious purposes*]: **and they** [*the scribes and Pharisees*] **come** [*came*] **and say** [*said*] **unto him** [*Jesus*], **Why do the disciples of John and of the Pharisees fast, but thy disciples fast not?**

19 **And Jesus said** unto them, **Can the children of the bridechamber fast, while the bridegroom is with them?** as long as they have the bridegroom with them, they cannot fast.

20 **But the days will come, when the bridegroom shall be taken away from them,** and **then shall they fast** in those days.

Understanding a bit of Jewish culture will help with verses 19–20, above. Wedding imagery is involved. Jesus is the "bridegroom," or groom, as we would say it. Faithful followers are the "bride." "Bridechamber" would be the place where the wedding feast is held and, symbolically, would be the land of Israel where the Savior was performing His mortal mission. While the groom and the bride are together, much celebrating and feasting—hearing and understanding the Savior's teachings—would take place. It would not make sense to mourn and fast at this time. But, when the Savior is crucified and taken from them, the "children of the bridechamber," the faithful Saints, will mourn and fast, including in the sense that they are "fasting" from His direct presence with them.

Next, Jesus will teach that people who are set in their ways do not usually accept new ideas, in this case, the true gospel.

21 **No man also seweth a piece of new cloth on an old garment**: else the new piece that filled it up taketh away [*tears away*] from the old, and the rent [*tear*] is made worse.

New Wine in Old Bottles

22 And **no man putteth new wine into old bottles** [*old, brittle leather wineskins*]: else the new wine doth burst the bottles [*the old, hardened leather containers*], and the wine is spilled, and the bottles will be marred [*damaged*]: but new wine must be put into new bottles [*new leather containers which are flexible*].

Jesus' Disciples Pluck Grain on the Sabbath

23 And it came to pass, that **he** [*Jesus*] **went through the corn** [*grain*] **fields on the sabbath** day; and **his disciples began**, as they went, **to pluck the ears of corn** [*to pick some heads of grain to eat*].

24 And **the Pharisees** [*very prominent Jewish religious leaders*] **said** unto him, Behold, **why do they** [*your disciples*] on the sabbath day **that which is not lawful** [*not legal according to Jewish law*]?

25 And **he said** unto them, **Have ye never read** [*haven't you read in the scriptures*] **what David did**, when he had need, and was an hungred [*was hungry*], he, and they that were with him?

26 **How he went into the house of God** [*the temple*] in the days of Abiathar the high priest, **and did eat the shewbread** [*the holy bread in the house of God*], which is not lawful [*legal*] to eat but for the priests, **and gave also to them** [*his soldiers*] **which were with him?**

The Sabbath Was Made for Man, Not Man for the Sabbath

27 And he [*Jesus*] said unto them [*the Pharisees*], **The sabbath was made for man, and not man for the sabbath:**

28 Therefore **the Son of man is Lord also of the Sabbath** [*in other words, I am Lord of the Sabbath*].

<u>JST Mark 2:26–27</u>
26 **Wherefore the Sabbath was given unto man for a day of rest; and also that man should glorify God, and not that man should not eat**;

27 For **the Son of Man made the Sabbath day** therefore the Son of Man is Lord also of the Sabbath.

In JST, verse 27, given above, it becomes clear that Jesus was telling these Pharisees that He, Himself made the Sabbath, as the Son of God, the promised Messiah, and thus is in charge of the Sabbath and makes the rules for it.

MARK 3

You have probably noticed already that Mark's account is moving along rather quickly through the mortal ministry of the Savior. In this chapter, we are already into the second year of the three year earthly ministry of the Master. Because Mark moves so rapidly, some members like to read it occasionally for the purpose of quickly refreshing their memory about the earthly ministry of Christ.

Healing of the Man with the Withered Hand, on the Sabbath

1 AND he [*Christ*] **entered again into the synagogue** [*Jewish church building*]; **and there was a man there which had a withered hand.**

Perhaps you can envision the scowls on the faces of these Jewish religious leaders as they look to see if Jesus will dare to violate the Sabbath by healing someone on this holy day.

2 And **they** [*the Pharisees*] **watched him, whether he would heal him on the sabbath day**; that they might accuse him. [*The Pharisees were looking for reasons to have Jesus arrested.*]

3 And **he saith unto the man which had the withered hand, Stand forth** [*stand up*].

4 And **he saith unto them** [*the Pharisees, who were trying to trap him*], **Is it lawful** [*legal*] **to do good on the sabbath days**, or to do evil? **to save life**, or to kill? **But they held their peace** [*they didn't answer His question*].

Imagine the tenseness among the people in the synagogue at this point!

5 And **when he had looked round about on them** [*Pharisees*] **with anger** [*this is often referred to as "righteous indignation"*], being grieved for the hardness of their hearts, **he saith unto the man, Stretch forth thine hand.** And he stretched it out: **and his hand was restored whole** as the other [*healed, as good as his other hand*].

6 And **the Pharisees went forth** [*left*], **and straightway** [*immediately*] **took counsel** [*plotted*] **with the Herodians against him, how they might destroy him.**

The Herodians were a political party among the Jews and were normally enemies of the Pharisees. (See Bible Dictionary, under "Herodians.") So here we have a situation where two groups who are normally enemies have joined together to destroy Jesus.

Next, Mark tells us that people came from several day's journeys in all directions to join the multitudes that were following the Master.

7 But **Jesus withdrew himself with his disciples to the sea**: and a great **multitude** from Galilee [*in northern Israel*] **followed him**, and from Judæa [*southern Israel, including Jerusalem*],

8 And **from Jerusalem**, and from **Idumæa** [*an area west of the southern end of the Dead Sea*], and **from beyond Jordan** [*east of the Jordan River*]; and they about **Tyre** [*on the Mediterranean Sea, northwest of the Sea of Galilee*] and **Sidon** [*north of Tyre*], a great multitude, when they had heard what great things he did, **came unto him.** [*Multitudes of people from all over the country are now following Jesus around.*]

9 And **he spake to his disciples, that a small ship should wait on him** [*ask them to get a small boat*

for Him] **because of the multitude**, lest they should throng him [*press in on Him too much*].

10 For he had healed many; insomuch that **they pressed upon him for to touch him**, as many as had plagues [*diseases*].

11 And **unclean** [*evil*] **spirits**, when they saw him, **fell down before him**, and cried, **saying, Thou art the Son of God**.

12 And **he straitly charged them** [*gave the evil spirits strict orders*] **that they should not make him known** [*that they should not bear witness of Him*].

An important message for us in verse 12, above, is that righteous testimony, accompanied by the witness of the Holy Ghost, cannot come from an unrighteous source.

The Calling and Ordaining of the Twelve Apostles

13 And **he goeth up into a mountain**, and **calleth unto him whom he would** [*those whom he wanted to come*]: and they came unto him.

14 And **he ordained twelve** [*Apostles*], that they should be with him, and that he might send them forth **to preach**,

15 And to have power **to heal sicknesses**, and to **cast out devils**:

16 And Simon he surnamed **Peter**;

17 And **James** the son of Zebedee, and **John** the brother of James; and he surnamed them Boanerges, which is, The sons of thunder:

18 And **Andrew**, and **Philip**, and **Bartholomew**, and **Matthew**, and **Thomas**, and **James** the son of Alphæus, and **Thaddæus**, and **Simon** the Canaanite,

19 And **Judas Iscariot**, which also betrayed him: and they went into an house.

Next, we see that the Savior continued to minister to the crowds to the point that the Apostles became worried that He would ruin His health.

20 And **the multitude cometh together again, so that they could not so much as eat bread** [*didn't even have time to eat*].

21 And when **his friends** heard of it, they **went out to lay hold on him** [*to take Him away from the crowds so He could eat and get some rest; see McConkie*, Doctrinal New Testament Commentary, Vol. 1, *p. 211*]: for they **said, He is beside himself** [*not being reasonable, working too hard, not taking care of Himself*].

Next, Mark informs us that the hypocritical Jewish religious have journeyed all the way from Jerusalem to discredit Jesus, and now preach that His miracles and preaching are done through the power of the devil.

22 And **the scribes** [*Jewish religious leaders, interpreters of the religious laws and rules for daily living*] which **came down from Jerusalem** [*they came all the way from Jerusalem to Galilee to try to trap Jesus*] **said, He hath Beelzebub** [*Satan; see Bible Dictionary,*

under "Beelzebub"], **and by the prince of the devils** [*by the power of Satan*] **casteth he out devils.**

Watch now as the Savior responds to their accusations with clear logic.

23 And **he called them** [*the scribes*] **unto him, and said** unto them in parables, **How can Satan cast out Satan?**

24 And **if a kingdom be divided against itself, that kingdom cannot stand.**

25 And **if a house be divided against itself, that house cannot stand.**

26 And **if Satan rise up against himself** [*fights against his own evil spirits*]**, and be divided, he cannot stand** [*will not continue as a powerful force*], but hath an end.

27 **No man can enter into a strong man's house, and spoil his goods, except he will first bind the strong man; and then he will spoil his house.**

In other words, Satan can't fight against himself and still maintain a strong force for evil.

Without the help of the JST, we are confused as we go from verse 27, above, to verse 28, next. But with the JST, we see that a verse has been left out here in the Bible. We will add it here, plus the one that follows it in the JST.

JST Mark 3:21–22

21 And then came certain men unto him, accusing him, saying, Why do ye receive sinners, seeing thou makest thyself the Son of God [*since You claim to be the Son of God*].

22 But he answered them and said, Verily I say unto you, All sins which men have committed, when they repent, shall be forgiven them; for I came to preach repentance unto the sons of men.

As you can see from JST verse 22, above, Jesus answers their question, telling them that He came to earth to teach sinners and invite them to repent, and that is why He associates with them.

Beginning with verse 28, next, the Savior continues by explaining that denying the Holy Ghost is not forgivable.

28 Verily I say unto you, All sins shall be forgiven unto the sons of men [*people*], and blasphemies [*speaking against God and holy things*] wherewith soever they shall blaspheme:

29 But **he that shall blaspheme against the Holy Ghost hath never forgiveness,** but is in danger of eternal damnation:

30 Because they said, He hath an unclean spirit. [*Christ's teachings in the above verses were in response to the claims of the scribes that Jesus was doing miracles by the power of Satan, including casting out evil spirits.*]

The JST adds much clarification for verses 28–30. Remember, as stated earlier in this study guide, the verses in the JST

(Joseph Smith Translation of the Bible) often have different numbers than their counterparts in the King James Version of the Bible (the one we use for English speaking Latter-day Saints).

JST Mark 3:22–25

23 And blasphemies, wherewith soever they shall blaspheme, **shall be forgiven them that come unto me, and do the works which they see me do.**

24 **But there is a sin which shall not be forgiven.** He that shall blaspheme against the Holy Ghost, hath never forgiveness; but is in danger of being cut down out of the world. And they shall inherit eternal damnation.

25 And this he said unto them because they said, He hath an unclean spirit.

Simply put, denying the Holy Ghost means knowing full well, by the power of the Holy Ghost, that God exists, that the Church is true, etc., then going completely against that sure knowledge, trying to destroy the Church and knowledge of God. In other words, it means becoming like Satan, thinking like he does and acting like he does. See D&C 76:31–35. See also *Teachings of the Prophet Joseph Smith*, p. 358.

31 There came then his brethren and his mother, and, standing without [*outside*], sent unto him, calling him.

JST Mark 3:26

26 **While he was yet with them, and while he was yet speaking, there came then some** of his brethren, and his mother; and standing without, sent unto him, calling unto him.

32 And the multitude sat about him, and they said unto him, **Behold, thy mother and thy brethren without** [*on the outside of the crowd*] **seek for thee.**

33 **And he answered** them, saying, **Who is my mother, or my brethren?**

34 And **he looked round about on them which sat about him, and said, Behold my mother and my brethren!** [*In other words, all of you are my family.*]

Verse 35, next, teaches us a major lesson.

35 For **whosoever shall do the will of God, the same is my brother, and my sister, and mother.**

JST Matthew 12:44, adds understanding to verse 35. "And he gave them charge concerning her [*asked them to take good care of His mother while He continued on His mission*], saying, I go my way, for my Father hath sent me. For whosoever shall do the will of my Father which is in heaven, the same is my brother, and sister, and mother."

MARK 4

Jesus is still in Galilee at this point. He will use many parables to teach the crowds that gather to Him now by the Sea of Galilee.

1 AND **he began again to teach by the sea side**: and there was gathered unto him a great multitude [*a large crowd of people had gathered*], so that **he entered into a ship**, and sat in the sea [*the ship in which He sat was just a little way off shore*]; and the whole multitude was by the sea on the land.

2 And **he taught them** many things **by parables**, and said unto them in his doctrine,

The Parable of the Sower

3 Hearken; Behold, **there went out a sower to sow** [*a farmer went out to plant seeds*]:

4 And it came to pass, as he sowed [*planted seeds*], **some fell by the way side** [*the footpath*], and the fowls [*birds*] of the air came and devoured it up [*ate the seeds*].

5 And **some fell on stony ground**, where it had not much earth [*the soil was very shallow*]; and immediately it sprang up [*started to grow*], because it had no depth of earth:

6 But when the sun was up, it was scorched; and because it had no root, it withered away [*dried up and died*].

7 And **some fell among thorns**, and the thorns grew up, and choked it, and it yielded no fruit [*did not produce food*].

> Sometimes in the scriptures, the word "thorns" is symbolic of wicked behaviors, false doctrines, wicked people, bad habits, and so forth.

8 And **other fell on good ground**, and did yield fruit that sprang up and increased; and brought forth, some thirty, and some sixty, and some an hundred.

> The Savior will explain this parable, starting in verse 13.

9 And he said unto them, **He that hath ears to hear, let him hear** [*people who are spiritually in tune should pay close attention to what I am teaching*].

10 And when he was alone, they that were about him with the twelve asked of him the parable [*asked Him to explain the parable*].

JST Mark 4:9

9 And when he was alone with the twelve, and **they that believed in him**, they that were about him with the twelve asked of him the parable.

As you saw in JST Mark 4:9, above, those who were asking Jesus for help in understanding the parable, were believers. This is an important fact as we move on to verse 11, next, where the Master explains why He teaches in parables to these people.

11 And he said unto them, **Unto you it is given to know the mystery** [*the basic teachings*] of the kingdom of God [*because you have a desire to learn spiritual things, you will be given understanding of the gospel*]: **but unto them that are without** [*those*

who are outside the Church and don't want to learn about these things], **all these things are done in parables:**

12 That seeing they may see, and not perceive [*not understand*]; and hearing they may hear, and not understand; lest at any time they should be converted, and their sins should be forgiven them.

> Verse 12 is a rather strong statement by Jesus indicating that there is truth all around us but if people don't want to pay attention to it, they won't understand it and won't be forgiven of their sins. The word "may," as used in the context of verse 12, above, seems to be saying that they have their agency.

13 **And he said unto them** [*the believers who asked the question in JST, verse 9*], **Know ye not this parable** [*don't you understand this parable*]? and how then will ye know [*understand*] all parables?

The Interpretation of the Parable of the Sower

14 **The sower** [*symbolic of the Savior, prophets, missionaries, members*] **soweth** [*plants*] **the word** [*teaches the gospel*].

15 And these [*this first group of people*] are **they by the way side**, where the word is sown [*where the gospel is taught*]; but **when they have heard, Satan cometh immediately, and taketh away the word that was sown in their hearts** [*Satan gets them to quickly disregard what they have heard of the true gospel; thus, the "seeds" don't even start to grow in their hearts*].

16 And these [*the second group of people*] are they likewise which are sown [*planted*] on **stony ground**; who, when they have heard the word [*the true gospel*], **immediately receive it with gladness;**

17 And **have no root** in themselves [*but don't do what is necessary for the gospel to take root in their hearts*], and so endure but for a time: afterward, **when affliction or persecution ariseth** for the word's [*gospel's*] sake, immediately **they are offended.** [*Peer pressure, social, family pressure, and so forth, causes them to reject the gospel and the beginning testimony which they had.*]

18 And these [*the third group of people*] are they which are **sown among thorns**; such as hear the word,

19 And **the cares of this world, and the deceitfulness of riches, and the lusts of other things entering in, choke the word**, and it becometh unfruitful. [*Worldliness, materialism, lustfulness etc. choke the gospel out of their lives so that it doesn't make righteous Saints out of them.*]

20 And these [*the fourth group*] are they which are sown on **good ground**; such as **hear the word** [*the gospel*], and **receive it** [*accept it and apply it in their lives*], and **bring forth fruit**, some thirtyfold,

some sixty, and some an hundred [*the gospel is very productive in their lives, and they are very productive in blessing the lives of others*].

The symbolism of a seed growing in one's heart and life reminds us that it takes time for the gospel to grow in our lives (as taught in Alma 32) and that we must nourish it by being faithful to the teachings of the gospel.

The Parable of the Candle under the Bushel

21 ¶ And he said unto them, **Is a candle** brought **to be put under a bushel**, or under a bed? and not to be set on a candlestick? [*In other words, should the light of the gospel be hidden from people? Answer: No!*]

The paragraph mark, ¶, at the beginning of verse 21 in our Bible indicates that there is now a change to a new topic.

22 For **there is nothing hid, which shall not be manifested**; neither was any thing kept secret, but that it should come abroad. [*All things will eventually be revealed to the righteous, who allow the "seed" to continue growing in their hearts and lives. See* Doctrinal New Testament Commentary, *Vol. 1, page 291.*]

23 **If any man have ears to hear, let him hear** [*you who are spiritually in tune, listen carefully to what I say*].

The Law of the Harvest

24 And he said unto them, Take heed what ye hear [*pay close attention to what I am teaching*]: **with what measure ye mete** [*the attention and obedience you give to what I am teaching*], **it shall be measured to you** [*will determine how much more truth you get—compare with Alma 12:10*]: and **unto you that hear** [*hear and apply it in your lives*] **shall more be given.**

25 **For he that hath, to him shall be given**: and he that hath not, from him shall be taken even that which he hath.

The JST combines verses 24 and 25, above, into one verse.

JST Mark 4:20
20 And he said unto them, Take heed what ye hear; **for** with what measure ye mete, it shall be measured to you; and unto you that **continue to receive,** shall more be given; for **he that receiveth, to him shall be given**; **but he that continueth not to receive**, from him shall be taken even that which he hath.

We will refer to the Book of Mormon for a moment to get more clarification. Alma summarizes what the Savior taught in verses 24–25 and JST verse 20, above:

Alma 12:9-11
9 And now Alma began to expound these things unto him, saying: **It is given unto many**

to know the mysteries ["*mysteries*" *are the basics of the gospel, which are mysteries to the unbelievers*] **of God**; nevertheless they are laid under a strict command that they shall not impart only according to the portion of his word which he doth grant unto the children of men, **according to the heed and diligence which they give unto him**.

10 And therefore, **he that will harden his heart, the same receiveth the lesser** portion of the word; and **he that will not harden his heart, to him is given the greater** portion of the word, until it is given unto him to know the mysteries of God **until he know them in full**.

11 And **they that will harden their hearts, to them is given the lesser portion of the word until they know nothing concerning his mysteries**; and then they are taken captive by the devil, and led by his will down to destruction. Now this is what is meant by the chains of hell.

The Parable of the Growing Seed

26 And he said, **So is the kingdom of God** [*this is like the Kingdom of God*], **as if a man should cast seed into the ground**;

27 And should sleep, and rise night and day, **and the seed should spring and grow up, he knoweth not how**.

28 For the earth bringeth forth fruit of herself; first the blade, then the ear, after that the full corn in the ear.

29 But **when the fruit is brought forth, immediately he putteth in the sickle, because the harvest is come.**

Interpretation of the Parable of the Growing Seed

This parable (verses 26–29) is only recorded in Mark. Apostle James E. Talmage interpreted it in his book *Jesus the Christ*, as follows:

"The sower in this story is the authorized preacher of the word of God; he implants the seed of the gospel in the hearts of men, knowing not what the issue shall be. Passing on to similar or other ministry elsewhere, attending to his appointed duties in other fields, he, with faith and hope, leaves with God the result of his planting. In the harvest of souls converted through his labor, he is enriched and made to rejoice. This parable was probably directed more particularly to the apostles and the most devoted of the other disciples, rather than to the multitude at large; the lesson is one for teachers, for workers in the Lord's fields, for the chosen sowers and reapers. It is of perennial value, as truly applicable today as when first spoken. Let the seed be sown, even though the sower be straightway called to other fields or other duties; in the gladsome harvest he shall find his recompense." (*Jesus the Christ*, pp. 289–290.)

The Parable of the Mustard Seed

30 And he said, **Whereunto shall we liken the kingdom of God?** or with what comparison shall we compare it?

31 **It is like a grain of mustard seed**, which, when it is sown in the earth, is less [*smaller*] than all the seeds that be in the earth:

32 But **when it is sown** [*planted*], **it groweth** up, **and becometh greater** [*larger*] **than all herbs**, and shooteth out great [*big*] branches; so that the fowls [*birds*] of the air may lodge under the shadow of it.

Interpretation of the Parable of the Mustard Seed

Joseph Smith explained this parable. "And again, another parable put He forth unto them, having an allusion to the Kingdom that should be set up, just previous to or at the time of the harvest, which reads as follows—'The Kingdom of Heaven is like a grain of mustard seed, which a man took and sowed in his field: which indeed is the least of all seeds: but, when it is grown, it is the greatest among herbs, and becometh a tree, so that the birds of the air come and lodge in the branches thereof.' Now we can discover plainly that this figure is given to represent the Church as it shall come forth in the last days."

For more of the Prophet's explanation, see *Teachings of the Prophet Joseph Smith*, pp. 98-99 and page 159.

33 And with many such parables [*stories that teach*] spake [*spoke*] he the word [*gospel*] unto them, **as they were able to hear it**.

The JST combines Bible verse 33 and part of Bible verse 34 into one verse, JST verse 26, next.

JST Mark 4:26
26 And with many such parables spake he the word unto them, as they were able to **bear; but without a parable spake he not unto them.**

34 But without a parable spake he not unto them [*the people*]: and when they were alone, he expounded [*explained*] all things to his disciples.

The Tempest Rages and the Sea Is Calmed

35 And the same day, when the even was come [*in the evening*], he saith unto them [*the disciples*], **Let us pass over unto the other side** [*of the Sea of Galilee*].

36 And when they had sent away the multitude, **they took him** even as he was **in the ship**. And there were also with him other little ships.

37 And **there arose a great storm** of wind, and **the waves beat into the ship**, so that it was now full [*of water*].

38 And **he was** in the hinder [*back*] part of the ship, **asleep on a pillow**: and **they awake him, and say** unto him, **Master, carest thou not that we perish** [*don't You care if we drown*]?

39 And **he arose, and rebuked the wind** [*commanded the wind to stop*]**, and said unto the sea, Peace, be still.** And the wind ceased, **and there was a great calm.**

40 **And he said unto them**, Why are ye so fearful? **how is it that ye have no faith?**

41 And they feared exceedingly, and said one to another, **What manner of man is this, that even the wind and the sea obey him?**

MARK 5

We are still studying the second year of the Savior's earthly mission, and are still in Galilee, as this chapter of Mark begins. First, you will see the Savior cast numerous evil spirits out of a man and then watch as these followers of Satan from the war in heaven enter into a herd of swine (pigs) and cause 2,000 of them to drown. By the way, remember that the Israelites were forbidden to eat pork (Leviticus 11:7–8).

1 AND **they came over unto the other side of the sea** [*east side of the Sea of Galilee*]**, into the country of the Gadarenes.**

Healing a Man Possessed with Evil Spirits

2 And when he was come out of the ship, **immediately there met him out of the tombs a man with an unclean spirit** [*who was possessed by evil spirits*],

3 Who had his dwelling among the tombs [*who lived among the tombs*]; and **no man could bind him**, no, not with chains:

4 Because that he had been often bound with fetters [*leg irons*] and chains, and the chains had been plucked asunder [*torn apart*] by him, and the fetters broken in pieces: **neither could any man tame him.**

5 And always, night and day, he was in the mountains, and in the tombs, crying, and cutting himself with stones.

6 **But when he saw Jesus afar off, he ran and worshipped him** [*bowed down in front of him*],

7 And cried with a loud voice, **and said, What have I** [*the evil spirit*] **to do with thee, Jesus**, thou Son of the most high God? I adjure [*beg*] thee by God, that thou torment me not.

8 **For he said** [*Jesus had said*] unto him, **Come out of the man, thou unclean spirit.**

9 And he [*Jesus*] asked him, **What is thy name?** And he [*the evil spirit who was speaking for all the evil spirits who possessed the man*] answered, saying, **My name is Legion: for we are many.**

10 **And he** [*the evil spirit spokesman*] **besought** him much [*pleaded*] **that he would not send them** [*the evil spirits*] **away out of the country.**